P9-CMO-811

The Sanctions Decade

A project of the International Peace Academy

The
SANCTIONS DECADE

Assessing UN Strategies
in the 1990s

David Cortright
George A. Lopez

with Richard W. Conroy, Jaleh Dashti-Gibson & Julia Wagler

LYNNE
RIENNER
PUBLISHERS

BOULDER
LONDON

149099

Published in the United States of America in 2000 by
Lynne Rienner Publishers, Inc.
1800 30th Street, Boulder, Colorado 80301
www.rienner.com

and in the United Kingdom by
Lynne Rienner Publishers, Inc.
3 Henrietta Street, Covent Garden, London WC2E 8LU

© 2000 by the International Peace Academy, Inc.
All rights reserved by the publisher.

Library of Congress Cataloging-in-Publication Data
The sanctions decade : assessing UN strategies in the 1990s / David Cortright
and George A. Lopez.
  Includes bibliographical references and index.
  ISBN 1-55587-891-1 (hc. : alk. paper)
  ISBN 1-55587-867-9 (pbk. : alk. paper)
    1. Economic sanctions. 2. Economic sanctions—Case studies. 3. United Nations.
Security Council. I. Cortright, David, 1946– II. Lopez, George A, 1950–.
  HF1413.5.S26   2000
  337—dc21
                                                                    99-089665
                                                                    CIP
British Cataloguing in Publication Data
A Cataloguing in Publication record for this book
is available from the British Library.

Printed and bound in the United States of America

The paper used in this publication meets the requirements
of the American National Standard for Permanence of
Paper for Printed Library Materials Z39.48-1984.

5 4 3 2

Contents

Foreword

David M. Malone

The International Peace Academy (IPA), a New York–based independent research and programming institution focusing on conflict prevention and management, has long followed trends in the United Nations Security Council with close interest. The 1990s was a busy decade for us, with the Council's initial euphoria following its authorizing role in Operation Desert Storm against Iraq succeeded by prolonged disorientation and drift after several of the conflicts it tackled proved resistant to its efforts.

As UN member states became increasingly risk-averse and also hesitant to shoulder the expense of large peacekeeping operations, the imposition of sanctions, seen in the Council's limited toolkit of instruments as a mild measure (and a cheap one for those imposing it), became widespread. The full humanitarian costs of several of the ensuing sanctions regimes came to be understood only much later. As consensus within the Council on how to deal with Iraq eroded, many of its members called for the lifting or extensive modification of the sanctions regime that had been imposed to encourage Iraqi compliance with Security Council decisions on its weapons-of-mass-destruction programs. However, the United States dug in its heels in defense of the regime, perhaps for lack of better ideas. These developments derailed much of the broader debate on sanctions at the United Nations, despite a great deal of thoughtful academic work and keen interest among the chairs of various Security Council sanctions committees at the UN Secretariat. An initiative by Switzerland, the so-called Interlaken process, helped focus attention on both the benefits and pitfalls of financial sanctions and proved to be a stimulus for further debate. The German government, in turn, picked up the torch in late 1999 and initiated similar work on arms embargoes and targeted sanctions.

The International Peace Academy worked hard to encourage informed discussion about sanctions on the margins of the United

Nations, drawing in many member states, leading figures in the non-governmental community, and interested members of the media. Elsewhere, the Canadian government had undertaken policy consultation and research on sanctions prior to its 1999–2000 term on the UN Security Council, and its foreign minister, Lloyd Axworthy, wanted to encourage active discussion in the Council on all aspects of sanctions as an enforcement instrument, including their past abuse. The coincidence of the IPA's and Canada's interest in improved Council policy on sanctions constitutes the genesis of this book.

We are grateful to Professors David Cortright and George A. Lopez, both eminent experts on sanctions, for undertaking to research and write *The Sanctions Decade*. The book seeks to inform Security Council and other UN members, the scholarly community, nongovernmental organizations focusing on peace and security, the media, and the broader public about experience during the 1990s with UN Security Council–mandated sanctions. Its far-reaching conclusions and recommendations aim to influence the Council's work in the future.

We are also grateful to Canada, and particularly to Lloyd Axworthy, for funding this effort to bring together scholarly research and policy prescription.

David M. Malone
President,
International Peace Academy

Foreword

Lloyd Axworthy

The word "sanctions" has become common in the international policy lexicon of our day. The authors of this study have called the past ten years the "sanctions decade," a period in which the United Nations imposed sanctions six times as often as in its previous forty-five years. Given the more frequent recourse to sanctions, Canada has made improving their efficacy a major focus of its Security Council agenda.

In some respects the increased use of sanctions could be seen as a welcome sign of greater Council responsiveness to global security challenges, but too often sanctions have been a substitute for more resolute action and sustainable solutions. Moreover, the results of the increased use of sanctions have been mixed, the consequence of checkered compliance and uneven enforcement.

We must all be concerned by the negative humanitarian impact sanctions can have. The suffering of innocent civilians, particularly children, is too high a price to pay for enforcing the Council's will. It is also unnecessary.

Sanctions regimes can and must be crafted in ways that shield civilians from harm. When imposing sanctions, the Council must give the same weight to protecting civilians as it does to attaining political objectives. Otherwise, the very legitimacy—and efficacy—of this tool of enforcement will be cast into doubt.

Getting sanctions right has often been a less compelling goal than getting sanctions adopted. The ad hoc and politically charged approach that often prevails can preclude reflection on how sanctions could be made more effective in each particular case. The fact that sanctions are increasingly used as an enforcement measure argues for a more circumspect and rigorous approach, particularly if the Council wishes to avoid having its authority flouted.

Canada favors narrowly targeted sanctions aimed at transgressing parties, whether they be in office or not, ruling elites or terrorists, rebel movements or other nonstate actors. The focus of sanctions must be on curtailing the target's ability to wage war and perpetuate human misery. They should harm the perpetrators, not their victims. Comprehensive economic sanctions have proven to be a blunt, indiscriminate tool whose limited political gains can exact an excessively high civilian toll.

The Council must also be fair when it comes to deciding when and against whom to impose sanctions. It is imperative that sanctions reflect the objectives of the international community, not just the national interests of its most powerful members. It is also important that the necessary will be present and resources forthcoming if sanctions are to be effective. This has been the impetus for Canada's work as chair of the Angola sanctions committee.

A solid empirical base of sanctions experience exists from which to draw lessons on what works and what does not. Academics, nongovernmental organizations, and concerned states have begun the requisite process of reflection and are creating important momentum for reforming the current practice of sanctions. Canada has been pleased to work in partnership with the International Peace Academy on this book, a comprehensive, independent study that would both refine the debate and provide practical recommendations for consideration by the Security Council. We hope in this way to contribute to Council effectiveness and also to advance human security.

I would like to express my appreciation to the International Peace Academy and its president, David Malone, for agreeing to undertake this project and ensuring its strategic relevance to the work of the Security Council. I also want to congratulate the coauthors of this volume, David Cortright and George Lopez, for producing this outstanding work. Their work is an important contribution to our understanding of sanctions and their impact.

The Honourable Lloyd Axworthy, P.C., M.P.
Minister of Foreign Affairs of Canada

Acknowledgments

No project of this scope can come to fruition without a team strategy of substantial magnitude. In the research and writing phases, and in the myriad of logistics associated with this project, we benefited enormously from the leadership of Julia Wagler, who served as project manager, logistics officer, interview coordinator, and chief editor of the final manuscript. She balanced multiple schedules, conducted a number of interviews of key figures, and answered many a footnote query. In truth, there is not a word in this book that is untouched by her.

As noted in their coauthorship of specific chapters, this book could not have been completed without the research skill and substantive expertise of Rich Conroy and Jaleh Dashti-Gibson. Our knowledge and assessment of specific cases benefited greatly from Conroy's earlier academic work on UN peacekeeping operations and arms embargoes in sub-Saharan Africa. His current research on travel sanctions has complemented our own work on smart sanctions. Dashti-Gibson provided background research materials that helped us to set the context and humanitarian concerns of sanctions in a number of the cases. She also contributed material on sanctions monitoring and administration from her ground-breaking dissertation on this topic.

Our goal in this book is to provide a definitive treatment of the impact of UN sanctions. While a portion of the work relies on our own assessment and judgment about specific sanctions cases, we cannot pretend to possess the expertise necessary to complete such a task. We relied heavily on the expertise of various practitioners and analysts during our research and writing. We engaged in interviews and follow-up conversations with many of the United Nations personnel and national officers who work on sanctions issues. We owe particular debts to Andrew Mack, director of strategic planning of the Office of the Secretary General, who posed challenging questions and offered insights into the thinking about sanctions that operated within the

Secretariat and Security Council. We are also extremely grateful to Joseph Stephanides, director of the Security Council Affairs Division and the senior UN official responsible for sanctions administration, who provided complete access to members of his staff and to numerous important documents and reports, and who constantly challenged us to think not only creatively but realistically about sanctions policy reform. Both Mack and Stephanides helped to provide access to chairs and staff members of the various sanctions committees.

We were privileged to interview, in a group setting and in one-on-one sessions, many of the senior professional staff within the UN Secretariat responsible for administering sanctions. Among those we interviewed were Steve Avedon, Tatiana Cosio, Rachid Gafez, Aleksandar Martinovic, Lorraine Rickard-Martin, and Jingzhang Wan. We especially thank the ambassadors and government representatives to the UN who shared their views with us: David Angell, Marie-Ann Coninx, João Madureira, Osvaldo Marsico, Per Norström, Elda Papapoulou, Ernst Sucharipa, Danilo Türk, Harry Verwey, and Peter van Walsum. Many other members of the United Nations community assisted us in our research and shared their time and knowledge, including Francesc Claret, Elizabeth Gibbons, Aleksandr Ilitchev, Ian Johnstone, and Hansjoerg Strohmeyer. We are grateful for their willingness to be interviewed and for their response to continued queries from us.

At various times in the spring and summer of 1999 we interviewed experts within the U.S. government engaged in sanctions work. We interacted with policymakers and researchers at the State Department, the CIA, and the Treasury Department. We acknowledge with gratitude the conversations we have had with Deborah Elliott, Betsy Fitzgerald, Jim McCracken, Dave Moran, and Carol Stricker.

We are grateful to a team of scholars and policy experts who participated in a May 1999 workshop that helped shape the early stages of this project. Among those colleagues were Claude Bruderlein, Richard Garfield, Jeff Laurenti, Ed Luck, and Sarah Zaidi.

Various academic experts and former policymakers provided critical feedback on specific sections of the book and responded to questions on particular cases. Among these generous people were Loretta Bondi, Frederick Brown, John Hirsch, James Paul, and William Reno.

As specific chapters took shape, we were well served by colleagues who read the manuscript and provided necessary correctives and questions. These included Thomas G. Weiss, Kimberly Ann Elliott, and Stephen Marks.

The final framing of the manuscript and the push for policy relevance were greatly assisted by a number of our students and academic colleagues who read the manuscript and joined us in a symposium in early September 1999, held at the Joan B. Kroc Institute for International Peace Studies. We are especially grateful for the substantive feedback on the manuscript provided by Sonia Cardenas, Denis Goulet, Fran Hagopian, Dan Lindley, Carolyn Nordstrom, Raimo Väyrynen, and Ann and Peter Walshe. A special thanks to our colleague Robert C. Johansen, acting director of the Kroc Institute, for sponsoring that session.

Of course this book would not exist at all were it not for the initiative and enthusiastic support provided by the International Peace Academy (IPA) and its spirited president, David Malone. David prodded us to produce a full study comparing all of the UN sanctions cases of the 1990s. Early in our research phase he helped to bring together various UN diplomats, practitioners, and other experts in luncheon dialogues that critiqued and further explored our initial ideas. This grounded our study in an appropriate set of policy concerns from the outset, and stimulated our thinking about the more complex political dimensions of sanctions.

Others at IPA, especially former U.S. Ambassador John Hirsh, Elizabeth Cousens, and Ameen Jan, readily lent their experience and their good will to this enterprise. So, too, did Marlye Gelin-Adams and Lucy Mair.

Without the financial support of the Ministry of Foreign Affairs of the Government of Canada, this research and the ability to utilize so many resource persons as critical commentators would never have been possible. We are especially grateful for the leadership of Foreign Minister Lloyd Axworthy. Among the staff of the Ministry of Foreign Affairs who assisted with and supported this project were Eric Hoskins, Heidi Hulan, and Patrick Wittmann. We were also inspired by the visionary leadership of Ambassador Robert Fowler, chair of the Angola sanctions committee, who broke new ground in his vigorous leadership to mobilize international support for tighter implementation of the sanctions in Angola.

This book would not have been possible without the herculean efforts of the staff of the Fourth Freedom Forum, who worked with us in conducting interviews, arranging travel, collecting documents and files, transcribing tapes, word processing the manuscript, assisting with editing, correcting endnotes, preparing maps and tables, and generally supporting us at every step along the arduous path of producing a work of this dimension on a very tight timeline. We were skillfully assisted by Jennifer Glick, publications director; Linda Gerber, executive assistant; Ann Pedler, administrative director; and by our very able student research assistants, Andre King and Steven P. Miller. We are most grateful to the board of directors of the Forum, who have given full support to this project and our other sanctions research efforts. We owe our greatest debt to the Forum's founder and chair, Howard Brembeck, whose vision of a more civilized and lawful world provides the essential inspiration for this and all of our work.

David Cortright
George A. Lopez

1

The Character of
the Sanctions Decade

The end of the Cold War brought with it a new willingness among the once contentious superpowers to use the Chapter VII instruments vested in the United Nations (UN) Security Council as the peace and security mechanisms originally envisioned in the UN Charter.[1] This new activism was visible in the sharp rise in the number of Security Council resolutions—647 in the first forty-five years of the organization, more than 620 in the last ten years—and the multiplication of major peace-keeping missions and humanitarian operations. The breakthrough in international cooperation also led to more frequent use of coercive economic sanctions. The utility of the sanctions instrument was tested early in the era when Iraq invaded Kuwait on 2 August 1990. Within four days the Council adopted comprehensive trade and financial sanctions that by December brought the Iraqi economy to a virtual standstill.[2] The sanctions decade had begun.

At the conclusion of the Gulf War in April 1991, the Council approved Resolution 687, which maintained economic sanctions as a stick over the Iraqi government to ensure its compliance with the eight major provisions of the cease-fire resolution.[3] Within two years of passing Resolution 687, the Council imposed partial or comprehensive economic sanctions against the Federal Republic of Yugoslavia, Libya, Liberia, Somalia, Khmer Rouge–controlled areas of Cambodia, Haiti, and the National Union for the Total Independence of Angola (UNITA) faction in Angola. The sanctions decade rapidly took shape.

Two aspects of this trend were particularly striking. The first was the proliferation of sanctions cases. Whereas the Council had only imposed sanctions twice in the first forty-five years of its existence, against Rhodesia in 1966 and South Africa in 1977, during the 1990s, the Security Council imposed comprehensive or partial sanctions against Iraq (1990), the former Yugoslavia (1991, 1992, and 1998), Libya (1992), Liberia (1992), Somalia (1992), parts of Cambodia

1

(1992), Haiti (1993), parts of Angola (1993, 1997, and 1998), Rwanda (1994), Sudan (1996), Sierra Leone (1997), and Afghanistan (1999). In addition, member states imposed unilateral, bilateral, or regional economic sanctions more than three dozen times during the 1990s.

The second noteworthy dimension was the diverse range of purposes for which sanctions were employed: to reverse territorial aggression, restore democratically elected leaders, promote human rights, deter and punish terrorism, and promote disarmament. Here again a parallel trend emerged in the deployment of UN peacekeeping troops, which were used for a broad range of purposes beyond the traditional interposing role of the period from 1945 to 1990.[4]

The new sanctions era of the 1990s appeared to offer the promise of effective Security Council action to resolve conflict and enforce international legal norms without the use of military force. But the use of sanctions was not without controversy. In Iraq, Yugoslavia, and Haiti, sanctions gave way to the use of military force. In the African cases, especially Angola, Liberia, Rwanda, and Sierra Leone, UN sanctions appeared to have little influence on the use of force by various national and regional parties. Only in Libya did sanctions appear to accomplish their objectives without military confrontation. The evidence for sanctions as a viable means of peacekeeping thus seemed ambiguous.

Moreover, the terrible humanitarian crisis within Iraq during the 1990s was related to, if not directly caused by, the economic stranglehold of sanctions. As the decade progressed, the increased visibility of suffering and death among Iraqi children and the deterioration of the social situation and health care systems in Haiti created a palpable sense of sanctions fatigue among Security Council members, generating caution about the imposition of new sanctions and outright condemnation of sanctions by some diplomats, scholars, and activists.[5]

Despite the debate and controversy, key actors within the UN community continued to portray sanctions as a necessary and important policy instrument. A subgroup of the UN General Assembly's Informal Open-Ended Working Group on "An Agenda for Peace" asserted in 1996 that "an effectively implemented regime of collective Security Council sanctions can operate as a useful international policy tool in a graduated response to threats to international peace and security."[6] Secretary-General Kofi Annan noted in his Africa report of 1998 that "sanctions, as preventive or punitive measures, have the potential to encourage political dialogue, while the application of rigorous economic and political sanctions can diminish the capacity of the protagonists to sustain a prolonged fight."[7] The Security Council confirmed the centrality of sanctions later in the decade when it voted in 1998 to approve new, comprehensive sanctions against UNITA and an arms embargo on the Milosevic regime in Serbia, and in 1999 when it imposed travel and financial sanctions on the Taliban regime in Afghanistan.

A Road Map of the Sanctions Decade

It is not surprising that these unprecedented activities generated substantial discussion in policy and academic circles.[8] Sanctions imposed by the Security Council at once charted new territory and left analysts wondering whether they represented a trend. The twelve cases of sanctions analyzed in this book did not develop in a vacuum. The assessment and derivation of "lessons" from each sanctions episode was an ongoing enterprise that shaped how subsequent cases unfolded. As each new episode progressed, the Security Council benefited from previous cases and made its own contributions to the emerging set of generalizations about the character of UN sanctions. These assumptions in turn set the parameters for understanding and evaluating UN sanctions policy.

We begin this book by highlighting six generalizations that dominated the sanctions discourse during the 1990s and that serve as a road map for viewing sanctions. Like other road maps, they delineate major locales, in this instance specifying the current state of consciousness regarding UN-mandated economic sanctions. They also provide a basis for scrutinizing the case studies that form much of this volume.

The economic success of sanctions does not guarantee political success. Whereas many of the embargoes of previous decades were extremely porous, several of the high-profile cases of the past decade have been very effective in economically isolating the targeted regime. Military interdiction and advanced monitoring and tracking technologies combined to create new possibilities for sealing national borders. This effectiveness was especially evident in the cases of Iraq and Yugoslavia. It was no small irony, then, that the ability to actually isolate an economy did not produce anticipated political outcomes. The United Nations demonstrated a remarkable ability in a world of economic interdependence to bring some of the targeted economies to a standstill. But to the dismay of decisionmakers, economic strangulation did not automatically or consistently lead to political compliance, that is, the decision by a targeted leadership to acquiesce to the dictates of the Security Council regarding the issues that generated economic sanctions.

This is not to suggest that sanctions regularly failed to achieve their political objectives. As we detail in the case studies, sanctions were often successful in applying bargaining pressure and in several instances contributed significantly to achieving the political purposes defined by the Security Council. But it is important to note that as the sanctions episodes unfolded, this disconnect between substantial economic effect and limited political impact led to frustration and the assumption that sanctions do not work. Some nations began to understand sanctions as instruments of punishment and retribution rather than as tools of diplomatic persuasion, which generated cynicism and further criticism of sanctions as a policy instrument.

Sanctions can have serious unintended consequences. Compounding the dilemma that economic success did not always produce the desired political compliance, it became clear very early in the decade that the sharpened economic bite of sanctions was wreaking havoc on the well-being of vulnerable populations within the targeted countries, especially in Iraq. Traditionally, concerns about the unintended effects of sanctions had focused on the disruption of trade. Article 50 of the UN Charter offered trading partners or neighboring states of a targeted nation the opportunity to seek compensation to offset the economic losses suffered due to their participation in Security Council sanctions. The discussion of adverse, unintended consequences focused almost exclusively on economic impacts, not on the average citizens living within a targeted state.

It did not occur to policymakers or analysts early in the decade that the unintended impacts of sanctions would harm those very social sectors within a targeted country that might be most supportive of the norms being protected by the UN Security Council. Consideration of these matters was somewhat skewed by the experience of South Africa, where the African National Congress supported economic sanctions even while acknowledging their deleterious effect on the majority population. By the decade's end, it was clear that sanctions carried with them the potential for bitter irony: often imposed to prevent human rights abuse and lawlessness, sanctions sometimes strengthened the centralized control of repressive regimes. At times they also disempowered those who were opposing from within policies that were being subject to isolation from without.

By the end of the decade decisionmakers and scholars alike embarked on a search for ways to increase the political effectiveness of sanctions while reducing unintended negative consequences. The resulting quest for targeted, or "smart," sanctions dominated the discussion of sanctions policy and led to intensive efforts by member states and the UN Secretariat to develop more precise and selective forms of economic coercion, as we detail in Chapters 11 and 12.

The United Nations system lacks the ability to administer sanctions. Throughout the 1990s the Security Council had to improvise mechanisms to effectively impose, administer, and monitor sanctions. The sanctions committees established in each case to oversee implementation varied in effectiveness according to the degree of politicization of the particular episode, its relative priority for the major powers, and the leadership provided by the committee chairs. But in all cases the UN's ability to enforce sanctions was woefully inadequate. In an era of financial constraint at the UN, the Security Council and its sanctions committees lacked sufficient resources to evaluate and implement sanctions.

Sanctions have been effective when valuable contributions to each effort have come from individual member states and regional organizations. An innovative interaction between the local and the global has evolved in a number of sanctions cases. The best example of this was the planning and implementation of the sanctions assistance missions (SAMs) deployed around the borders of Yugoslavia, where member states and European agencies cooperated with the Security Council in the successful implementation of comprehensive trade sanctions. One of the worst examples was the incomplete and ineffectively implemented sanctions on Haiti.

A substantial amount of learning and adaptation occurred during the past decade as the UN system began to find other innovative approaches to improving implementation. Sanctions became more tightly focused, had clearer objectives, and even began to feature preassessments of likely impacts. Strategies for mitigating adverse humanitarian impacts on vulnerable populations were incorporated into sanctions policies and considered essential for their success. At the policy level, a variety of creative proposals circulated by the end of the decade for better targeting of sanctions. The most important of these was the two-year initiative of the Swiss government, the Interlaken process, that produced serious and far-reaching proposals for refining targeted financial sanctions. In 1999 the German government sponsored a similar initiative to develop proposals for improving the implementation of arms embargoes and travel sanctions. As the 1990s ended the Security Council also grappled with strategies for how to end sanctions in cases of partial or ambiguous compliance. Thus, the concept of "suspension" emerged as a halfway point between continuing and ending sanctions. It may be a precursor to the development of other concepts and strategies that permit greater bargaining within a sanctions environment.

There are tensions between the goals of the Security Council and those of member states. Early in the decade Lisa Martin published a detailed theoretical study demonstrating that the cooperation that sustains sanctions tends to change among states as the sanctions episode progresses.[9] Larger and more powerful states, especially the five permanent members of the Security Council (China, France, Great Britain, Russia, and the United States), have tended historically to steer or capture the sanctions enterprise to meet their particular foreign policy objectives, which may or may not match the goals of the broader UN community. The history of the Iraqi and Libyan cases in particular reflects tensions between UN objectives and those of major states like the United States and Great Britain. A related concern is the manner in which major states tend to "move the goalposts" regarding criteria for the removal of sanctions once a Security Council resolution is in place. The letter of the law, as imbedded in the text of resolutions, loses prominence, while the most powerful states, especially the United States, interpret the spirit of the resolutions to meet their own particular interests.

Sanctions are sometimes used as an alternative and sometimes as a prelude to war. For many member states and UN officials, the attraction of sanctions lies in their potential utility as an alternative way of responding to threats to peace. They comprise a middle ground between doing nothing and authorizing the use of military force. Others view sanctions as a peaceful means of coercion or as a powerful means of persuasion but, in any case, as an alternative to the use of force. Under this rubric, sanctions were not to be followed by the use of force. In the cases of Iraq, Haiti, and Yugoslavia, however, sanctions gave way to military force, with the conclusion easily derived from the first two cases that military force accomplished what sanctions could not. Some analysts suggested that sanctions seemed to be used as a way of softening public opinion for the subsequent use of force, as a first step toward war that crippled the targeted economy and psychologically intimidated its population.

Apart from this debate on intentionality in the use of sanctions, it is important to recognize that sanctions *are* extreme measures that can have effects in some cases equal to or more severe than those of war. The perception of sanctions as a peaceful, or "soft," tool of persuasion does not reflect the harsh reality of the economic and social devastation that can result, especially from general trade sanctions. The fact is that sanctions represent a forceful measure of coercive pressure. To some analysts, sanctions are a form of economic warfare and should be guided by strategies and operational principles equivalent to those applied in the military realm. Those who view sanctions as a purely peaceful means of persuasion have used a different and somewhat inadequate yardstick for comparison. Sanctions were not meant to be a fragile or gentle approach to dealing with international threats to peace. They are often a biting and devastating tool of economic coercion and need to be understood as instruments of forceful diplomacy. As one sanctions committee chairperson noted to us, the best understanding of sanctions may be that they are three-quarters of the way toward the use of force, and that they may have their greatest impact when it is clear to the targeted state that the senders will resort to military force if sanctions fail to achieve their stated goal.

We currently learn about sanctions effectiveness by using case studies and statistical method. During most of the 1990s, analysts have been preoccupied with the question of sanctions effectiveness (which is where we begin in Chapter 2). The prior methodological challenge, however, is in some ways more important. How do we know what we think we know about sanctions effectiveness? Those who operate within a tradition of comparative case analysis cite specific examples to validate their claim. For optimists, South Africa demonstrates that sanctions can achieve their stated objectives if the senders are consistent, patient, and stay the course. At the opposite end of the spectrum are the UN sanctions against the UNITA faction in Angola, applied over a seven-year period, twice strengthened by the Security Council, yet utterly ineffective in constraining the military capability of the targeted entity or preventing continued warfare. Also on the extreme end of the analytic spectrum is the case of Iraq, where sanctions are seen as purely an instrument of punishment against a civilian population, with no hope for changing the leadership or its policies.

The alternative to case analysis, of course, exists in the statistical method employed by the Institute for International Economics (IIE) in its classic study *Economic Sanctions Reconsidered.* We discuss this study and its examination of 116 cases of sanctions from 1914 to 1990 in Chapter 2. The IIE analysis argues that sanctions have been effective, albeit at a lower rate of success than might be desired. The IIE method relies on case analysis as well, however, and it must make sometimes uncertain judgments about the degree of compliance by a targeted regime and the role of sanctions in such compliance. As a result, this study has been subjected to varying interpretations about the actual rate of effectiveness.[10] Each approach, the empirical and the case study method, has created its own controversies, and each poses opportunities and challenges for understanding sanctions impacts.

Our Plan in This Book

In this book, we explore the effectiveness of the twelve cases of UN Security Council sanctions imposed during the 1990s. Following the sketch of the sanctions era in this chapter, we present in Chapter 2 a general framework for analyzing the political impact and humanitarian consequences of sanctions. The chapter synthesizes the best available scholarship on how and under what conditions sanctions are likely to be effective. In Chapter 2 we also offer a "bargaining model" framework that focuses more on the process of negotiation that might accompany sanctions than on the accomplishment of declared policy objectives. We explore this model in the context of reviewing other theories of sanctions and present it as a template for scrutinizing the various cases.

The ordering of the cases reflects the different types of sanctions and the different settings in which they have been imposed over the past decade. Although we attempt to present a dispassionate summary of the twelve cases and let the facts speak for themselves, we also attempt to cast new light on the cases by interpreting them within the framework of our bargaining model of effectiveness. We begin with Iraq, which is in a class by itself as the longest, most comprehensive, and most severe multilateral sanctions regime ever imposed. We explore the controversy over the humanitarian consequences of these sanctions and assess the complicated but crucial question of whether these measures have been successful in exerting pressure on the Iraqi regime. We argue, contrary to conventional wisdom, that the sanctions against Iraq have been partially effective, notwithstanding the misuse of the instrument by the major powers and the manipulation of their impacts by authorities in Baghdad.

The Yugoslav case (actually two separate episodes) stands out as one of the most important for understanding the requirements for effective enforcement and the significant role sanctions can play in bargaining dynamics. The arms embargo of 1991–1995 and comprehensive sanctions imposed during the Bosnian war predated the more limited arms embargo applied in 1998 in response to the crisis in Kosovo. The elaborate and highly effective sanctions monitoring and enforcement procedures developed during the Bosnian episode are contrasted with the limited and halfhearted measures applied three years later. Sanctions in Haiti are examined as a case in which hesitation, inconsistency, and a lack of enforcement undermined the potential effectiveness of sanctions. UN sanctions were highly successful initially in sparking a bargaining process, but the agreement that resulted from these negotiations was deeply flawed. By the time the United States and the Security Council subsequently strengthened the sanctions and tightened enforcement, the decision was being made to opt for a military solution.

The cases of Libya, Sudan, and Afghanistan are grouped together as examples of the use of travel bans and aviation sanctions as forms of actual (Libya and Afghanistan) or threatened (Sudan) coercive pressure to address the problem of international terrorism. In the case of Libya, sanctions contributed to a resolution of the crisis, although only after a prolonged stalemate and when international cooperation with the sanctions began to erode. More important, UN sanctions may have played a role in deterring Tripoli's support for international terrorism. In Sudan, travel sanctions were threatened but never imposed and played no role in resolving the immediate issue that prompted UN action or in altering the government's involvement in international terrorism. In Afghanistan, travel and financial sanctions were applied in November 1999 to end the Taliban's support for terrorism and force the extradition of Usama bin Laden, indicted in the United States for the August 1998 bombings of U.S. embassies in Africa. The case of Cambodia is presented as an example of selective sanctions applied against a terrorist rebel movement within a country. Sanctions combined with a large UN peacemaking operation to isolate and weaken the Khmer Rouge, contributing to its demise a few years later.

The cases of Sierra Leone and the UNITA areas of Angola were attempts to apply more focused coercive pressure as part of a "smart sanctions" policy. In each case the Security Council sought to impose sanctions on specific leadership groups and factions while avoiding measures that would add to already severe humanitarian problems for vulnerable populations. In neither case were sanctions effectively monitored or enforced, however. Sanctions did not contribute in either instance to pressuring the parties to negotiate a peaceful settlement or constraining the military capabilities of the rebel movements against which they were targeted. Liberia, Rwanda, and Somalia are examples of ineffective arms embargoes applied against failed states in circumstances of war, genocide, and famine. They reflect the crisis of violence and human rights abuse that has plagued sub-Saharan Africa, as addressed in Secretary-General Kofi Annan's report on Africa.[11] They also illustrate the inability of the Security Council or any other international body to provide meaningful solutions.

In Chapter 11 we attempt to identify trends and patterns of experience from the cases, draw conclusions about sanctions effectiveness, and summarize the accomplishments of the sanctions decade. We find that the limits to sanctions effectiveness are due less to inherent shortcomings in the instrument itself than to flaws in the design, implementation, and enforcement of specific policies. In the final chapter we present a series of policy recommendations, based on our interpretation of the cases, to guide UN policymakers toward the development of more effective and humane multilateral sanctions. Along the way we integrate the concerns about humanitarian consequences and argue that minimizing unintended negative impacts is not only compatible with but necessary for improving political effectiveness.

Our approach in this book is a comparison across cases. Our analysis and generalizations are empirical, acknowledging that each case of Security Council sanctions has been unique, even as we aim to identify general trends from these unique realities. Our goal is to contribute greater clarity to an understanding of how sanctions work and to explore how sanctions can be made to function both more effectively and more humanely.

Notes

1. For a helpful review of the thinking that informed the founders of the UN Charter as they framed the role and power of sanctions, see John Stremlau, "Sharpening International Sanctions: Toward a Stronger Role for the United Nations," a report to the Carnegie Commission on Preventing Deadly Conflict, Carnegie Corporation of New York, November 1996.

2. U.S. CIA director William H. Webster, remarks in "Iraq: The Domestic Impact of Sanctions," testimony of the director of the Central Intelligence Agency before the House Armed Services Committee, 5 December 1990, reprinted in the *Congressional Record,* 10 January 1991, S123–124.

3. No one associated with that action, nor the many who observed it, assumed that the sanctions would be in place for more than a few months and certainly not longer than two years. At the time of this writing, however, economic sanctions against Iraq are entering their tenth year.

4. For a comprehensive survey of UN peacekeeping missions and their broadened mandates, see William J. Durch, ed., *The Evolution of UN Peacekeeping: Case Studies and Comparisons* (New York: St. Martin's Press, 1993).

5. One of the best summaries of the ethical critique of sanctions can be found in Joy Gordon, "A Peaceful, Silent, Deadly Remedy: The Ethics of Economic Sanctions," *Ethics and International Affairs* 13 (1999): 123–142.

6. United Nations, General Assembly, Subgroup on the Question of United Nations Imposed Sanctions of the Informal Open-Ended Working Group of the General Assembly on "An Agenda for Peace," *Provisionally Agreed Texts,* 10 July 1996.

7. Kofi Annan, *The Causes of Conflict and the Promotion of Durable Peace and Sustainable Development in Africa: The Secretary-General's Report to the United Nations Security Council* (New York: United Nations, 16 April 1998), 25.

8. To illustrate this point: by 1998 major study commissions within the Carnegie Commission on Preventing Deadly Conflict, the Center for Preventive Action of the Council on Foreign Relations, and the Brookings Institution had all undertaken studies of sanctions policy either in general or toward a particular country.

9. Lisa L. Martin, *Coercive Cooperation: Explaining Multilateral Economic Sanctions* (Princeton, N.J.: Princeton University Press, 1992).

10. Robert A. Pape, "Why Sanctions Do Not Work," *International Security* 22, no. 2 (Fall 1997): 90–136.

11. Annan, *The Causes of Conflict.*

2

How to Think About the Success and Impact of Sanctions

Amid the various issues in sanctions performance and evaluation that we have highlighted in Chapter 1, none is more difficult and perplexing than the simple question: Do sanctions work? Given the frequency with which sanctions have been imposed in the last decade, policymakers seem to be answering in the affirmative. More than fifty new episodes have occurred during the 1990s, including twelve instances of UN Security Council sanctions, with the rest imposed primarily by the United States and the European Union.[1] Yet the conventional belief, seemingly supported by the scholarly research, is that sanctions do not work. In the words of one reporter, sanctions are considered "an ineffective bromide intended to placate public demands for action but incapable of achieving real results."[2]

Eminent scholars, from quite different positions on the political spectrum, share this skepticism about the effectiveness of sanctions. Margaret Doxey, the dean of sanctions scholars, argued that sanctions can achieve modest gains of the "slap on the wrist" variety but that "a major change in policy is . . . harder to come by."[3] Richard Falk, who often eschews military intervention and advocates more nonviolent means of peacemaking, concedes that "the difficulty with economic sanctions is that they cannot be effective, or that it is hard to make them effective."[4] Nearly all academic studies share this gloomy assessment of sanctions efficacy. As a recent paper by UN analysts observed, the only real disagreement among sanctions scholars "relates to the degree to which sanctions fail."[5]

In this chapter, we address the critical question of whether sanctions work by applying three distinct angles of vision, each broader than the preceding one. First, we examine and evaluate the literature that has formed the basis for calculating and understanding sanctions success. Here we suggest a few criteria for success that encompass a broader range of options for attaining policy goals but that have seldom been recognized in the current debate about sanctions effectiveness.

Then we move the analysis a step "backward" so that the inquiry might focus on the *impact* of sanctions and less on success. We are concerned with specifying both the political and the humanitarian impacts of sanctions because these embody the two central missions affirmed under the United Nations Charter. Political impacts include international and domestic peace and security, and humanitarian impacts address the mandate to enhance the condition and quality of life of the citizens of member states. These two categories of impacts will guide the information collection and analysis of trends and indicators for the twelve sanctions cases we investigate.

Finally, having critiqued the narrow approach to success that pervades the consideration of sanctions and having presented a framework for scrutinizing the impacts of sanctions, we note the tension that exists between the two basic though often unarticulated "models" for the operation of sanctions. We sketch the contours of the punishment model and the bargaining model and suggest criteria for assessing which model is likely to be most effective in achieving the operational goals of sanctions.

Definitions of Success

The most influential and widely cited study of sanctions' effectiveness, from the Institute for International Economics, examined 116 cases spanning the years 1914 through 1990. Through a rating system that attempted to determine whether the target complied with the sender's goals and whether sanctions were the primary cause of this change, the authors of the IIE study calculated an overall success rate for the 116 cases of 34 percent.[6] That is, sanctions contributed to achieving their articulated goals in approximately one-third of the cases. According to the IIE study, the success rate declined to approximately 26 percent for the years 1970 through 1989. A 1997 article that recoded and reevaluated the IIE data in *International Security* found an even lower rate of sanctions effectiveness. By disputing many of the successes claimed by the IIE authors and identifying different causes for the successes that did take place, Robert Pape concluded that the actual success rate in the cases examined was less than 5 percent.[7] However, a leading Dutch scholar, Peter van Bergeijk, argued in a paper that same year that the

IIE study sets too high a benchmark for success and that when measured against the multiple objectives that sanctions serve, the effectiveness rate is higher than the 1990 study suggests.[8]

In 1999 the IIE authors produced a revised and updated version of
their study, incorporating the fifty new sanctions cases of the 1990s.
This latest edition, encompassing 170 sanctions episodes from 1914
through 1999, gives an overall success rate of approximately 35 percent.[9] This rate of effectiveness is comparable to that of the previous
study and suggests that the average rate of sanctions success remains
modest, at least as measured by the empirical methods employed by the
IIE authors.

Many observers consider these success rates paltry, especially
when compared to the presumed higher effectiveness rate of military
force. It is important to note, however, that the use of military power
is not always as successful as some would assume. During the 1990s,
the multilateral use of military force was rated a success in Kuwait
and Kosovo (although some question the presumed success in
Kosovo), but failed in Somalia.[10] Economic sanctions have their limitations, but the use of military force is no panacea either. And attempting to measure military success is fraught with an equal number of
difficulties.

Two major weaknesses plague the utility of empirical analyses,
such as the IIE study, for the systematic analysis of United Nations
sanctions. First, these statistical generalizations are arrived at by combining unilateral, bilateral, and regional sanctions cases with multilateral episodes. The latter set of examples constitute the "universe" of cases
most relevant to the UN Security Council, but no separate systematic
analysis has been conducted yet on these cases, by the IIE or any other
group. William Kaempfer and Anton Lowenberg have recently argued
that unilateral sanctions are more likely to achieve their goals than multilateral sanctions, but their careful, theoretical study does not match the
analysis of theory to the review of actual data from multilateral cases.[11]
The truth may be that neither academic scholars nor political practitioners yet hold sufficient analytic data to validly assess the success rate of
multilateral sanctions.

A second major weakness of using the IIE study as a benchmark for
sanctions success is that the data focus exclusively on the stated policy
objectives of sanctions, ignoring the other purposes sanctions may
serve. Analyses that focus too narrowly on instrumental objectives create a misleading impression of ineffectiveness and undervalue the

broader political impact of sanctions. As Alan Dowty noted, the success of sanctions "depends on what goals they are measured against."[12] In addition to their official or publicly declared objectives, sanctions can be imposed for symbolic purposes. These may include deterring future wrongdoing, demonstrating resolve to allies or domestic constituencies, upholding international norms, and sending messages of disapproval in response to objectionable behavior. All these multiple purposes need to be considered in evaluating the political effectiveness of sanctions.

The symbolic or signaling purposes of sanctions may be less measurable than instrumental goals, but they can be important to achieving the sender's goals and may even contribute to instrumental objectives. As a report by the United Nations Association of the United States observed, "even if prospects for bringing the transgressor to heel are dim, an operational sanctions regime is worth imposing in order to stigmatize, contain, and punish the offender and thus uphold international standards."[13] At times symbolic sanctions may be imposed as an initial response to wrongdoing and as an implied threat of stronger, more coercive measures to follow if the targeted regime does not alter its policies. In this role they may help to change a targeted decisionmaker's perception of the choices available and of the relative costs and benefits of those choices. Defining effectiveness in this context is fairly easy. On the positive side, when sanctions are meant as a signal of disapproval or as a gesture of support for international norms, the very fact of nations joining together to impose such sanctions is in itself a manifestation of success. On the negative side, to impose weak sanctions, especially after a divisive debate and as an alternative to more forceful action, will likely communicate a lack of resolve. Of the various purposes that sanctions can serve, this signaling function is the simplest to understand and the most likely to be effective.[14]

One way of evaluating the symbolic function of sanctions is to employ a counterfactual line of reasoning to international incidents and consider the consequences if the international community were to pursue options other than imposing sanctions.[15] At the first level of counterfactual reasoning, one can ask, "What would the consequences of using military force have been in this case?" In several of the episodes examined, sanctions ultimately led to the application of military force. In some of these cases the prior imposition of sanctions facilitated the subsequent use of force, but it is highly implausible that the political will and resources for the use of force could have been mobilized and employed in many of the other cases where sanctions were employed.

In some instances sanctions were a prelude to war, but in many others they were a substitute for the use of armed force.

The second counterfactual option would be to consider the consequences if the international community were simply to do nothing, that is, take no responsive actions to the violation of an international norm. When nations engage in severe human rights abuses, violate treaties, or take other actions contrary to widely accepted norms, a failure to respond has tended to further weaken those norms and embolden other would-be transgressors. If multilateral institutions or major states fail to respond to violations of international norms, or if they react pusillanimously with mere words rather than action, wrongdoers may interpret this inaction as a form of consent. The importance of a forceful response is especially crucial in the area of human rights policy, where political and moral norms are the very foundation of policy and where the activation of public opinion is a key element of enforcement. Regardless of whether sanctions achieve their immediate objective of changing policy within the targeted nation, the statement of support for principles of peace and human rights that they embody can have important long-term effects in reinforcing international norms.

A full accounting of sanctions success must take into account both instrumental and symbolic purposes. Separating the different functions creates a false dichotomy that ignores the positive effects of expressive sanctions and expects too much in terms of immediate policy impact. Even if the sanctions measures are modest, they can be effective in isolating those who violate accepted standards of international behavior. Symbolic and instrumental purposes are mutually reinforcing and together appear to enhance effectiveness.

Conditions for Success:
Analyzing the Impact of Sanctions

The most important factor for determining the likely success of sanctions is the nature of the objectives being sought. The available evidence suggests that sanctions by themselves are seldom able to achieve major policy changes in a targeted regime. In this regard, they are no different than other tools of external policy influence. The more ambitious the instrumental objectives, the less likely that sanctions by themselves will be able to achieve these goals. According to the IIE study, "Sanctions are seldom effective in impairing the military potential of an important power, or in bringing about major changes in the policy of the targeted country."[16] If the goal is rolling back military aggression, impairing the military capacity of an adversary, or forcing a change in the leadership of a regime, sanctions alone are unlikely to be effective. These realities led the U.S. General Accounting Office to conclude that "the primary goal of sanctions is usually the most difficult to achieve."[17] However, if the goals are more modest, especially if they are used to bring the targeted regime to the bargaining table, the prospects for success are greater.

The success of sanctions also depends on a range of objective economic factors. Most major studies agree that sanctions are most likely to be successful under the following conditions: when the economic cost of sanctions on the targeted country is substantial, exceeding 2 percent of gross domestic product (GDP); when the targeted country has a high degree of trade dependency on the principal sender countries; and when the sender countries are much larger economically than the targeted regime.[18] There is more debate regarding the economic cost to the sender as a criteria for success, with the IIE study supporting the notion that senders do not need to sustain high costs in cases of successful sanctions, whereas Lisa Martin argues that substantial sender costs are crucial in order for sanctions to send the desired signal.[19] Timing is also a factor in the effectiveness of sanctions. According to the IIE analyses, successful sanctions require on average nearly three years to achieve their political objectives.[20] The greatest impact of sanctions typically occurs in the first year, however, and it is therefore important for maximizing effectiveness that bargaining with the targeted regime begin in the initial period of sanctions enforcement.[21]

Another consideration in assessing effectiveness, especially in the case of UN multilateral sanctions, is that the major states that dominate sanctions policy may have purposes in mind that differ from the officially stated objectives. In the case of Iraq, for example, the declared purpose of the continuing UN sanctions is to gain Iraqi compliance with Resolution 687. For the United States, Great Britain, and other countries, however, maintaining comprehensive sanctions has served other purposes, including the political and military containment of the regime of Saddam Hussein. Policymakers in the United States, including President Bill Clinton, have asserted that the sanctions will remain in place until Hussein is removed from office.[22] Although the official UN objective of gaining Iraqi compliance with Resolution 687 remains only partially fulfilled, the goal of containing Baghdad's potential for military aggression has been achieved. Does the Iraq case rate as a failure or a success?

In the case of Libya, the UN-imposed sanctions were imposed to force the extradition of suspected terrorists and to end Libyan support for international terrorism. An agreement to turn over the suspects was eventually attained after more than six years of frustrating and often fruitless negotiations. More important, Libyan support for international terrorism declined, according to the U.S. State Department.[23] Whether the latter result was due to the impact of sanctions is a matter of debate, but officials in Washington contend that the combination of U.S. and UN pressures was effective. Rating the success of this case is also uncertain. The calculation of effectiveness is a highly complex and nuanced process that must take into account all the purposes that sanctions may serve, stated and unstated, instrumental and symbolic. Such a process does not lend itself to convenient quantification or simple conclusions of success or failure.

Toward a Framework of Sanctions Analysis

Progress in calculating the success of sanctions can be made by assessing impacts in two critical areas, the political and the humanitarian. With the exception of David A. Baldwin's seminal early work, discussions of the political impact of sanctions have traditionally focused on target compliance, narrowly defined.[24] The analysis of effectiveness has been confined to indicators of economic and social deterioration and the subsequent political choices made by a target nation's leadership in the allocation of increasingly scarce goods.[25] In this framework, sanctions are supposed to exact political change that is directly proportionate to the economic hardship experienced. The greater the economic pain inflicted, the more the political gain realized. According to this theory, when sanctions exercise sufficient "bite," citizens in the targeted country will exert political pressure on their government to force either a change in policy or a removal of wrongdoers from office. More than thirty years ago, Johan Galtung termed this the "naïve theory" of sanctions, for it failed to account for the efforts of the targeted state to adjust to or counteract the impact of sanctions.[26] The naïve theory erroneously assumes that a "societal transmission belt" exists that turns economic damage into political change.[27] As Baldwin and other scholars observed, however, "the economic effects of sanctions do not necessarily translate into political impact."[28] There is no assurance that a sanctioned population will redirect the pain of external coercion onto political leaders and force a change in policy, especially with the authoritarian or dictatorial regimes that are the usual targets of sanctions. When civilian populations are terrorized and lack basic democratic rights, they have few means of influencing government policy. On the contrary, they are more likely to be victimized by sanctions, as the leadership of a targeted regime redirects external pressure onto isolated or repressed social groups while insulating and protecting itself.

A similar, narrow focus has pervaded the assessment of how sanctions alter internal political dynamics within the targeted state. Various analysts have concluded that sanctions generate an unintended "rally 'round the flag effect." The targeted leadership invokes a siege mentality among the general population to redirect the discontent created by sanctions hardships away from the regime that maintains the sanctioned policies and toward the external actors that have imposed sanctions. Rather than causing political disintegration, sanctions may enflame nationalist sentiments and generate greater autarky in the targeted country.

Sanctions sometimes enrich the very power elites who are responsible for wrongdoing. They may create a "perverse vested economic interest" among these elites and their supporters, who often control and profit from black market smuggling and illicit trade activities.[29] In the former Yugoslavia, hard-line militia groups used their control of border checkpoints and transportation routes to enrich themselves and consolidate political power. In Haiti as well, members of the military junta took advantage of their position of power and control over resources to profit from sanctions busting and black marketing. At the same time, sanctions may undermine the economic position of middle-class professionals who often support democracy and political reform. In the case of the former Yugoslavia, sanctions forced many middle-class opponents of Belgrade's war policies to flee the country and also undermined the economic and social position of those who remained. As Elizabeth Gibbons has argued, sanctions may redound to the benefit of an autocratic regime because it is in the best position to control economic activity and the allocation of scarce resources.[30]

A rally 'round the flag effect does indeed emerge in some sanctions cases, but other, contrary political responses are also possible. Systematically underrepresented in many analyses of sanctions impact has been the extent to which sanctions affect the political capabilities and power of domestic opposition groups within the targeted nation. At times sanctions may empower internal political forces and render more effective their opposition to a regime's objectionable policies, thus generating an "internal opposition effect."[31] Prior attempts to scrutinize the impact of sanctions and colleagues along these lines have been minimal. Thomas G. Weiss provides the category for impact on civil society but does not dwell on this area in any depth in his analyses of the humanitarian impact of sanctions.[32] The more recent work of Neta C. Crawford and Audie Klotz highlights the sectors of society other than elite decisionmakers who feel the effects of sanctions, but they also do not delve into the societal or political dimensions for these groups to any detailed extent.[33] In the end, we know relatively little about the circumstances under which sanctions will rally people or divide them.

As a report of the U.S. General Accounting Office observed, "If the targeted country has a domestic opposition to the policies of the government in power, sanctions can strengthen this opposition and improve the likelihood of a positive political response to the sanctions."[34] In the case of South Africa, the opposition African National Congress actively encouraged stronger international sanctions and gained moral and political legitimacy from the solidarity thus expressed by the world community.[35] In Haiti as well, the opposition Lavalas movement supported and took encouragement from sanctions and lobbied for stronger and more forceful external coercive measures. Although sanctions were applied unevenly and managed poorly in Haiti, the support for these measures that existed within the population suggests that properly implemented sanctions could have contributed substantially to the restoration of democracy.

The prospects for internal opposition depend substantially on the degree of support for sanctions within the targeted nation. When credible civil society groups and human rights organizations in the targeted country support international sanctions, the moral legitimacy and likely political effectiveness of those measures are enhanced. In its 1993 study, *Dollars or Bombs,* the American Friends Service Committee argued that sanctions are morally justified when there is "significant support for sanctions within the targeted country among people with a record of support for human rights and democracy or by the victims of injustice."[36] Lori Fisler Damrosch emphasized a similar point in highlighting the significance of internal opposition in both the South African and Rhodesian cases: "I attach great significance to the fact that the authentic leadership of the majority populations called for the imposition, strengthening, and perpetuation of sanctions." When legitimate opposition voices plead for sanctions as a strategy for political transformation, according to Damrosch, that plea should carry great weight.[37]

The political impact of sanctions ultimately depends on internal political dynamics within the targeted country. Sanctions succeed when targeted decisionmakers change their calculation of costs and benefits and determine that the advantages of cooperation with Security Council resolutions outweigh the costs of continued defiance of expressed global norms. One of the key considerations in a leadership's calculation of costs is the degree of opposition from domestic political constituencies. To the extent that sanctions strengthen or encourage these opposition constituencies, they are more likely to achieve success.

These factors help to explain why sanctions are more likely to be effective in societies where there is some degree of democratic freedom than in rigidly totalitarian states.[38] Recent scholarly analyses suggest that sanctions are more successful when directed against multiparty states than against one-party dictatorships. A 1997 analysis by van Bergeijk found a statistically significant correlation between the success of sanctions and the degree of democracy within the targeted regime.[39] A 1998 assessment by Canadian scholar Kim Richard Nossal also found that sanctions are most successful against states with a functioning multiparty electoral system, whereas they almost always fail when imposed against dictatorial regimes.[40] Kaempfer and Lowenberg find that unilateral sanctions are more effective than multilateral ones in part because high volume trading states tend to be more democratic and vulnerable to economic coercion.[41] Although these studies are limited and tend to focus solely on the declared instrumental purposes of sanctions, they are valuable in confirming that sanctions are more likely to succeed against open societies than closed regimes. They also highlight the importance of internal political dynamics to the prospects for sanctions success and the need to design sanctions policies in ways that benefit, or at least do not harm, reform constituencies within the targeted society.

More than simply establishing a new category for assessing sanctions impact is at issue here. In fact, according to one recent view, the very success of sanctions may depend less on the economic deprivation they cause to the target and more on the relative power gain that accrues to oppositional and civil society forces as a result of the way that sanctions affect internal political dynamics. In a challenging article that compares the effectiveness of multilateral sanctions with unilateral or bilateral sanctions, Kaempfer and Lowenberg state:

> International sanctions, even if multilateral, can only have a favorable impact on policymaking in a target country if there exists within that

country a reasonably well organized opposition group whose political effectiveness potentially could be enhanced as a consequence of sanctions.[42]

If this analysis is correct, it has substantial implications for evaluating the relative significance of the bargaining model of sanctions as opposed to a punitive model, as we discuss below.

Assessing the effectiveness of UN sanctions thus requires an examination of their impact on both leadership elites and oppositional groups. The decisions a leader takes in response to sanctions can significantly affect the economic and social well-being of the civilian population. Governments may use the adverse impacts of sanctions (1) to rally public support and deflect their economic effects, (2) to further centralize control of the economy and increase the repressive power of the ruling elite, or (3) to dole out resources in a "political" manner to reward supporters and punish real or potential adversaries. It is important to know which domestic groups gain or lose in a given sanctions episode and how sanctions affect the ability of opposition groups to challenge the policies of the targeted state. Of particular importance is whether these domestic groups support the imposition of sanctions and how this affects a population's willingness to endure the resulting hardships. The extent to which civil society benefits or suffers from sanctions and how this affects a population's support for the targeted leadership are crucial questions in the assessment of sanctions impact.

Humanitarian Impacts

During the 1990s, concerns about the impact of sanctions shifted increasingly to their humanitarian consequences. As Secretary-General Kofi Annan noted, sanctions pose a dilemma for the United Nations' dual mandate of preserving peace and protecting human needs: "Humanitarian and human rights policy goals cannot easily be reconciled with those of a sanctions regime."[43] As the Secretary-General stated, economic sanctions are "too often a blunt instrument" and may impose hardships on a civilian population that are disproportionate to likely political gains.[44] Former Secretary-General Boutros Boutros-Ghali expressed similar concerns about the humanitarian impact of sanctions and questioned "whether suffering inflicted on vulnerable groups in the targeted country is a legitimate means of exerting pressure on political leaders."[45] He called for a new UN "mechanism" that would monitor and assess sanctions impacts, ensure the delivery of humanitarian assistance to vulnerable groups, and help maximize the political impact of sanctions while minimizing unintended negative consequences. The permanent members of the Security Council have also expressed concerns about humanitarian impacts. In 1995 the ambassadors of China, France, the Russian Federation, Great Britain, and the United States wrote to the president of the Security Council that "further collective actions in the Security Council within the context of any further sanctions regime should be directed to minimize unintended adverse side effects of sanctions on the most vulnerable segments of targeted countries."[46]

Numerous studies have documented the severe social and humanitarian consequences that can result from the imposition of sanctions. According to a statement by the UN Inter-Agency Standing Committee, sanctions "often have negative consequences for vulnerable groups and often directly affect the poorest strata of the population."[47] A 1995 report from the International Federation of Red Cross and Red Crescent Societies (IFRC) observed that the major cases of comprehensive sanctions "have paid only minimal political dividends at a very high price in human terms."[48] Damage to the social safety net has been most severe in the cases of Iraq and Haiti, but some degree of humanitarian hardship has occurred in other recent sanctions cases as well. Under sanctions the quality of life for citizens in strife-torn countries may deteriorate from difficult to unbearable. Unemployment and inflation increase, commodity shortages develop, and economic production declines. The most vulnerable members of society may be forced from a precarious marginal status to full-scale emergency. In some cases, especially in Iraq, sanctions have contributed to a genuine public health crisis, leading to malnutrition, illness, and death. In addition to these direct effects, sanctions also make the work of humanitarian organizations more difficult, increasing the number of people in need and making it harder for relief agencies to import necessary supplies into the targeted society.[49]

The social impacts of sanctions relate not only to humanitarian and ethical concerns but are directly connected to the issue of sanctions effectiveness. When sanctions cause severe humanitarian hardships and impose unacceptable suffering on the most vulnerable, political support for these measures declines, which may erode the international cooperation that is so vitally necessary for the effective implementation and enforcement of sanctions. Mitigating adverse humanitarian consequences is thus linked to the challenge of improving sanctions effectiveness. To be more effective, sanctions must also be more humane.[50]

Some degree of civilian pain is probably inevitable with the application of sanctions. The question is not whether humanitarian impacts occur but how serious they are and whether they exceed ethical bounds of proportionality and civilian immunity. As noted in the Iraqi case study, UN sanctions against the Baghdad regime have grievously violated these ethical standards. More than 200,000 children under the age of five have died prematurely during the Iraq sanctions.[51] In Haiti, sanctions impacts were also severe. Although the scale of the impact was far below that of Iraq, the evidence suggests that child mortality rates increased in Haiti during the period of UN sanctions.[52] Sanctions against Yugoslavia during the Bosnian war also caused social hardships, but there is no evidence of major loss of life or severe humanitarian suffering.[53] In all these cases the Security Council took action to address the needs of vulnerable populations and mitigate humanitarian hardships. The success of these remedial efforts varied, but each was an attempt to meet the UN's responsibility to protect human rights while simultaneously pursuing action under Chapter VII to preserve peace.

Critics have charged that the major powers have misused the Security Council to impose needless suffering on innocent civilians.[54] This accusation may be true in the case of Iraq, as we document in Chapter 3. In most other cases, however, UN officials have learned lessons over the past decade and have responded to the humanitarian challenge by adapting mitigating measures and new sanctions strategies that seek to limit adverse social consequences. The UN Department of Humanitarian Affairs and its successor agency, the Office for the Coordination of Humanitarian Affairs, have played leading roles in raising awareness about unintended consequences and developing reform measures for avoiding such impacts. The Security Council and the UN Secretariat have responded positively to the calls for more humane sanctions policies and, as we will note later, have increasingly used more selective targeted sanctions. These developments have helped to address some of the concerns about UN culpability for sanctions-related suffering.

Responsibility for the humanitarian impacts of sanctions also rests with the leaders of targeted countries. These leaders cause the imposition of sanctions in the first place through their violation of international norms. They also control much of the negative humanitarian impact of sanctions through their allocation of scarce resources (often to protect their power base rather than to assist vulnerable populations) and through decisions about whether or not to comply with UN demands. Iraq is the classic example of a leadership that has rejected opportunities to relieve humanitarian suffering in the pursuit of narrow political ambitions. These realities, however, do not absolve sanctioning authorities of ethical responsibility for mitigating unintended consequences. It is not simply enough, as in Iraq, to create the oil for food relief program and then assume that humanitarian needs are being met. If malnutrition and preventable deaths continue, as has been the case, the principles of proportionality and civilian immunity require that sanctioning authorities take further action to relieve suffering. If decisionmakers in war are bound by just-war moral criteria, those imposing sanctions must be similarly bound by ethical constraints. The principle of civilian immunity applies no less in the application of sanctions than in the conduct of war. This suggests that sanctioning authorities bear the fundamental responsibility for mitigating unintended consequences and for ensuring that the measures enacted to uphold international norms do not cause suffering disproportionate to the ends served.

Political gain and civilian pain cannot be separated from one another or analyzed in isolation. The connection between the two is often viewed as a tension or contradiction, but it is more accurately represented as a continuum. On one end of the scale, sanctions are expected to generate some level of inconvenience and discomfort within the targeted society to help persuade targeted political leaders to alter objectionable policies, but they do not cause widespread hardships. Toward the middle of the continuum, the bite of sanctions is intensified sufficiently to cause serious disruption within the targeted country and to induce compliance by regime leaders, but civilian suffering stays within ethically tolerable limits and does not threaten life or cause severe deprivation. At the far end of the continuum, sanctions pressures intensify beyond the point of necessary political impact and cause intolerable suffering among vulnerable populations. The art of sanctions statecraft lies in applying sanctions that are sufficiently forceful to persuade targeted leaders to move toward political compliance while avoiding severe humanitarian impacts that undermine the viability of the policy and of the instrument itself.

Incremental Versus Rapid Imposition

One of the tensions between the sanctions literature and sanctions practice lies in whether sanctions are more effective when imposed incrementally, with a gradual ratcheting up of pressure, or in an immediate and comprehensive manner. The authors of the IIE study argue that when sanctions are imposed slowly and incrementally, they are more likely to invite evasion and failure. The gradualist approach may allow the targeted authorities time to adapt to sanctions pressures, and the prolongation of the sanctions regime may lead to the erosion of support among senders and a steady decline in their effectiveness. The IIE authors conclude that "if sanctions can be imposed in a comprehensive manner, the chances of success improve."[55]

UN sanctions practitioners appear to have a different view. The chairs of the UN sanctions committees, in their important 1998 issue paper, argued for a more flexible strategy: "The experience of recent years and the practice of the Security Council confirm that in many situations—although not necessarily in all—it is preferable to use the approach of a targeted and 'flexible response' as opposed to massive retaliation."[56] This preference for a more graduated application of pressure has solid backing in the early scholarly literature on persuasive coercion. Thomas Schelling provided the classic argument for this approach in calling for the incremental application of force, combined with the clear and imminent threat of inflicting additional pain in the future. The escalatory nature of such policies, linked to the threat of further action, leaves the target a sense of impending "pain beyond endurance."[57] Faced with this prospect, according to Schelling, the targeted authorities will be more inclined to alter their behavior to avoid the threatened escalation of pressure. This strategy of incremental pressure is shared by those who emphasize peaceful conflict resolution and preventive diplomacy, but it may not be suitable in every instance. In some cases where there is an immediate threat to peace or gross violation of human rights, a hard and fast approach may be necessary. In other situations where the crisis is less urgent, an incremental strategy may be more appropriate. Through our examination of the cases, we expect to determine whether incrementalism or the rapid, comprehensive application of sanctions leads to success and how that success is related, if at all, to certain types of political or humanitarian impacts.

Bargaining or Punishment?

Underpinning the search for success and the assessment of impact are implicit models for how sanctions presumably work. Traditionally, sanctions have been forged, implemented, and maintained in a manner consistent with a "punishment" model. In this approach, sanctions serve as a means to coerce and isolate, to force a targeted regime into capitulation. Both the means of influencing the target and the criteria for lifting pressure are set in terms of demand, compliance, and ostracism. Multiple interactions are discouraged, and compliance is considered the only legitimate behavior and diplomatic response from the target. If immediate compliance does not occur, the usual response is further punishment in the form of stronger sanctions or the use of military force.[58]

A rather different approach considers sanctions a form of persuasion, a tool for encouraging targeted regimes to reevaluate their policy options. In this model, sanctions increase the costs of defiance while offering benefits for cooperation. This approach places sanctions within the broader context of economic statecraft and diplomacy in general. We term this the "bargaining model" of sanctions. It assumes that sanctions work best as tools of persuasion, that they are most effective when applied as part of a carrot-and-stick diplomacy designed to bring about a negotiated solution. It views sanctions not as a policy unto themselves but as part of a continuum of policy instruments from the negative to the positive, designed to encourage political compromise and spark a process of dialogue and negotiation.

Of course, bargaining and punishment are related. They are not as distinct as this discussion might imply. Punishment, or at least the threat of such, can be considered an element of the bargaining process. Sometimes only coercive pressure can induce a willingness to negotiate, and it may be necessary as well to ensure compliance with the resulting agreement. In a number of cases during the 1990s, sanctions were effective in sparking negotiations, but the resulting bargaining process collapsed from a lack of compliance with the agreed-upon settlement. A bargaining process is usually necessary but not always sufficient for the resolution of conflict. Compliance is the ultimate objective, and it often requires the continued exertion, or at least threat, of coercive pressure. Coercion becomes dysfunctional, however, when it is unconditional, when it demands total submission as the price for an easing of pressure. For bargaining to be successful, punitive pressures must be eased as well as imposed.

The effectiveness of sanctions in the bargaining model does not derive primarily from their ability to punish or coerce. Their impact comes not from the severity of the economic damage they cause, but from their ability to encourage dialogue and bargaining. From this perspective, sanctions can be considered successful if they contribute to a bargaining process and become the basis around which a negotiated settlement is reached. They do not require the imposition of draconian economic pressure to have persuasive influence. Sanctions need only cause sufficient hardship and discomfort to motivate the targeted authorities to enter into a bargaining process. Their bite is determined not by an objective measurement of economic pain but by the subjective response of targeted political leaders. Sanctions work if the desire for a lifting of coercive pressure serves as an inducement for negotiation and compliance.

Within this bargaining model, the question of when and how to lift sanctions becomes pivotal. The desire to escape coercive pressures is a major concern for targeted authorities, as evidenced by the frequency with which the issue is raised in public statements and diplomatic dialogue. In such circumstances the senders can use the offer to ease or lift sanctions pressure as an incentive to extract concessions from the targeted regime. The desire by targeted leaders for a lifting of sanctions pressure is present in nearly every case examined. When this desire is harnessed to a carrot-and-stick bargaining process, success is more likely. The bargaining process may be more effective when the offer to lift sanctions is linked to concrete steps toward compliance by the targeted authorities.

Carrots as Well as Sticks

The bargaining framework highlights the importance of incentives for conflict prevention and resolution. A sanctions policy can become counterproductive when it leans too heavily on punitive pressures, with little or no prospect for positive incentives. As Alexander George has emphasized, coercive diplomacy requires a mix of inducements for cooperation as well as punishments for noncompliance.[59] What the stick cannot accomplish by itself can be achieved by combining it with a carrot. Baldwin has also noted the connection between carrots and sticks, observing that the use of negative sanctions can lay the groundwork for the subsequent application of positive incentives to enhance the prospects for compliance.[60] A study from the University of California at Los Angeles suggests that a mixed use of incentives and sanctions is more effective than relying on coercive pressures alone. An examination of twenty-two cases of attempts to influence a targeted state's behavior through either coercive strategies or a mixture of sanctions and incentives found that mixed strategies were three times more effective than the use of coercive measures alone.[61]

In recent years a number of studies have highlighted the role of inducement strategies in resolving and preventing conflict. A major study by the Carnegie Commission on Preventing Deadly Conflict (edited by one of the authors of this book) reviewed recent examples of incentives use and identified the most important variables and conditions for the effective use of positive measures.[62] The Carnegie study also addressed the objections that are often raised against inducement strategies. Incentives are sometimes criticized as a form of appeasement, a payment for objectionable behavior that may encourage others to engage in similar forms of wrongdoing. To avoid this moral hazard, senders can offer benefits incrementally in response to specific concessions from the target. At times incentives may not be appropriate at all, especially if a regime has committed a major act of aggression or has engaged in massive human rights abuses. In other cases, combining sanctions with incentives not only helps to avoid the moral hazard problem but encourages the bargaining process that is necessary to resolve conflict.[63]

Most examples of the use of inducement strategies involve international financial institutions, regional organizations, or member states working alone or with others. The Security Council lacks the ability to provide direct financial benefits or to offer security assurances. The Council can still play a role, however, by urging international organizations and member states to offer inducements as part of a coordinated carrot-and-stick policy. Most important, the Security Council can design sanctions policies that provide incentives for cooperation. The more effective approach, according to former Australian foreign minister Gareth Evans, is the tit-for-tat strategy of progressively lifting sanctions pressure as an incentive for compliance.[64] In a 1997 resolution, the UN General Assembly called for a similar strategy of gradually easing sanctions pressures as a means of encouraging compliance with UN demands:

> The Security Council could also provide for imposing sanctions that may be partially lifted, in the event the targeted country or party complies with previously defined requirements imposed by specific resolutions. It could also consider the possibility of introducing a range of sanctions and lifting them progressively as each target is achieved.[65]

Combining sanctions and incentives as part of a carrot-and-stick bargaining process can contribute significantly to the success of economic statecraft.

Cooperation theory teaches that the reciprocation of conciliation is likely to generate additional steps toward compliance.[66] In the case of sanctions, a partial easing of pressure in response to steps toward compliance by the target regime can induce additional gestures of cooperation and facilitate a diplomatic settlement. However, a failure to reciprocate concessions may squander opportunities for additional compliance and generate dynamics of deepening distrust and animosity that make a negotiated solution more difficult.

The UN's contrasting experiences in implementing sanctions against Yugoslavia and Iraq illustrate these dynamics. As noted in Chapter 4, some observers credit UN sanctions with moderating Belgrade's war policies in Bosnia and helping to spark a bargaining process that led to the Dayton peace accord. In August 1994, under the pressure of intensifying sanctions, Belgrade severed political and economic relations with the Bosnian Serbs and invited UN monitors to verify its action. In response to this gesture of partial compliance, the UN Security Council eased some of the sanctions imposed against Serbia and Montenegro while extending the previous sanctions to territories under the control of the Bosnian Serbs. The Security Council's actions sent a message of encouragement to the Milosevic regime, suggesting that further compliance with UN demands would result in additional easing of coercive pressures. In Iraq, by contrast, Baghdad received no encouragement or sanctions relief when it made partial concessions to UN demands in 1993 and 1994, accepting UN weapons monitoring on its territory and recognizing the redrawn borders with Kuwait. If these concessions had been met with a partial easing of sanctions pressure, the Baghdad regime might have responded with further measures toward compliance. The failure to reciprocate Iraqi concessions and the policy of unyielding punitive pressure (largely dictated by the United States and Great Britain) undermined the prospects for political compromise and needlessly prolonged both the political confrontation with Baghdad and the humanitarian suffering of the Iraqi people.

When senders refuse to reciprocate concessions, the bargaining leverage gained through the use of sanctions is lost. The advantages of carrot-and-stick bargaining are also wasted when sanctions are lifted prematurely, before actual compliance has occurred. Offering the carrot of eased sanctions before the other side has reciprocated may squander the advantages gained through successful bargaining dynamics. In the case of Haiti, sanctions were effective in inducing the military junta to negotiate and accept the return of deposed president Jean-Bertrand Aristide. The resulting Governors Island agreement was flawed, however, in lifting sanctions pressure two months before the date of Aristide's scheduled return to office. The junta reneged on its part of the bargain, and the agreement collapsed. The offer to lift sanctions can be an effective inducement to negotiations and political compromise, but it is most successful when linked to concrete measures of compliance by the target.

Conclusion

In this chapter we have argued that the traditional criteria for assessing the success of sanctions have been too narrow. To appreciate fully the potential significance of sanctions requires a broader view of how they impact the economic, social, and political dynamics of the targeted regime, and a fuller consideration of the diverse goals that sanctions may serve. In contrast to the conventional understanding of sanctions as a punitive instrument, we speculate about the utility of a bargaining process that places sanctions within the context of carrot-and-stick diplomacy. In our consideration of the cases that follow, we examine each episode with an eye toward its political and humanitarian impacts and how these affect the prospects for success broadly defined. We review the dynamics of punishment and bargaining and attempt to determine the extent to which, if at all, sanctions contributed to the prevention and resolution of conflict.

Notes

1. Kimberly Ann Elliott and Gary Clyde Hufbauer, "Ineffectiveness of Economic Sanctions: Same Song, Same Refrain? Economic Sanctions in the 1990s," papers and proceedings of the 111th Annual Meeting of the American Economic Association, 3–5 January 1999, *American Economic Review* (May 1999): 403.

2. Jim Hoagland, "The Sanctions Bromide," *Washington Post,* 12 November 1993, A25.

3. Margaret P. Doxey, *International Sanctions in Contemporary Perspective,* 2d ed. (New York: St. Martin's Press, 1996), 65.

4. Richard Falk, "The Use of Economic Sanctions in the Context of the Changing World Order," paper delivered at the Conference on International Economic Sanctions in the Post–Cold War Era, Philadelphia, 17 October 1992, 1.

5. Andrew Mack and Asif Kahn, "A Glass Half Empty? UN Sanctions in the 1990s," Strategic Planning Unit, Executive Office of the Secretary-General, United Nations, New York, March 1999.

6. Gary C. Hufbauer, Jeffrey J. Schott, and Kimberly Ann Elliott, *Economic Sanctions Reconsidered: History and Current Policy,* 2d ed. (Washington, D.C.: Institute for International Economics, 1990), 93.

7. Robert A. Pape, "Why Economic Sanctions Do Not Work," *International Security* 22, no. 2 (Fall 1997): 90–136; for a rebuttal, see Kimberly Ann Elliott,

"The Sanctions Glass: Half Full or Completely Empty?" *International Security* 23, no. 1 (Summer 1998): 50–65.

8. Peter van Bergeijk, "Economic Sanctions, Autocracy, Democracy and Success," paper presented at the Conference on the Effectiveness and Effects of UN Sanctions, Tilburg, Netherlands, 1997.

9. Elliott and Hufbauer, "Ineffectiveness of Economic Sanctions," 403–404; Kimberly Ann Elliott, comments on manuscript in letter to authors, 20 September 1999.

10. See Michael Mandelbaum, "A Perfect Failure," *Foreign Affairs* 78, no. 5 (September–October 1999): 2–8.

11. William Kaempfer and Anton Lowenberg, "Unilateral Versus Multilateral International Sanctions: A Public Choice Perspective," *International Studies Quarterly* 43, no. 1 (March 1999): 37–58.

12. Alan Dowty, "Sanctioning Iraq: The Limits of the New World Order," *Washington Quarterly* 17, no. 3 (Summer 1994): 192.

13. Lisa L. Martin and Jeffrey Laurenti, "The United Nations and Economic Sanctions: Improving Regime Effectiveness," paper of the United Nations Association–USA International Dialogue on the Enforcement of Security Council Resolutions, United Nations Association of the United States of America, New York, August 1997, 19.

14. Miroslov Nincic and Peter Wallensteen, eds., *Dilemmas of Economic Coercion: Sanctions and World Politics* (New York: Praeger, 1983), 8.

15. Philip E. Tetlock and Aaron Belkin, *Counterfactual Thought Experiments in World Politics* (Princeton, N.J.: Princeton University Press, 1996).

16. Hufbauer, Schott, and Elliott, *Economic Sanctions Reconsidered*, 94.

17. U.S. General Accounting Office, *Economic Sanctions: Effectiveness as Tools of Foreign Policy* (Washington, D.C.: GAO, 1993), 11.

18. The sources for these generalizations include Hufbauer, Schott, and Elliott, *Economic Sanctions Reconsidered*, 97–102; Margaret P. Doxey, *Economic Sanctions and International Enforcement* (New York: Oxford University Press, 1980), 77–83; and James M. Lindsay, "Trade Sanctions as Policy Instruments: A Reexamination," *International Studies Quarterly* 30 (June 1986): 153–173.

19. Hufbauer, Schott, and Elliott, *Economic Sanctions Reconsidered;* Lisa L. Martin, *Coercive Cooperation: Explaining Multilateral Economic Sanctions* (Princeton, N.J.: Princeton University Press, 1992).

20. Hufbauer, Schott, and Elliott, *Economic Sanctions Reconsidered*, 101.

21. Nincic and Wallensteen, *Dilemmas of Economic Coercion,* 109.

22. In November 1997, Clinton remarked: "Sanctions will be there until the end of time, or as long as [Hussein] lasts." Quoted in Barbara Crossette, "For Iraq, a Doghouse with Many Rooms," *New York Times,* 23 November 1997, 4.

23. U.S. Department of State, *Patterns of Global Terrorism 1996,* Publication 10535 (Washington, D.C.: Government Printing Office, 1996).

24. David A. Baldwin, *Economic Statecraft* (Princeton, N.J.: Princeton University Press, 1985); for the indicators literature, see David M. Rowe, "Surviving Economic Coercion: Rhodesia's Responses to International Economic Sanctions," Ph.D. diss., Duke University, 1993.

25. David M. Rowe, "Surviving Economic Coercion."

26. Johan Galtung, "On the Effects of International Sanctions," in Miroslov Nincic and Peter Wallensteen, eds., *Dilemmas of Economic Coercion: Sanctions and World Politics* (New York: Praeger, 1983), 22–27.

27. Claudia von Braunmühl and Manfred Kulessa, *The Impact of UN Sanctions on Humanitarian Assistance Activities: Report on a Study Commissioned by the United Nations Department of Humanitarian Affairs,* Berlin, Gesellschaft für Communication Management Interkulter Training, December 1995, 30.

28. David A. Baldwin, *Economic Statecraft,* 63.

29. Mack and Kahn, "A Glass Half Empty?" 5.

30. Elizabeth Gibbons, *Sanctions in Haiti: Human Rights and Democracy Under Assault,* Center for Strategic and International Studies, Washington Papers 177 (Westport, Conn.: Praeger, 1999), 38–39.

31. U.S. General Accounting Office, *International Trade: Issues Regarding Imposition of an Oil Embargo Against Nigeria: Report Prepared for the Chairman, Subcommittee on Africa, Committee on Foreign Relations, U.S. House of Representatives,* 103rd Cong., 2d Sess., GAO/GGD-95-24 (Washington, D.C.: GAO, November 1994), 12.

32. Thomas G. Weiss, David Cortright, George A. Lopez, and Larry Minear, eds., *Political Gain and Civilian Pain: Humanitarian Impacts of Economic Sanctions* (Lanham, Md.: Rowman and Littlefield, 1997).

33. Neta C. Crawford and Audie Klotz, eds., *How Sanctions Work: Lessons from South Africa* (New York: St. Martin's Press, 1999).

34. U.S. General Accounting Office, *International Trade,* 12.

35. Jennifer Davis, "Sanctions and Apartheid: The Economic Challenge to Discrimination," in David Cortright and George A. Lopez, eds., *Economic Sanctions: Panacea or Peacebuilding in a Post–Cold War World?* (Boulder, Colo.: Westview Press, 1995): 173–186.

36. American Friends Service Committee, Working Group on International Economic Sanctions, *Dollars or Bombs: The Search for Justice Through International Economic Sanctions* (Philadelphia: American Friends Service Committee, 1993), 9.

37. Lori Fisler Damrosch, "The Civilian Impact of Economic Sanctions," in Lori Fisler Damrosch, ed., *Enforcing Restraint: Collective Intervention in Internal Conflicts* (New York: Council on Foreign Relations, 1993), 302.

38. Mack and Kahn, "A Glass Half Empty?" 4.

39. Van Bergeijk, "Economic Sanctions, Autocracy, Democracy and Success."

40. Kim Richard Nossal, "Liberal Democratic Regimes, International Sanctions, and Global Governance," in Raimo Väyrynen, ed., *Globalization and Global Governance* (Lanham, Md.: Rowman and Littlefield, 1999), 127–149.

41. Kaempfer and Lowenberg, "Unilateral Versus Multilateral International Sanctions."

42. Ibid.

43. Kofi Annan, *Annual Report of the Secretary-General on the Work of the Organization (1998),* A/53/1, United Nations, New York, 27 August 1998, 64.

44. Kofi Annan, *The Causes of Conflict and the Promotion of Durable Peace and Sustainable Development in Africa, Secretary-General's Report to the United Nations Security Council* (New York: United Nations, 16 April 1998), 25.

45. Boutros Boutros-Ghali, *Supplement to An Agenda for Peace: Position Paper of the Secretary-General on the Occasion of the 50th Anniversary of the United Nations,* A/50/60 (New York: United Nations, 3 January 1995), 17–18.

46. United Nations Security Council, *Letter Dated 13 April 1995, Addressed to the President of the Security Council,* S/1995/200, Annex 1.

47. United Nations Inter-Agency Standing Committee, *Report for Humanitarian Mandates in Conflict Situations,* 1996, sec. 12.

48. Peter Walker, "Sanctions: A Blunt Instrument," *Red Cross, Red Crescent,* no. 3 (1995): 19.

49. For a detailed assessment of these impacts, see Weiss et al., *Political Gain and Civilian Pain,* especially chap. 1.

50. Some analysts argue that humane sanctions are impossible due to the inherent limitations of the instrument. See, for example, Joy Gordon, "A Peaceful, Silent, Deadly Remedy: The Ethics of Economic Sanctions," *Ethics and International Affairs* 13 (May 1999). Gordon's argument may be correct in the case of comprehensive sanctions applied in a purely punitive manner, but we believe that most UN officials have moved beyond this approach to the use of more targeted and selective sanctions that are designed in large part to avoid unintended consequences. See George A. Lopez, "More Ethical Than Not: Sanctions as Surgical Tools," *Ethics and International Affairs* 13 (May 1999): 143–148.

51. Richard Garfield, *Morbidity and Mortality Among Iraqi Children from 1990 to 1998: Assessing the Impact of Economic Sanctions,* Occasional Paper Series 16:OP:3, paper commissioned by the Joan B. Kroc Institute for International Peace Studies at the University of Notre Dame and the Fourth Freedom Forum, March 1999.

52. Elizabeth Gibbons, *Sanctions in Haiti,* 61.

53. See Julia Devin and Jaleh Dashti-Gibson, "Sanctions in the Former Yugoslavia: Convoluted Goals and Complicated Consequences," in Weiss et al., eds., *Political Gain and Civilian Pain,* 149–188.

54. See, for example, Center for Economic and Social Rights, *UN Sanctioned Suffering: A Human Rights Assessment of United Nations Sanctions on Iraq,* May 1996. This is a self-published report by the Center for Economic and Social Rights in New York City.

55. Hufbauer, Schott, and Elliott, *Economic Sanctions Reconsidered,* 102.

56. United Nations Security Council, Chairs of the Sanctions Committees, "Issue Paper Concerning the Sanctions Imposed by the Security Council," 30 October 1998, par. 13.

57. See especially Thomas Schelling, "The Diplomacy of Violence," *Arms and Influence* (New Haven, Conn.: Yale University Press, 1966), 66ff.

58. Patrick Clawson, "Sanctions as Punishment, Enforcement, and Prelude to Further Action," *Ethics and International Affairs* 7 (1993): 17–38.

59. Alexander L. George, *Forceful Persuasion: Coercive Diplomacy as an Alternative to War* (Washington, D.C.: United States Institute of Peace, 1991), 11.

60. David Baldwin, "The Power of Positive Sanctions," *World Politics* 24, no. 1 (October 1971): 25.

61. Gitty M. Amini, "A Larger Role for Positive Sanctions in Cases of Compellence?" Working Paper no. 12, Center for International Relations, University of California at Los Angeles, May 1997.

62. David Cortright, ed., *The Price of Peace: Incentives and International Conflict Prevention* (Lanham, Md.: Rowman and Littlefield, 1997).

63. David Cortright, "Incentives Strategies for Preventing Conflict," in Cortright, ed., *The Price of Peace,* 277–280.

64. Gareth Evans, *Cooperating for Peace* (Sydney: Allen and Unwin, 1993), 139.

65. United Nations General Assembly, *Supplement to An Agenda for Peace,* A/RES 51/242, 26 September 1997, par. 8.

66. Robert Axelrod, *The Evolution of Cooperation* (New York: Basic Books, 1984).

3

Sanctions Against Iraq

The United Nations mission in Iraq has been by far the largest in the history of the organization. In many respects it has also been the most important, with significant implications for the future of sanctions policy. The sanctions that were imposed in response to Iraq's invasion and occupation of Kuwait (United Nations Security Council Resolution 661, 1990) were the most comprehensive economic measures ever devised by the UN. They have remained in place for more than nine years, making them the longest of the cases examined. The consequences of this prolonged economic strangulation, combined with the destruction resulting from the 1991 Gulf War, created one of the worst humanitarian crises of the decade, resulting in hundreds of thousands of premature deaths among Iraqi children. In an attempt to ameliorate this crisis, the UN mounted the largest humanitarian relief operation in its history, the oil for food program. By 1999 this program had dispensed more than $4.5 billion worth of food and medicines to the Iraqi people.

Yet for all this effort, the political results of the UN sanctions seemed meager. Resolution 661 did not achieve its original objective of forcing Iraqi withdrawal from Kuwait and gave way in January 1991 to war. Nor have sanctions succeeded in forcing full compliance with Gulf War cease-fire Resolution 687 (1991), especially its disarmament mandate for the "destruction, removal or rendering harmless" of Iraq's weapons of mass destruction.[1] For many observers this is a dismal performance, suggesting that sanctions do not work and in themselves violate human rights. Our perspective is different. We argue that in fact sanctions applied effective pressure against the Baghdad regime, leading to some Iraqi steps toward compliance and the partial fulfillment of many of the UN's objectives in Iraq. But continuing political animosities between Iraq and the West (including ongoing U.S./British bombing raids) prevented the development of a bargaining dynamic and unnecessarily prolonged both the political crisis and the agony of the Iraqi

37

TURKEY

40° 42° Hakkâri 44° Orūmiyeh 46° Diryāchch-ye 48°
Zākhū (Urmia) Oriumiyeh Mīāneh
DAHŪK Lake Urmia
Al Qāmishlī Dahūk
'Aqrah Rāyāt Mīāndowab
Al Mawşil Zanjān
Sinjār (Mosul)
Ar Raqqah 36° Tall 'Afar ARBĪL 36°
NĪNAWÁ Arbīl
Al Qayyarah Kūysanjaq
SYRIAN ARAB Makhmūr As
REPUBLIC Al Hadr Sulaymānīyah Sanandaj
Dayr az Zawr AT TA'MĪM Kirkūk Hālabjah
Bayjī Tāwūq ISLAMIC REPUBLIC OF
Tharthā Hamādān
Abū Kamāl 'Ānah ŞALĀH AD IRAN
Al Qā'im DĪN Qaşr-e Shīrīn
Al Hadīthah Sāmarrā' Khānaqīn Kermānshāh
34° Tharthā DIYĀLÁ 34° Borūjerd
Lake Ba'qūbah
Akāshāt Al Habbānīyah Īlam Khorramābād
Hīt
Ar Ramādī Baghdad
Habbānīyah Mehrān
Ar Ruţbah AL ANBĀR Lake BAGHDAD
Wādī al Ghadaf Al Fallūjah
Razzāza WĀSIT Dehlorān
Lake Karbalā' BĀBIL Shaykh Sa'd
KARBALĀ' Al Hillah Al Kūt 'Alī al Gharbī Dezfūl
32° Wādī al Ubayyiḑ Al Hayy 32°
An Najaf Ad Dīwānīyah MAYSĀN
Abū Şukhayr AL QĀDISĪYAH Qal'at Sukkar Al 'Amārah
Qaryat al Gharab DHĪ QĀR Qal'at Şālih Ahvāz
AN NAJAF An Nāşirīyah Al Qurnah
Ar'ar As Samāwah Euphrates Hawr al Hammār
As Salmān Jalībah
AL MUTHANNÁ Al Başrah
30° Makhfar al Buşayyah Umm Qaşr 30°
Al Fāw

IRAQ KUWAIT
Rafhā' Al Jahrah
○ National capital Kuwait Persian
◉ Provincial capital Gulf
○ City, town Al Ahmadī
International boundary
Provincial boundary IRAQ
Main road Hafar al Bāţin
Secondary road
Railroad
28° Major airport SAUDI ARABIA 28°

The boundaries and names shown and the designations used
on this map do not imply official endorsement or acceptance
by the United Nations.

40° 42° 44° 46° 48°

0   100   200   300 km
0   100   200 mi

Map No. 3835 Rev. 2   UNITED NATIONS
August 1996

Department of Public Information
Cartographic Section

people. The failings of sanctions were not due to the limitations of the instrument itself but to the flaws in the overall U.S./UN policy toward Iraq.[2]

The Response to Invasion

When Iraqi forces invaded and illegally occupied Kuwait on 2 August 1990, the Security Council met just eleven hours later to condemn the invasion and demand that Iraq immediately and unconditionally withdraw its forces. Opposition to Iraqi aggression was nearly universal, coming not only from the UN but the Gulf Cooperation Council, the League of Arab States, the Organization of the Islamic Conference, the European Community, and many other regional organizations and individual nations. Four days later the Security Council adopted Resolution 661 under Chapter VII of the UN Charter, imposing comprehensive, mandatory sanctions on Iraq and creating a sanctions committee to monitor implementation of the sanctions. The sanctions included a ban on all trade, an oil embargo, the suspension of international flights, an arms embargo, a freezing of Iraqi government financial assets, and a prohibition on financial transactions. Exemptions were allowed for "supplies intended strictly for medical purposes, and, in humanitarian circumstances, food stuffs."[3] Since the Security Council did not formally acknowledge the humanitarian emergency in Iraq until April 1991, food imports were also banned for the first several months.

Strong measures were quickly taken to enforce the sanctions. On 25 August 1990 the Council called upon member states to impose a sea blockade, urging action to "halt all inward and outward maritime shipping."[4] A month later the Security Council also asked member states to block all aviation links to Iraq.[5] The naval and air blockades were enforced by a substantial force led primarily by the United States, with support from Great Britain and other countries. All shipping on the Shatt-al-Arab waterway in the south of Iraq was intercepted, and all vessels approaching the Jordanian port of Aqaba were boarded and inspected. Enforcement of the oil embargo was facilitated by the cooperation of neighboring states. Pipeline shipments through Turkey and Saudi Arabia were cut off immediately after the imposition of sanctions and remained closed until the oil for food program began in late 1996. The Security Council gave permission for Jordan to import Iraqi oil, as compensation for the economic burden it was shouldering from sanctions on its principal trading partner and as a reward for its cooperation with UN efforts in Iraq. Enforcement of the trade sanctions and oil

IRAQ, Security Council Resolutions

Resolution Number	Action
661	**6 August 1990*** Imposed comprehensive, mandatory sanctions Created sanctions committee Banned all trade Imposed oil embargo and arms embargo Suspended international flights Froze Iraqi government financial assets/prohibited financial transactions
678	**29 November 1990** Authorized member states to liberate Kuwait Gave Iraq "pause of goodwill" to comply with UN demands
687	**3 April 1991** Established terms of cease-fire Established set of eight specific conditions for the lifting of sanctions
706	**15 August 1991** Authorized oil for food program Permitted sale of up to $1.6 billion in Iraqi oil over six-month period Directed that proceeds be deposited in UN escrow account to finance humanitarian imports, war reparations
712	**19 September 1991** Established basic structure for oil for food program implementation Iraq rejected Resolutions 706 and 712
778	**2 October 1992** Called on member states to transfer Iraqi oil funds from pre–Gulf crisis to UN escrow account
986	**14 April 1995** Established new formula for oil for food Permitted sale of up to $1 billion in Iraqi oil every three months Gave Baghdad primary responsibility for distribution of humanitarian goods Came into force December 1996

1111	**4 June 1997**
	Extended oil for food program
	Baghdad withheld distribution plans and oil sales
1153	**20 February 1998**
	Extended oil for food program again
	Raised oil sales to $5.25 billion every six months
	Permitted revenues to finance urgent development
	needs (electricity sector)
1284	**17 December 1999**
	Established new UN Monitoring, Verification and
	Inspection Commission (UNMOVIC)
	Outlined procedures for the completion of weapons
	verification process
	Expanded humanitarian provisions
	Declared Council's intention to suspend sanctions for
	renewable 120-day periods if Iraq cooperated with
	UNMOVIC and IAEA

* Dates indicate time of Security Council decision. In some cases actual imposition may be later. Lists for this and all subsequent case studies include sanctions-related resolutions only.

embargo benefited greatly from the cooperation of neighboring countries, especially Iran and Turkey, which were either military adversaries of Baghdad or allies of the West. Some sanctions violations inevitably occurred, through a modest traffic of overland trucks and smaller ships along the southern waterway, but Iraqi revenues from these shipments were limited and paled in comparison with previous earnings.

As the Security Council progressively tightened the sanctions, the United States and other countries began to deploy substantial military forces to the region. Various attempts to mediate the dispute and negotiate an Iraqi withdrawal failed, and pressure increased for a military solution to the crisis. Some argued that sanctions were economically effective and should have been given more time to produce political compliance. Others, particularly the U.S. and British governments, dismissed the prospects for sanctions success and pressed for prompt military action. On 29 November 1990 the Security Council adopted Resolution 678 authorizing member states to use "all necessary means" to liberate Kuwait and giving Iraq "a pause of goodwill" until 15

January 1991 to comply with UN demands.[6] On 16 January 1991, the day after the ultimatum expired, the United States and its coalition partners launched a massive air campaign, followed by an intensive ground war that drove Iraqi forces out of Kuwait and effectively achieved the UN's principal objective of reversing Baghdad's aggression.

About a month after the end of the Gulf War, on 3 April 1991 the Security Council adopted Resolution 687, establishing the terms of the cease-fire and laying out an extensive set of conditions for the lifting of sanctions. Sometimes referred to as "the mother of all resolutions," Resolution 687 was the longest and most complicated resolution ever approved by the Security Council. It contained twenty-six preambular paragraphs and thirty-four operative paragraphs. The resolution set out eight specific conditions that the Iraqi government needed to meet for sanctions to be lifted:[7]

- Recognition of Kuwait's territorial integrity and newly demarcated international borders with Kuwait
- Acceptance of a demilitarized zone with UN peacekeepers along the Iraqi-Kuwaiti border
- The monitoring and destruction of all chemical, biological, and ballistic missile weapons and acceptance of a permanent ongoing monitoring program managed by the United Nations
- The monitored elimination of nuclear weapons materials and capabilities, supervised by the International Atomic Energy Agency (IAEA)
- The return of all property stolen from Kuwait
- Acceptance of war damage liability and a compensation fund managed by the UN
- Repatriation of all Kuwaiti and third-party nationals
- A pledge not to commit or support any act of international terrorism

A week later the government of Iraq announced its acceptance of Resolution 687. Baghdad harshly criticized the resolution, however, labeling it an unjust assault on Iraqi sovereignty. Although the Iraqi government pledged to comply with the resolution, its actions told a different story and reflected a deep reluctance to actually implement the stated terms. Thus began a grueling contest of wills between Iraqi leader Saddam Hussein and Western leaders over the interpretation and implementation of Resolution 687 that has continued for more than nine years.

Most of the controversy in the confrontation between Iraq and the UN has centered on the disarmament provisions of Resolution 687. The resolution required Iraq to present within fifteen days a full declaration of all its nuclear, ballistic missile, chemical, and biological weapons materials and capabilities. More than nine years later, a full accounting of Iraq's prohibited weapons had not yet been received. The resolution established the UN Special Commission (UNSCOM), which was to carry out immediate on-site inspections and assure the dismantling of all materials, systems, and capabilities related to weapons of mass destruction. In the implementing letters Iraq agreed to grant UNSCOM "unrestricted freedom of entry and exit . . . and freedom of movement" throughout Iraq.[8] In fact, however, Iraq consistently denied access to UN monitors, interfered with inspections, and provided false and misleading disclosures. UNSCOM nonetheless succeeded over the years in locating and dismantling much of Iraq's weapons capability, but this progress came in the face of repeated Iraqi attempts to disrupt and complicate UNSCOM's work.

The Potential of Sanctions

During the December 1990 U.S. Senate debate over using force against Iraq, many prominent senators declared that war was not necessary and that sanctions, if given enough time, would be able to force Iraqi withdrawal from Kuwait. Reports at the time confirmed that sanctions were having a devastating impact on Iraq's economy. Oil exports, accounting for more than 95 percent of Iraq's foreign currency earnings and 60 percent of its GDP, dropped by more than 90 percent.[9] It was estimated that Iraq's GDP fell by nearly two-thirds in 1991. Due to these huge impacts, many believed that a continuation of sanctions, especially in combination with more creative and flexible diplomacy, might have been sufficient to achieve UN goals.

In some respects conditions in Iraq were favorable for the effective use of sanctions. The Iraq crisis produced unprecedented unanimity within the international community. Rarely before and not since has the international community been as united in condemning an act of aggression and cooperating to reverse it. This extraordinary degree of solidarity resulted in a high degree of compliance with Security Council sanctions and substantial participation in the U.S.-led military campaign against Iraq. Although the cohesion of the coalition arrayed against Iraq frayed over the years, mostly due to the severe humanitarian costs of the sanctions, enforcement of the sanctions remained remarkably effective. This substantial degree of international cooperation was a significant factor in favor of the likely success of sanctions.

Iraq's economic dependence on oil exports also made it extremely vulnerable to sanctions. The experience of the last decade has demonstrated that an effective oil embargo against Iraq is an easily manageable operation when it is enforced by major powers and backed by a broad international consensus. The oil embargo cost Iraq more than $18 billion per year in lost oil revenues, with the cumulative loss over the nine years of the sanctions reaching more than $130 billion.[10] Iraq has also been vulnerable to the effects of a well-enforced arms embargo. At the time of the invasion of Kuwait, Iraq was in the midst of a major arms-buying spree to replace its extensive losses during the Iran-Iraq War and to rebuild its military capabilities. The denial of weapons-related imports prevented the regime from strengthening its principal power base, the armed forces. From a purely economic and military perspective, therefore, Iraq was highly susceptible to sanctions pressures.

However, Iraq's rigidly autocratic political governance was a strong factor mitigating against the likely effectiveness of sanctions. Iraq has been and continues to be one of the most ruthlessly repressive and undemocratic governments on the planet. As noted in Chapter 2, past experience suggests that sanctions are more likely to succeed against regimes with some degree of democracy and political openness. In dictatorships, by contrast, sanctions are less effective, because domestic opposition groups and reform constituencies are unable to exert pressure for political change. Regime type matters significantly. In the case of Iraq, the tyrannical nature of the regime limited the prospects for a successful application of sanctions.

The success of sanctions also depended on the objectives being sought. In the prewar period the goal was to force Iraqi withdrawal from Kuwait. The evidence from past episodes suggests that sanctions almost never succeed in achieving such major objectives as reversing an act of military aggression. Given these inherent limitations, it was probably unrealistic to expect in the initial stages of the Gulf crisis that sanctions alone would have been sufficient to force a complete Iraqi withdrawal from Kuwait. Sanctions and a more flexible diplomacy might have encouraged a negotiated settlement, but it is unlikely that this would have produced the complete and unconditional withdrawal from Kuwait that resulted from military action. In the postwar phase of the conflict, the prospects for sanctions success were greater. The record of previous cases suggests that sanctions can be effective for precisely the kind of more limited goals outlined in the provisions of Resolution 687. The vast scope of the cease-fire resolution became a problem, however, for it mandated Iraqi compliance across a very broad range of requirements. An alternative approach would have been to place the different mandates in separate resolutions and thereby allow a partial easing of sanctions pressure in response to progress in each area of concern. This approach would have allowed sanctions to be combined with incentives and linked to a give-and-take bargaining process. The carrot-and-stick strategy was rejected in the Iraqi case, however, mostly at the insistence of the United States. As a result, the bargaining leverage gained through sanctions was not effectively utilized to achieve the UN's cease-fire objectives.

The Humanitarian Crisis

On 1 March 1991 Secretary-General Javier Pérez de Cuéllar dispatched Under-Secretary-General Martti Ahtisaari to Iraq and Kuwait to report on humanitarian conditions and recommend actions that the UN could take to avoid further human suffering. The report of the Ahtisaari mission described "near apocalyptic" destruction and observed that war damage had relegated Iraq to a "pre-industrial age" in which the means of modern life had been "destroyed or rendered tenuous."[11] The report stated that virtually all of Iraq's power plants, oil refineries, and water-pumping facilities had been destroyed by the war. The destruction of electrical generation capacity and pumping stations led to a virtual collapse of the water supply system. A World Health Organization (WHO)/United Nations Children's Fund (UNICEF) mission to Iraq in February 1991 found the available piped water supply in Baghdad at less than 5 percent of prewar levels.[12] Waste treatment plants also ceased to function, and raw sewage was pumped directly into the Tigris River, the main source of Iraq's drinking water. Many people were thus forced to rely on water contaminated with untreated sewage. The result was a public health crisis, leading to a major increase in infectious diseases, including cholera and typhoid. The Ahtisaari mission concluded that the people of Iraq faced "imminent catastrophe, which could include epidemic and famine."[13] The report recommended the immediate lifting of sanctions on food supplies and agricultural goods and called for the urgent provision of equipment and materials for agricultural production, sanitation systems, water supply, and health care. The report also noted the need to permit emergency oil imports and the urgency of repairing electricity generation and oil-refining capacity. It provided the basis for the Security Council's decision in Resolution 687 to lift all restrictions on food imports and to establish a "no objection" procedure in the Iraq sanctions committee for the approval of specified imports.

The Ahtisaari report was one of the first in a long series of studies that have documented the devastating impact on Iraq of war and sanctions. This book is not the place for a detailed rendering of those humanitarian impacts, which have been thoroughly documented elsewhere.[14] We offer here only a glimpse of some of the social and humanitarian impacts, to illustrate the order of magnitude and severity of the crisis.

In the aftermath of the Gulf War, unemployment and inflation skyrocketed, while economic production plummeted.[15] With market prices for food beyond the reach of most families, the government's food-rationing program became an essential source of nutrition for many Iraqis, although the ration provided less than half a person's average daily dietary requirements. Malnutrition steadily increased in Iraq and remained at alarmingly high levels for years. The percentage of underweight children rose sharply, as did rates of stunting and wasting among children.[16] Infectious diseases that had virtually disappeared in Iraq reappeared and spread widely. Poorly nourished children were especially vulnerable and suffered rising mortality rates.

By 1995 some reports from international agencies such as the Food and Agricultural Organization (FAO) reported a major increase in the death rate among children five years of age and younger.[17] The United Nations Population Fund reported an increase in maternal mortality rates from 50 per 100,000 births in 1989 to 117 per 100,000 births in 1997.[18] In 1996 UNICEF reported that 4,500 children under the age of five were dying every month in Iraq from preventable hunger and disease.[19] In March 1999 Richard Garfield of Columbia University published an independent study of mortality among Iraqi children, based on a comparative analysis and correlation of malnutrition and mortality figures. According to the Garfield report, the number of excess deaths among children under five years of age for the period August 1991 through March 1998 was at least 100,000 and most likely 227,000. Approximately three-quarters of these deaths were associated with the consequences of economic sanctions.[20]

Although the existence of a severe humanitarian crisis in Iraq is undeniable, considerable uncertainty exists about the extent of the crisis and the reliability of some of the mortality figures that have been reported.[21] A controversy developed in 1996, when the *New York Times* published an article asserting that "Iraq sanctions kill children" and the popular CBS television documentary program *60 Minutes* broadcast an episode depicting sanctions as a murderous assault on children. These news reports were based in part on a December 1995 letter to the *Lancet,* the journal of the British Medical Association, in which researchers from the FAO study team to Iraq asserted that the sanctions were responsible for the deaths of 567,000 Iraqi children.[22] Doubts about these assertions were raised by researchers at the London School of Hygiene and Tropical Medicine and by scholars in Canada. In 1997 one of the authors of the original letter to the *Lancet* published another communication to that journal casting grave doubt on the most important findings of the 1995 FAO report.[23]

Whatever the exact details, there can be no doubt that the people of Iraq have suffered grievously during the sanctions regime. The dismal picture of Iraqi social conditions was summarized in a November 1997 report to the Security Council by Secretary-General Kofi Annan:

> United Nations observers regularly report an exceptionally serious deterioration in the health infrastructure: a high infant mortality rate and high rates of morbidity and mortality in general, poor and inadequate storage conditions for supplies, an unreliable supply of electricity and backup generators, faulty or non-functioning air conditioning, defective cold storage, interrupted water supplies, broken/leaking sewage systems and non-functioning hospital waste disposal systems.[24]

Annan concluded: "One-third of children under five years of age and one-quarter of men and women under 26 years of age are malnourished."[25] A November 1998 report by the Secretary-General noted that general malnutrition rates had declined slightly but remained alarmingly high: 14.7 percent among infants and 25 percent among children under five.[26] These rates were far above the levels that prevailed prior to 1990.

Sanctions caused most of these humanitarian hardships, but other causal factors were also at work. The most important of these was the lingering impact of the massive bombing of Iraq during the Gulf War. More than 90,000 tons of explosives were dropped on Iraq and Kuwait during the Gulf War. The bombing and short-lived ground campaign resulted in the deaths of thousands of Iraqi soldiers and civilians. The peculiar nature of the bombing campaign, which targeted vital electrical, water, and sanitation systems, greatly magnified the destructive consequences of the war and increased the civilian death toll. Many of these consequences continued into 1992 and beyond, contributing significantly to humanitarian suffering. The imposition and maintenance of comprehensive sanctions compounded and exacerbated these impacts, making it extremely difficult to rebuild economic infrastructure and repair war-related damage. The combination of war and years of comprehensive sanctions magnified Iraq's misery. The result has been an appalling humanitarian tragedy.

The Oil for Food Humanitarian Program

As reports documented the overwhelming needs of the Iraqi people, it became evident that the required scale of humanitarian relief was far beyond what could be available through conventional UN programs.[27] In response, UN officials developed a plan for using Iraqi oil revenues to finance humanitarian relief. On 15 August 1991, the Security Council adopted Resolution 706, which spelled out the procedures for the proposed oil for food program. The resolution permitted the sale of up to $1.6 billion worth of Iraqi oil over a six-month period, with the proceeds to be deposited in a UN escrow account and used to finance humanitarian imports. Thirty percent of the oil revenues would be deposited in a war reparations fund, with additional sums set aside for the costs of UN operations in Iraq. Resolution 712, passed a month later, established a basic structure for the implementation of the oil for food program. The government of Iraq refused to accept Resolutions 706 and 712, however, asserting that the proposed procedures for providing humanitarian relief were a violation of Iraqi sovereignty.[28] Iraq also objected to using some of its oil revenues to finance war reparations and UN activities. Despite several rounds of negotiations in which UN officials attempted to persuade Baghdad to accept the oil for food operation, Iraqi officials remained adamant in their rejection of the program, objecting that it compromised their national independence and interfered with internal affairs.[29]

Faced with Iraq's refusal to cooperate in the provision of humanitarian aid but confronted with continuing reports of the deteriorating humanitarian situation in Iraq, the Security Council adopted Resolution 778 in October 1992, calling on all member states in which there were funds from the sale of Iraqi oil prior to the Gulf crisis to transfer those funds to the UN escrow account established under Resolutions 706 and

712. This attempt to raise humanitarian relief funds was a failure, with only two countries indicating that they held assets that could be transferred to the escrow account. Approximately $100 million was later deposited in the escrow account, but most of this came from voluntary contributions by Saudi Arabia and Kuwait and from the transfer of $50 million in frozen Iraqi assets from the United States.[30] These funds were used to implement provisions of Resolution 687 and to provide humanitarian assistance.

UN officials continued their efforts to provide relief and in April 1995 adopted Resolution 986, establishing a new formula for the oil for food program. Resolution 986 permitted the sale of up to $1 billion of Iraqi oil every three months. The resolution made a concession to Iraqi concerns about sovereignty by giving Baghdad primary responsibility for the distribution of humanitarian goods, although the UN maintained direct control over the provision of humanitarian assistance in the three predominantly Kurdish governorates in northern Iraq. Again the Iraqi government balked, but after months of negotiations Baghdad finally accepted the program in May 1996. Preparations for implementation of the operation were in their final stages in August 1996 when Iraqi military forces marched north into the Kurdish zone, an event that led to a suspension of negotiations with UN officials. Talks resumed a few weeks later, and arrangements were finally completed in November. Resolution 986 officially came into force in December 1996, and deliveries of food and medicine began a few months later.

The oil for food program was a serious attempt by the Security Council to address the needs of the Iraqi people, but the humanitarian operation was plagued from the outset by bureaucratic problems at the UN and an unwillingness in Baghdad to participate fully in implementing the program. Administrative difficulties at the UN stemmed from the sanctions committee's case-by-case review of applications for humanitarian imports and the frequent holds placed on items that could be considered dual use. Iraqi officials complained that the sanctions committee too often placed arbitrary holds on vitally needed humanitarian supplies. Even the UN's director of the Iraq program, Benon Sevan, expressed concern in a July 1999 report about the "excessive number of holds placed on supplies and equipment for water and sanitation and electricity."[31] Distribution problems also hampered the program. A February 1999 UN report noted that approximately one-half of all medicines and medical supplies imported under the program remained in warehouses and had not been distributed to local clinics and hospitals.[32]

Some observers attributed these distribution delays to a lack of equipment and transportation in Iraq, but others cited the worsening political tensions between Baghdad and the UN.

The government of Iraq was never comfortable with the oil for food program, as evidenced by its five-year delay in accepting the operation and the numerous roadblocks it placed in the way of its implementation. For the first few months of the program in 1997, Iraq cooperated with the relief operation. When the Security Council extended the program in June 1997 with Resolution 1111, however, Baghdad failed to submit the required distribution plan for humanitarian goods and withheld oil sales. From 8 June to 13 August 1997, Iraq halted oil exports. Because of this refusal to sell oil, a substantial shortfall in revenues for humanitarian relief developed, causing delays and difficulty in the purchase and delivery of supplies. The Secretary-General reported that Iraq's decision to forgo oil deliveries was the major factor in slowing the pace of aid deliveries.[33] UN officials also acknowledged the slow and cumbersome procedures of the sanctions committee and took steps in 1997 to improve the processing of contracts and the distribution of purchased goods.

In response to continuing reports of severe malnutrition and the evident inability of the oil for food program to stem the health emergency in Iraq, the Security Council adopted Resolution 1153 in February 1998, extending the program again and raising the level of authorized oil sales to $5.25 billion every six months.[34] For the first time the Council also agreed to use revenues from the program for urgent development needs, particularly in the electricity sector, where power generation stood at only 40 percent of prewar levels.[35] When Resolution 1153 was passed, Iraqi officials and independent experts pointed out that the country was incapable of pumping enough oil to meet the higher revenue target because of disrepair and a lack of spare parts in the oil industry. Low oil prices in the world market also hampered Iraq's ability to generate sufficient revenue. In response to these concerns, the Security Council adopted Resolution 1210 in November 1998, authorizing the purchase of spare parts and pumping equipment for the oil industry as part of the humanitarian relief program.

Despite the difficulties involved in its implementation, the oil for food program can be rated a partial success. An April 1999 review of the program by Secretary-General Kofi Annan observed that the program "has met its priority objective in making available basic food items and health supplies."[36] According to the review, food availability improved, water contamination rates dropped, and the "availability of life-saving drugs . . . increased."[37] According to the March 1999 experts panel report, the oil for food program "played an important role in averting major food shortages and to a considerable extent has helped to alleviate the health situation, especially in the North."[38] In the northern Kurdish governorates, where the UN rather than the government of Iraq managed the relief operation (and where a greater number of private relief organizations operate), the nutritional levels and health conditions of vulnerable populations improved considerably. But the experts report also observed that the program "has not been able to fully achieve its objectives" and even if fully implemented could "meet but a small fraction of the priority needs of the Iraqi people."[39] Annan's review also noted that the "overall health situation has not improved" and that "the magnitude of the humanitarian needs is such that they cannot be met within the parameters" of the relief operation.[40] Despite the vast scale of the oil for food program and the enormous effort UN officials have made to meet the humanitarian needs of the Iraqi people, the relief operation has not been able to overcome the humanitarian crisis resulting from war and sanctions. Nonetheless, the oil for food program helped to avert an even greater disaster and by 1999 succeeded in stabilizing humanitarian conditions and generating some slight improvement in the overall health and nutritional status of the Iraqi people.

Unacknowledged Progress

The official purpose of the continuing UN sanctions was to achieve Iraqi compliance with Resolution 687. Public attention focused primarily on the disarmament provisions of this resolution, but the other terms of the resolution were also important. The excessive focus on weapons issues distracted attention from the progress achieved in realizing many of the UN's objectives. To be sure, Baghdad did not comply fully with each provision of Resolution 687, and it frequently resisted and obstructed the UN mission in Iraq, but substantial progress did occur. Unfortunately, the failure to acknowledge and respond to Iraqi concessions undermined UN objectives.

Two of Iraq's concessions were significant. In November 1993, Baghdad accepted the creation of ongoing UN weapons monitoring facilities on Iraqi soil. Iraq formally agreed to the installation of cameras and chemical detection equipment at numerous sites and industries to verify the destruction of weapons of mass destruction and monitor any resumption of prohibited activities.[41] The equipment and personnel were installed in early 1994 and became operational by the end of that year. This was an important breakthrough that enabled UNSCOM to establish baseline data on Iraq's weapons capabilities and monitor future compliance with the weapons elimination program. The second major concession came in November 1994, when Baghdad accepted the findings of the UN Boundary Demarcation Commission and declared its irrevocable and unqualified recognition of the sovereignty of Kuwait and the redrawn international borders.[42] This decision was widely seen as an encouraging development and was described by the Security Council as "a significant step in the direction towards implementation of the relevant Security Council resolutions."[43]

In addition to inducing Iraqi concessions on weapons monitoring and border demarcation, sanctions contributed to a significant weakening of Iraq's military capabilities. Military containment was not one of the declared objectives of Resolution 687, but it is a widely shared goal among nations in the region and around the world. Sanctions were a major factor in isolating Iraq and denying it the resources to maintain and strengthen its once formidable armed forces. The loss of more than $130 billion in oil revenues and the ban on all weapons-related imports severely constrained Baghdad's ability to rebuild its war machine after the heavy losses sustained during the Gulf War. To be sure, the Iraqi government prioritized military purposes over the needs of the people in spending the resources available to it, but these limited means were not sufficient to reverse a steady erosion of military capability. According to a February 1998 report from the Center for Strategic and International Studies (CSIS) in Washington, D.C., Iraqi armed forces suffered from "decaying, obsolete, or obsolescent major weapons."[44] Because of sanctions, Iraq was unable to import weapons, spare parts, and specialized equipment. Although Baghdad pursued various weapons-smuggling efforts, these black market operations provided only "an erratic and inefficient substitute for large-scale resources," according to the CSIS report.[45] Because of sanctions, Iraq's ability to commit military aggression against its neighbors diminished.

Dismantling Weapons of Mass Destruction

Sanctions also contributed to the considerable progress achieved in the UN weapons inspection and dismantlement effort. Although Baghdad impeded UNSCOM's efforts and expelled the weapons inspectors altogether following the U.S./British bombing raids of December 1998, substantial progress was achieved toward eliminating Iraq's chemical, biological, ballistic missile, and nuclear weapons programs. U.S. secretary of state Madeleine Albright admitted as much in a Georgetown University speech in March 1997 when she called the progress reported to date "stunning."[46] The greatest successes occurred in the nuclear realm. Baghdad's uranium enrichment and other nuclear production facilities were identified and destroyed early in the inspection program. The International Atomic Energy Agency reported in 1998 that "Iraq has satisfactorily completed . . . its full, final and complete declaration of its clandestine nuclear program."[47] UNSCOM also reported that "there are no indications that any weapons-usable nuclear materials remain in Iraq" and "no evidence in Iraq of prohibited materials, equipment, or activities."[48] Although concerns remained about gaps in the information Baghdad provided and components that were unaccounted for, most observers agreed that the Iraqi nuclear threat had been effectively neutralized.[49]

Iraq's ballistic missile programs were also largely eliminated. According to UNSCOM reports, efforts to inspect and dismantle missile capabilities yielded "significant results."[50] All but two of the 819 SCUD missiles known to have existed at the start of the Gulf War were accounted for, and no evidence was uncovered of the successful development or testing of indigenous Iraqi ballistic missiles. Much of Iraq's chemical weapons capability was located and destroyed as well. According to the March 1999 report of the UN experts panel, inspectors "supervised or . . . certif[ied] the destruction, removal or rendering harmless of large quantities of chemical weapons (CW), their components and major chemical weapons production equipment. . . . The prime CW development and production complex in Iraq was dismantled and closed under UNSCOM supervision and other identified facilities have been put under monitoring."[51] UNSCOM also reported "significant progress" in this area.[52] According to a 1998 report by the British Foreign Office, UNSCOM destroyed 38,000 chemical weapons and 480,000 liters of live chemical agents.[53]

Much less headway was achieved in locating and eliminating Iraq's biological weapons threat. A panel of international experts, convened at Baghdad's request, reported in April 1998 that Iraq's disclosures on biological weapons were "incomplete, inadequate and technically flawed."[54] Even in this area, however, some progress was achieved. UNSCOM supervised the destruction of Iraq's main biological weapons production and development facility, Al Hakim, and destroyed equipment and growth media at four other facilities.[55] The March 1999 experts panel report noted that Iraq retained the capability and knowl-edge base for producing biological warfare agents "quickly and in vol-ume" but also observed that "some uncertainty is inevitable" in such a verification effort.[56] As weapons experts acknowledge, absolute assur-ances against the threat of biological weapons are impossible. Because of the dual-use character of many biological agents, verifying the pres-ence of a biological warfare capability is inherently more difficult than monitoring nuclear or ballistic missile programs. The attempt to verify the definitive destruction of all Iraqi biological weapons capabilities is a hopeless chimera, a formula for permanent confrontation.

Sanctions played a role in UNSCOM's partial success. According to former UNSCOM director Rolf Ekeus, sanctions were "very impor-tant" in pressuring Iraqi officials to accept UN weapons inspections.[57] Although it is impossible to separate the role of economic sanctions from that of military pressure and other factors influencing the Iraqi government, it is safe to say that the continuing weight of sanctions had at least some impact in pressuring Baghdad to accept some of the weapons inspections provisions of Resolution 687.

The expulsion of UNSCOM and the end of weapons inspections following the December 1998 bombing created a new dilemma for the Security Council that further delayed a resolution of the crisis. U.S. officials initially expressed concern that Iraq would take advantage of the hiatus in monitoring to rebuild its weapons of mass destruction, but intelligence reports found no evidence of a major rearmament program. According to a U.S. official quoted in the *Washington Post,* "We have seen no evidence of reconstruction of weapons of mass destruction."[58]

After the expulsion of UNSCOM, various proposals were offered by France, Great Britain, and other countries for the creation of a new weapons organization and the resumption of monitoring and dismantle-ment efforts. The major powers had difficulty agreeing on a common program, however. U.S. officials opposed any easing of sanctions pres-sure. Meanwhile, many countries, including members of the Security Council, grew weary of the seemingly endless confrontation with Iraq and, motivated by a desire to relieve human suffering and resume trade relations, called for a lifting of sanctions altogether.

Lost Bargaining Opportunities

According to the bargaining model of sanctions, the partial concessions made by Iraq and the progress achieved in disarmament would merit a partial easing of sanctions pressure. A scorecard of the eight conditions identified in Resolution 687 shows that Baghdad complied fully or in part with seven out of eight Security Council demands. This is reflected in Table 3.1.

Within the two categories related to weapons dismantlement, three out of the four objectives were met. The most dangerous programs,

Table 3.1   Scorecard of Iraqi Compliance with Resolution 687

Conditions of Resolution 687	Compliance Status	Comments
Recognition of Kuwaiti territorial integrity and newly demarcated border	Yes	November 1994 recognition of Kuwaiti sovereignty and borders
Acceptance of demilitarized zone	Yes	Established soon after end of Gulf War
Ongoing monitoring and dismantlement of ballistic missile, chemical, and biological weapons of mass destruction	Partly yes	Acceptance of permanent monitoring in November 1993; much progress by UNSCOM on ballistic missiles and chemical weapons; unanswered questions remain on biological capabilities and other issues
Elimination of nuclear weapons capabilities	Yes	IAEA certifies that no nuclear weapons capabilities remain
Return of stolen property	Partly yes	Some state property returned; military equipment and private assets stolen
Acceptance of war damage liability	Partly yes	No formal admission of responsibility, but acceptance of Resolution 986 provides for compensation fund, which has paid war damages
Repatriation of missing persons	Partly yes	Many prisoners returned, but several hundred Kuwaitis remain missing
Renunciation of terrorism	No	No formal pledge, but no evidence of actual Iraqi support for international terrorist acts

Source: Based on Eric Hoskins, "The Humanitarian Impact of Economic Sanctions and War in Iraq," in Thomas G. Weiss, David Cortright, George A. Lopez, and Larry Minear, eds., *Political Gain and Civilian Pain: Humanitarian Impacts of Economic Sanctions* (Lanham, Md.: Rowman and Littlefield, 1997).

nuclear weapons and ballistic missiles, were effectively contained. In recognition of this progress, a number of member countries on the Security Council favored a formal certification of Iraqi compliance and a closing of the nuclear, ballistic missile, and chemical weapons inspections files. Russia and other countries urged the gradual lifting of sanctions pressure in response to the progress achieved on weapons inspection as a means of encouraging further Iraqi cooperation.

Proposals for reciprocating Iraq's partial compliance with an easing of sanctions pressure fit within the framework of the bargaining model of sanctions. The theory and practice of coercive diplomacy emphasize the importance of reciprocating concessions. An easing of economic pressure in response to partial compliance can produce further concessions. In part, this is a recognition of the limits of what sanctions realistically can be expected to accomplish. It is also an essential step in encouraging dialogue and negotiation. As emphasized in Chapter 2, sanctions work best in combination with incentives and other forms of external influence as part of a carrot-and-stick diplomacy designed to resolve conflict through negotiation. In the Iraqi case, however, sanctions were used almost exclusively in a punitive manner. There was no reciprocation of Baghdad's concessions and thus no incentive for the Iraqi government to take further steps toward compliance.

The Security Council's refusal to reciprocate Iraqi concessions resulted primarily from the unyielding position of the United States. In effect, the Security Council was held hostage by Washington's belligerent and unyielding posture toward Baghdad, which included not only unrelenting sanctions pressure but frequent military attacks and, beginning in December 1998, ongoing bombing raids against Iraqi targets. For the United States the purpose of the continuing confrontation with Iraq was no longer (or perhaps was never merely) to enforce Resolution 687. The political goalposts were moved. Resolution 687 states explicitly that the ban on Iraqi exports will be lifted when Iraq complies with UN weapons inspections, but Secretary of State Albright declared in March 1997 that the United States does not accept this view.[59] The larger objective became the permanent containment of the regime of Saddam Hussein, which was implicit in the many statements from U.S. officials that the sanctions would not be lifted while Saddam Hussein remained in office. In November 1997 President Bill Clinton remarked that "sanctions will be there until the end of time, or as long as [Hussein] lasts."[60] Although many UN member states strongly disagree with this approach, they have been unable to prevent the United States from using its position on the Security Council to block an easing of sanctions pressure.

Under these conditions, sanctions lost the bargaining leverage so crucial to their effectiveness. If Baghdad's conciliatory gestures had been reciprocated earlier, a different political dynamic might have evolved between the United Nations and Iraq. Instead, political hostilities and distrust persisted and, with the ongoing bombing raids in 1999, deepened. With no hope or expectation of possible conciliation, Baghdad relied instead on strategies of obstruction and confrontation, attempting to wear down UN resolve and widen the growing political differences within the Security Council. The result was a steady weakening of the political commitment to continued sanctions within the Security Council, especially among China, Russia, and France, with even Great Britain at times distancing itself from the U.S. position. The Council became deadlocked, unable to agree on a plan for resolving the current impasse and equally unable to ease sanctions pressures or end the sanctions-related suffering of the Iraqi people.

The Search for an Endgame

Despite more than nine years of comprehensive sanctions, the United Nations has been unable to complete its mission in Iraq. Through 1999 Iraq and the UN remained far apart on finding a solution to the crisis. Within the international community and among nongovernmental organizations (NGOs), a palpable sense of "sanctions fatigue" has set in, generating a political backlash not only against the policy in Iraq but against sanctions in general. Because of the Iraqi ordeal, the United Nations has become wary of imposing general trade sanctions, and concerns about humanitarian consequences have become paramount. The trend toward more targeted and selected sanctions identified in Chapter 12 emerged in very large part as a result of the Iraqi experience.

Several major attempts were made in 1999 to find a solution to the impasse in Iraq. In January France proposed lifting the oil embargo and UN financial controls in exchange for the development of a new, less intrusive weapons inspection program.[61] U.S. and British opposition to lifting the oil embargo scuttled the French proposal. Also in January, acting on a proposal from the Canadian government, the Security Council established three expert panels to explore options for resolving the most critical outstanding issues: weapons inspections, humanitarian

needs, and missing persons and property. The panels reported their recommendations in March, but the Security Council was unable to agree
on a formula for implementing any of the various recommendations.[62]

In June 1999, Great Britain and the Netherlands circulated a draft
resolution that called for lifting the ban on Iraqi exports, in exchange
for Iraqi acceptance of a new weapons inspection and monitoring
agency. The proposal was similar to the earlier French plan, except that
the British-Dutch proposal called for maintaining strict financial controls on Iraqi oil revenues. Russia and China drafted an alternative proposal, backed by France, that called for ending all sanctions and the creation of a less intrusive weapons monitoring system. Iraq declared that
it would refuse to accept the British-Dutch proposal, and the United
States signaled its opposition to the Russian-Chinese plan.

In December 1999 the Council attempted to break the impasse
when it approved a new weapons inspection system and offered to suspend all nonmilitary sanctions if Baghdad accepted the return of
weapons inspectors. Security Council Resolution (SCR) 1284 (1999)
established a new UN Monitoring, Verification and Inspection
Commission (UNMOVIC) to replace UNSCOM and outlined procedures for the completion of the weapons verification process.[63]
Resolution 1284 also removed the ceiling on the volume of Iraqi oil
exports for humanitarian purchases, eased some of the restrictions on
medical and agricultural imports, and exempted Hajj pilgrimage flights.
The Council declared its intention to suspend sanctions for renewable
periods of 120 days if Iraq cooperated with UNMOVIC and the IAEA.
If Iraq did not cooperate or was found importing prohibited military
goods, the suspension would automatically cease.

When the final vote on SCR 1284 came, after weeks of delicate negotiations, four members of the Security Council abstained, including
France, Russia, and China. Only two of the permanent five, the United
States and Great Britain, voted for the resolution, a fact that some analysts
believed would embolden Iraqi resistance to the plan.[64] Indeed, when
Resolution 1284 was adopted, Iraq immediately rejected the resolution,
reiterating its previous refusal to permit the return of UN inspectors and
demanding a complete lifting of sanctions. The prospects for an end to the
Iraq standoff thus remained uncertain as the decade came to a close.

Notes

    1. United Nations, *Security Council Resolution 687,* S/RES/687 (1991), 3
April 1991, par. 13.

2. David Cortright and George A. Lopez, "Are Sanctions Just? The Problematic Case of Iraq," *Journal of International Affairs* 52, no. 2 (Spring 1999): 735–755; and George A. Lopez and David Cortright, "Trouble in the Gulf, Pain and Promise," *Bulletin of the Atomic Scientists* 54, no. 3 (May–June 1998): 39–43.

3. United Nations, *Security Council Resolution 661*, S/RES/661 (1990), 6 August 1990, par. 3, c.

4. United Nations, *Security Council Resolution 665*, S/RES/665 (1990), 25 August 1990, par. 1.

5. United Nations, *Security Council Resolution 670*, S/RES/670 (1990), 25 September 1990.

6. United Nations, *Security Council Resolution 678*, S/RES/678 (1990), 29 November 1990, par. 1.

7. United Nations, *Security Council Resolution 687*, S/RES/687 (1991), 8 April 1991.

8. United Nations, *The United Nations and the Iraq-Kuwait Conflict 1990–1996*, United Nations Blue Book Series, vol. 9 (New York: United Nations Department of Public Information, 1996), 77.

9. William H. Webster, "Iraq: The Domestic Impact of Sanctions," testimony of the director of the Central Intelligence Agency before the House Armed Services Committee, 5 December 1990, reprinted in *Congressional Record*, 10 January 1991, S123–24.

10. Milton Leitenberg, interview by author, 12 December 1997. Leitenberg based his estimates on figures for lost oil revenues used by former UNSCOM Director Rolf Ekeus. See also Richard Haass, "Time to Revisit Sanctions," *Financial Times*, 12 January 1998, p. 14. Haass has estimated Iraq's lost oil revenues at $100 billion.

11. United Nations Security Council, *Report to the Secretary-General on Humanitarian Needs in Kuwait and Iraq in the Immediate Post-Crisis Environment by a Mission to the Area Led by Mr. Martti Ahtisaari, Under Secretary-General for Administration and Management, 10–17 March 1991*, S/22366, 20 March 1991, par. 8.

12. World Health Organization and United Nations Children's Fund, *Joint WHO/UNICEF Team Report: A Visit to Iraq* (New York: WHO and UNICEF, 16–21 February 1991).

13. United Nations Security Council, *Report to the Secretary-General on Humanitarian Needs in Kuwait and Iraq*, par. 37.

14. One of the most comprehensive recent studies is Richard Garfield, *Morbidity and Mortality Among Iraqi Children from 1990 to 1998: Assessing the Impact of Economic Sanctions*, Occasional Paper Series 16:OP:3, paper commissioned by the Joan B. Kroc Institute for International Peace Studies, University of Notre Dame and the Fourth Freedom Forum, March 1999, available at http://www.fourthfreedom.org/sanctions/garfield.html.

15. Eric Hoskins, "The Humanitarian Impact of Economic Sanctions and War in Iraq," in Thomas G. Weiss, David Cortright, George A. Lopez, and Larry Minear, eds., *Political Gain and Civilian Pain: Humanitarian Impacts of Economic Sanctions* (Lanham, Md.: Rowman and Littlefield, 1997), 91–147.

16. Food and Agricultural Organization, *Evaluation of Food and Nutrition Situation in Iraq* (Rome: FAO, 1995).

17. Ibid.

18. As reported in United Nations Security Council, *Letters Dated 27 and 30 March 1999, Respectively, from the Chairman of the Panels Established Pursuant to the Note by the President of the Security Council of 30 January 1999,*

S/1999/100, Addressed to the President of the Security Council, S/1999/356, 30 March 1999, 35.

19. UNICEF press release, "Disastrous Situation of Children in Iraq," United Nations, New York, 4 October 1996.

20. Garfield, *Morbidity and Mortality Among Iraqi Children,* 1, 42, 43.

21. Lopez and Cortright, "Trouble in the Gulf."

22. Sarah Zaidi and Mary C. Smith-Fawzi, "Health of Baghdad's Children," *Lancet* 346, no. 8988 (2 December 1995): 1485.

23. For references on these sources and our commentary on the controversy, see our foreword to Richard Garfield's study on *Morbidity and Mortality Among Iraqi Children.*

24. United Nations Security Council, *Report of the Secretary-General Pursuant to Paragraph 3 of Resolution 1111 (1997)* 28 November 1997, S/1997/935, par. 72.

25. Ibid., par. 81.

26. United Nations Security Council, *Report of the Secretary-General Pursuant to Paragraph 10 of Security Council Resolution 1153 (1998),* S/1998/1100, 19 November 1998, par. 29.

27. United Nations, *Report to the Secretary-General Dated 15 July 1991 on Humanitarian Needs in Iraq, Prepared by a Mission Led by the Executive Delegate of the Secretary-General for Humanitarian Assistance in Iraq,* S-22799, 17 July 1991.

28. United Nations, *The United Nations and the Iraq-Kuwait Conflict,* 100.

29. Ibid., 101.

30. Ibid.

31. United Nations Office of the Iraq Programme, *Briefing by Benon Sevan, Executive Director of the Iraq Programme, at the Informal Consultation Held by the Security Council on Thursday, 22 July 1999,* 3.

32. United Nations Security Council, *Report of the Secretary-General Pursuant to Paragraph 6 of Security Council Resolution 1210 (1998),* S/1999/187, 22 February 1999, par. 30.

33. United Nations Security Council, *Report of the Secretary-General Pursuant to Paragraph 7 of Resolution 1143 (1997),* S/1998/90, 1 February 1998, 5.

34. See *Special Report: FAO/WFP Food Supply and Nutrition Assessment Mission to Iraq,* (Rome: FAO, 3 October 1997).

35. United Nations, *Report of the Secretary-General,* S/1998/90, 6.

36. United Nations Security Council, *Review and Assessment of the Implementation of the Humanitarian Programme Established Pursuant to Security Council Resolution 986 (1995) December 1996–November 1998,* S/1999/481, 28 April 1999, par. 53.

37. Ibid.

38. United Nations Security Council, *Letters Dated 27 and 30 March 1999,* S/1999/356, 39.

39. Ibid., 45.

40. United Nations, *Review and Assessment,* S/1999/481, pars. 80 and 116.

41. United Nations, *The United Nations and the Iraq-Kuwait Conflict,* 95–96.

42. Ibid., 54–55.

43. Ibid.

44. Anthony H. Cordesman, "The Iraq Crisis: Background Data" (Washington, D.C.: Center for Strategic and International Studies, 1998), 15.

45. Ibid., 17.

46. Madeleine K. Albright, "Preserving Principle and Safeguarding Stability: United States Policy Toward Iraq," speech at Georgetown University, Washington, D.C., 26 March 1997.

47. United Nations Security Council, *Letter Dated 9 April 1998 from the Secretary-General Addressed to the President of the Security Council, appendix: Fifth Consolidated Report of the Director General of the International Atomic Energy Agency Under Paragraph Sixteen of Security Resolution 1051 (1996),* S/1998/312, United Nations, New York, 11.

48. United Nations Security Council, *Letter Dated 22 November 1997 from the Executive Chairman of the Special Commission Established by the Secretary-General Pursuant to Paragraph Nine (b)(i) of Security Council Resolution 687 (1991) Addressed to the President of the Security Council,* S/1997/922, 24 November 1997, 3.

49. Steven Dolley, "Iraq and the Bomb: The Nuclear Threat Continues" (Washington, D.C.: Nuclear Control Institute, 19 February 1998).

50. United Nations Security Council, *Report of the Executive Chairman on the Activities of the Special Commission Established by the Secretary-General Pursuant to Paragraph 9(b)(i) of Resolution 687 (1991),* S/1998/332, 16 April 1998, 10.

51. United Nations Security Council, *Letters Dated 27 and 30 March 1999,* S/1999/356, 10.

52. United Nations Security Council, *Letter Dated 22 November 1997,* S/1997/922, 4.

53. British Foreign Office, "Foreign Office Paper on Iraqi Threat and Work of UNSCOM," London, 4 February 1998.

54. United Nations Security Council, *Report of the Executive Chairman of the Special Commission,* S/1998/332, 17; see also United Nations, *Report of the United Nations Special Commission Team to the Technical Evaluation Meeting on the Proscribed Biological Warfare Programme,* S/1998/308, 8 April 1998.

55. United Nations, *Letters Dated 27 and 30 March 1999,* S/1999/356, 12.

56. Ibid., 12–13.

57. Rolf Ekeus, speech given at the Carnegie Endowment for International Peace, Conference on Nuclear Nonproliferation and the Millennium: Prospects and Initiatives, Washington, D.C., 13 February 1996.

58. Karen de Young, "Baghdad Weapons Programs Dormant; Iraq's Inactivity Puzzles U.S. Officials," *Washington Post,* 15 July 1999.

59. Albright, "Preserving Principle and Safeguarding Stability."

60. Barbara Crossette, "For Iraq: A Doghouse with Many Rooms," *New York Times,* 23 November 1997, A4.

61. Barbara Crossette, "France, in Break with U.S., Urges End to Iraqi Embargo," *New York Times,* 14 January 1999.

62. United Nations, *Letters Dated 27 and 30 March 1999,* S/1999/356.

63. United Nations, *Security Council Resolution 1284,* S/RES/1284 (1999), 17 December 1999.

64. Barbara Crossette, "Divided UN Council Approves New Iraqi Arms Inspection Plan," *New York Times,* 18 December 1999, A1.

4

Sanctioning Yugoslavia

The United Nations Security Council imposed sanctions against the Federal Republic of Yugoslavia three times during the 1990s: an arms embargo in September 1991 in response to the war between Serbia and Croatia; comprehensive economic sanctions in May 1992 during the war in Bosnia-Herzegovina; and an arms embargo in March 1998 in response to the Kosovo crisis. The sanctions during the Bosnian war were by far the most important. The episode that took place between 1992 and 1995 featured unprecedented international cooperation in sanctions monitoring and enforcement. Along with the Iraq embargo, the Yugoslavia sanctions were the most effectively implemented in history. Also like those in Iraq, they had devastating impacts on the target's economy and society. The Yugoslavia sanctions had a significant impact on the bargaining process that led to the Dayton peace accord, helping to convince Slobodan Milosevic and the rest of the Serbian leadership to abandon their war aims and accept a negotiated peace. By contrast, the arms embargo during the Kosovo crisis was halfhearted at best, and no effort was made to impose stronger sanctions.

In this chapter, we examine the sanctions of 1992 through 1995 in depth, highlighting the innovations in sanctions enforcement that were introduced during this case. We review the economic and social impacts of the sanctions, and assess their political effectiveness. We conclude the chapter with a review of the limited arms embargo during the Kosovo crisis and a consideration of whether the lessons learned during the Bosnian war could have been applied to the conflict in Kosovo.

The Arms Embargo: Unequal Effects

In September 1991, as fighting between Serbia and Croatia intensified, the Security Council adopted Resolution 713, imposing an arms embar-

THE FORMER YUGOSLAVIA

Legend:
- International boundary
- Republic boundary
- Autonomous province boundary
- ⊚ National capital
- ◉ Administrative capital
- Railroad
- Principal road
- Secondary road

0   50   100   150 km
0   50   100   150 mi

Department of Public Information
Cartographic Section

The boundaries and names shown and the designations used on this map do not imply official endorsement or acceptance by the United Nations.

THE FORMER YUGOSLAVIA

go on Yugoslavia. The resolution called for an immediate cease-fire and gave full support to ongoing efforts by the European Community (EC) and the Conference on Security and Cooperation in Europe (CSCE) to negotiate an end to the war in Croatia.[1] The Security Council embargo reinforced action already taken by the United States and the EC in July 1991 to suspend all arms sales and transfers to Yugoslavia. As in the case of other arms embargoes adopted by the Security Council, Resolution 713 did not restrain the escalating levels of armed conflict in the region. It had no discernible effect on the political dynamics of the worsening Yugoslav crisis. The resolution was passed in part as an attempt to do something in the face of demands for action and in part as a signal of stronger measures to come if the contending parties did not negotiate a settlement. As the fighting continued into the fall, the Security Council adopted Resolution 724 in December 1991, creating a sanctions committee with a mandate to ensure implementation of the embargo. This same sanctions committee continued during the much more comprehensive measures to follow. The European Community and the United States began to impose broader economic sanctions against Serbia. The arms embargo remained in place as tensions in Bosnia heated up and continued in force throughout the war. It was not lifted until after the signing of the Dayton peace accord in November 1995.

The arms embargo of 1991 through 1995 was criticized for con- tributing to political and military chaos in Yugoslavia and inadvertently conferring a military advantage to Serbian forces.[2] The embargo applied to all parties, regardless of their responsibility for the conflict, and had the effect of preserving a balance of military power that significantly favored the Serbs. When Yugoslavia began to break up, Serbia retained effective control of the vast resources of the Yugoslav People's Army (YPA), which was one of the best equipped armed forces in Europe, even exporting $2 billion worth of weapons in 1990.[3] A study from the Stockholm International Peace Research Institute (SIPRI) estimated that the forces of the government of Bosnia-Herzegovina were out- gunned nine-to-one by Serbian units.[4] The arms embargo tended to lock in place this imbalance and impeded the ability of the emerging Bosnian state to defend itself. Many voices in the United States and Europe called for exempting Bosnia from the arms embargo. Islamic states mounted a substantial weapons supply effort for the beleaguered Bosnian forces in violation of the UN embargo. The Security Council did not respond to the calls for lifting the arms embargo on Bosnia, but it quietly looked the other way as prohibited arms flowed into Bosnia.

YUGOSLAVIA, Security Council Resolutions

Resolution Number	Action
713	**25 September 1991** Imposed arms embargo on Yugoslavia Called for immediate cease-fire Gave full support to EC and CSCE efforts to negotiate end to war in Croatia
724	**15 December 1991** Created sanctions committee
757	**30 May 1992** Imposed sanctions Banned all international trade with Yugoslavia Prohibited air travel Blocked financial transactions Banned sports and cultural exchanges Suspended scientific and technical cooperation Allowed transshipment of goods through Yugoslavia Exempted humanitarian goods
787	**15 November 1992** Prohibited transshipment of strategic goods through Yugoslavia Halted all maritime shipping on Danube River
820	**17 April 1993** Froze Yugoslav government financial assets Prohibited the transit through any country of vessels owned by or registered in Yugoslavia Further limited the transshipment of goods through Yugoslavia
942	**23 September 1994** Extended full range of sanctions to Bosnian Serb–controlled territory
943	**23 September 1994** Eased some restrictions on Serbia Suspended sanctions on air and ferry service between Montenegro and Italy Suspended ban on sporting and cultural events
1160	**31 March 1998** Imposed arms embargo on Yugoslavia Established new sanctions committee to monitor member state compliance

Bargaining Leverage

When war broke out in Bosnia, the Security Council imposed comprehensive trade sanctions on the Federal Republic of Yugoslavia (Serbia and Montenegro). On 15 May 1992, the Security Council adopted Resolution 752 demanding that all parties end military hostilities and cease interference in each other's affairs and that units of the YPA be withdrawn. Two weeks later on 30 May 1992, the Council adopted Resolution 757 imposing sanctions. It banned all international trade with Yugoslavia, prohibited air travel, blocked financial transactions, banned sports and cultural exchanges, and suspended scientific and technical cooperation. The resolution did not prohibit the transshipment of goods through Yugoslavia, and it exempted humanitarian goods, including medicines and foodstuffs.

As the conflict worsened and evidence of the porosity of the sanctions mounted, the Security Council took action to strengthen the restrictions on Serbia and Montenegro. On 15 November 1992, the Council adopted Resolution 787 to prohibit the transshipment through Yugoslavia of designated strategic goods. The resolution called upon states to halt all inward and outward maritime shipping on the Danube River. A few months later, in response to continuing atrocities and military violence, the Security Council took further steps to strengthen the sanctions and to increase pressure on the Bosnian Serbs. On 17 April 1993 the Council approved Resolution 820, which froze Yugoslav government financial assets, prohibited the transit through any country of vessels owned by or registered in Yugoslavia, and strictly limited the transshipment of goods through Yugoslavia. Implementation of the sanctions was delayed nine days to give the Bosnian Serb authorities time to sign the Vance-Owen plan. Although Slobodan Milosevic endorsed the Vance-Owen plan and spoke on its behalf, the Bosnian Serb assembly voted it down at Jahorina in early May. The stronger sanctions of Resolution 820 were implemented as scheduled and remained in force until the signing of the Dayton peace accord in November 1995.

The Security Council made one more important adjustment in the sanctions regime in September 1994. The actual change in the structure of the sanctions was slight, but its implications for the bargaining process with Serbia were great. In September 1994 the Security Council voted to ease some restrictions on Serbia while extending the full range of sanctions to the territory controlled by Bosnian Serbs. These simultaneous actions (Resolutions 942 and 943) were a reward for Milosevic's agreement to cut off support for the Bosnian Serbs and a tightening of pressure on Republika Srpska for its refusal to accept the Contact Group peace plan. Serbia announced its break with the Bosnian Serbs in August 1994 and invited a monitoring mission of 135 UN observers to verify compliance with the blockade. This was a significant shift in Belgrade's position, although its importance was more symbolic than real. Serbia's decision did not stem the flow of support to the Bosnian Serbs nor impede their war-making abilities.[5] But it was another diplomatic blow against the authorities in Pale and further alienated them from their uncertain patron in Belgrade. Milosevic's blockade was a more serious step than the May 1993 attempt to win Bosnian Serb support for the Vance-Owen plan, and it signified a deepening determination to secure a peace agreement regardless of Bosnian Serb concerns.

The official UN report on sanctions in Yugoslavia described these events of September 1994 as "the turning point."[6] Milosevic's actions "signaled the effectiveness of the United Nations sanctions," according to the UN report, and "contributed to the decision of the government in Belgrade to sever links with the Bosnian Serb party."[7] Evidence from the memoirs of the principal Western negotiators confirmed that sanctions provided crucial leverage over Serbian leaders. According to former U.S. ambassador Warren Zimmerman, Milosevic strongly backed the 1994 Contact Group plan in order to get the sanctions lifted from Serbia.[8] Chief U.S. negotiator Richard Holbrooke put it this way: "Milosevic hated the sanctions . . . and he wanted them lifted. This gave us a potential lever over him."[9] The desire to lift sanctions was a driving force of Serb diplomacy. The Security Council's decision to reciprocate Serbia's blockade of the Bosnian Serbs was an acknowledgment of that force and an encouragement of further steps toward compliance with UN demands. Although some knowledgeable experts question the utility of sanctions in the Bosnian peace process, the diplomatic record shows that sanctions were a central element in the bargaining process that eventually led to the Dayton peace accord. We review the debate over the impact of these sanctions and further examine the memoirs of the negotiators below.

The SAMs Experience

One of the most important features of the Yugoslavia sanctions was the introduction of an elaborate, multinational monitoring and enforcement system. A network of sanctions assistance missions (SAMs) was organized by the CSCE and the European Community. The SAMs system represented a significant innovation in the implementation of UN Security Council sanctions, and the lessons learned from this experience have relevance to future sanctions regimes.

Soon after sanctions were imposed, the CSCE and the EC formed a Sanctions Liaison Group to provide technical assistance for sanctions implementation, concentrating on the states immediately surrounding Yugoslavia. In October 1992 customs officials were dispatched to Bulgaria, Hungary, and Romania to form the first SAMs. SAMs were also established in Albania, Croatia, the Former Yugoslav Republic of Macedonia (FYROM), and Ukraine. The European Commission established a Sanctions Assistance Missions Communications Center (SAM-COMM) at its headquarters in Brussels and created the post of sanctions coordinator. By March 1995, the SAMCOMM staff had grown to twenty-six people.[10] SAMCOMM developed a computerized satellite communications system linking its headquarters in Brussels with the UN sanctions committee in New York. This system, made available and maintained by the United States, enabled customs officers in the field to verify shipping documents and prevent the use of forged or falsified documents.[11] These measures established a substantial institutional capacity for monitoring and enforcing sanctions. For the first time in history, major regional organizations stepped in to assist the United Nations in providing staff and financial resources for the implementation of UN sanctions.

Other European institutions also contributed to the enforcement of sanctions. In April 1993, the Western European Union (WEU) established a Danube Patrol Mission of eight patrol boats staffed with customs and police officers to inspect riparian traffic. The North Atlantic Treaty Organization (NATO) also joined the effort, teaming with WEU in June 1993 to establish a combined naval task force in the Adriatic Sea. Fourteen nations provided ships, crews, and resources to the Sharp Guard operation, which was responsible for checking all vessels entering or leaving the Adriatic and diverting ships to Italian harbors when necessary to inspect cargoes and documents.[12] According to a U.S. State Department report, this international naval force "prevented large merchant vessels from calling at Bar—Serbia's only significant port" and had a significant impact on trade.[13]

The contributions of the CSCE, EC, WEU, and NATO made the Yugoslavia sanctions among the most effective in history. The Iraq sanctions were also well enforced, but the burden of policing those restrictions fell predominantly on the United States. In the Yugoslavia case, major regional organizations participated collectively to enforce the sanctions. According to the official UN report, "this unique and unprecedented formula of coordinated interinstitutional cooperation at the regional level . . . was identified as the main reason for the effectiveness of the sanctions in the case of the former Yugoslavia."[14] The U.S. State Department report concluded that "the presence of monitors bolsters frontline state enforcement by exerting pressure on the host government and its police, customs, and military to minimalize violations."[15] International monitors also help frontline states by providing training, equipment, and technical coordination. The main lesson of the Yugoslavia experience, according to the UN report, was that "adequate arrangements for international cooperation and assistance can enhance sanctions effectiveness."[16] The requisite resources for establishing such arrangements, however, are likely to be available only in cases where the interests of the wealthiest states are at stake. In Africa, where Western efforts to resolve conflict have been minimal, such monitoring mechanisms have been nonexistent. In the cases of Liberia and Sierra Leone, for example, the Economic Community of West African States (ECOWAS) imposed sanctions and attempted to establish a regional monitoring system, but a lack of resources and the absence of assistance from the United States and Europe undermined the effectiveness of these efforts. If the SAMs system is to have relevance beyond Europe, a system for sharing resources and technical capacity will be necessary.

The Work of the Sanctions Committee

The SAMs system and other enforcement efforts effectively blocked most riparian and seagoing commerce with Yugoslavia. They also reduced road and rail traffic, especially at major crossing points. Despite these efforts, however, a great deal of unauthorized trade took place. A major concern was the flow of truck and rail traffic from FYROM. As the Danube Patrol and SAMs system closed off supply routes in the north, illegal shipments shifted increasingly southward to the Macedonian border.[17] According to the report of the sanctions committee, "the situation noticeably deteriorated in 1994," with illegal shipments crossing the border in both directions.[18] The committee documented more than 300 companies in FYROM involved in sanctions violations.[19] Chief European negotiator David Owen cited figures of more than 1,000 trucks and hundreds of railway cars going each direction every week across the Macedonian border in the summer of 1994. Labeling this "an intolerable situation," Owen called for sealing the border with Macedonia and providing generous financial support to FYROM through Article 50 to compensate for the economic losses that would result.[20]

Another major concern was the shipment of oil to Serbia. According to the SIPRI report, Greece, Romania, and Russia were involved in delivering fuel to Serbia.[21] One of the biggest problems was the supply of oil from the UN-protected area of eastern Slavonia in Croatia to Serbia. The sanctions committee tabulated fifty-five reports from the UN Protection Force (UNPROFOR) of illegal tanker truck crossings into Serbia.[22] David Owen reported that twelve oil wells were operating in eastern Slavonia, producing 300 to 400 tons per day, most of it shipped via a pipeline under the Danube to Serbia.[23] Halting this flow of oil would have required military action, but UNPROFOR, with its limited rules of engagement, was not capable of such a task, and no action was taken.

Enforcement of the UN financial sanctions was uneven. The United States and Great Britain imposed financial sanctions on both individual Serbian leaders and government-controlled entities, but the financial sanctions imposed by the Security Council were more limited. The UN restrictions applied only to government assets and did not target the personal accounts of Milosevic and other Serbian political leaders and militia commanders. Nor is there evidence that the sanctions committee produced a list of Serbian designated entities whose assets were to be frozen. Serbian authorities reportedly avoided much of the impact of the freeze on Yugoslav financial assets by shifting funds to Cyprus and other unregulated banking centers. As a former banking official, Milosevic was adroit at creating front companies and moving assets to safer locations. The sanctions committee was aware of these maneuvers and urged Cypriot authorities to cooperate with sanctions enforcement, but it had no power to investigate or take enforcement action.[24]

Although Serbian authorities no doubt sheltered many of their bank accounts, the assets freeze nonetheless seriously depleted Yugoslavia's financial reserves. The United States, Great Britain, and other countries acted quickly and decisively in imposing sanctions and freezing Yugoslav assets. The total amount of overseas Yugoslav financial assets frozen during the Bosnian war has been estimated at approximately $2.8 billion. According to U.S. estimates, this left Milosevic with less than $1 billion available in hard currency. A Belgrade newspaper put the figure for remaining assets at only $268 million.[25] The economic impact of the assets freeze was significant and over time contributed to the mounting economic pressure on the Belgrade government.

As the functioning of the SAMs system improved, European officials and neighboring states were able to crack down on smuggling operations. Bulgarian officials disrupted a large-scale fuel-smuggling operation at the Kalotina border crossing in December 1993. Authorities in Romania were especially vigorous in blocking potential shipments on the Danube, seizing some 1,200 vessels involved in smuggling operations.[26] With the participation of the riparian states and technical assistance from European regional organizations, illegal shipments on the Danube "virtually ceased."[27]

A major priority for the sanctions committee was processing applications from member states and international humanitarian organizations for exports of foodstuffs, medicines, and essential humanitarian goods. The committee received approximately 140,000 applications for the shipment of exempted goods.[28] With its very limited staff resources, the committee was overwhelmed by the huge volume of applications. In 1994 and early 1995 complaints about the increasing backlog mounted. The committee took a number of steps to simplify the review process. In February 1995, the committee decided that applications from recognized international humanitarian agencies would be processed on a priority basis.[29] It also established a standardized list of humanitarian items that would be approved automatically on a no objection basis. Blanket exemptions were granted to humanitarian requests from the International Committee for the Red Cross (ICRC) and the United Nations High Commissioner for Refugees (UNHCR).[30] As a result, the backlog of exemption applications disappeared. Although the expedited review process did not always work smoothly in practice, the system was a considerable improvement over previous arrangements.

These improvements in the functioning of the sanctions committee were another important innovation in the Yugoslavia sanctions experience. The precedent of providing institution-specific exemptions to major UN humanitarian organizations was significant. So was the practice of providing automatic approval for designated humanitarian items. The Yugoslavia case demonstrated that the humanitarian exemptions process can be streamlined and that doing so is fully consistent with an effective monitoring and enforcement system against prohibited commerce.

Economic Devastation

Yugoslavia's economy was already in a steep decline when economic sanctions were imposed. Susan Woodward and other analysts have argued that the debt crisis and economic downturn that began in the late 1970s and continued into the 1980s were responsible for the country's dissolution and descent into ethnic violence. By the time trade sanctions were enacted in May 1992, Yugoslavia was experiencing severe economic dislocation. The causes of the economic crisis were many: the breakup of interrepublic trade, which previously accounted for 40 percent of commerce; uneven and halfhearted attempts at market reform; the wars in Croatia and Bosnia; and massive flows of displaced persons and refugees. Any one of these factors would have been sufficient to cause economic turmoil. The combination of these factors along with the imposition of strictly enforced comprehensive trade sanctions caused a virtual collapse of the Yugoslav economy.

According to Serbian data reported by the U.S. State Department, the Serbian economy contracted by 26 percent in 1992 and 28 percent in 1993. Real income declined 50 percent across the board.[31] Industrial production fell 22 percent in 1992 and 37 percent in 1993.[32] Capacity utilization in 1993 stood at only 35 percent.[33] Officially acknowledged unemployment reached 23 percent in 1993, although private economists estimated that actual joblessness, counting those not working but on "paid leave," was approximately 40 percent.[34] The portion of the population classified as poor rose from 14 to 44 percent.[35]

The economic crisis in Yugoslavia touched off an uncontrolled inflationary spiral that by late 1993 led to the complete collapse of the dinar. Inflation was 122 percent in 1991 and increased to 9,000 percent in 1992. As production and incomes dropped, the government resorted to the desperate act of printing currency to make ends meet. As prices skyrocketed in late 1993, inflation was recorded daily, not yearly. Consumers tried to buy goods early in the day to beat the inevitable increases in price by afternoon. Yugoslavia experienced a rate of inflation not seen in the world since the days of the Weimar Republic in Germany during the 1920s. By the end of 1993, the inflation rate reached an astonishing 100 trillion percent.[36] Shopkeepers increasingly abandoned the dinar and resorted to either bartering or the use of the German mark.

In response to this virtual economic meltdown, the government instituted an economic reform program in January 1994. The emergency program introduced a new dinar linked to the German mark with parity at 1:1. Government expenditures and budget deficits were slashed.[37] These reforms had an immediate stabilizing effect, as incomes rose, production rebounded, and prices moderated. The limits of the recovery program were soon reached, however. By the end of 1994, production began to decline again, and prices resumed their climb, although less steeply. During the last year of sanctions, industrial production declined by about 4 percent, and the rate of inflation averaged 120 percent.[38]

One of the consequences of the economic reform program was a reduction in the level of Serbian government support and subsidies for Bosnian Serb forces waging war in Bosnia. In an attempt to overcome the effects of sanctions, Belgrade had to limit the volume of resources devoted to the war in Bosnia. Assistance to Republika Srpska was curtailed. These economic necessities no doubt made it easier for Belgrade to impose its blockade on the Bosnian Serbs in August and September 1994. Because of sanctions and the near collapse of the Yugoslav economy, the Milosevic regime became less able to support the Bosnian Serbs.[39]

Humanitarian and Social Impacts

In Yugoslavia as elsewhere, sanctions caused the greatest hardships for the most vulnerable populations. The government and economic elites and a narrow band of militia leaders prospered, while the vast majority of the population suffered. Many middle-class households were forced into poverty, and the poor, the disabled, the elderly, and children faced extreme hardships. But Yugoslavia did not experience anything like the humanitarian catastrophe that gripped Iraq. Serbia traditionally has produced plenty of food, including large surpluses of grain for export. Although agricultural production declined during the sanctions period, food production was sufficient to prevent hunger or serious malnutrition. Yugoslavia is also blessed with ample fresh water supplies and is self-sufficient in hydroelectric power. The country's natural bounty enabled it to survive the ravages of war and sanctions without a humanitarian disaster.

Unpublished UNICEF reports confirm that humanitarian hardships nonetheless mounted during sanctions.[40] The health care system in Yugoslavia, once one of the most specialized in Europe, suffered significantly during the period of war and sanctions. According to Duk

Stambolovic, medical coordinator for the Soros Foundation, the health care services were "surviving on humanitarian aid," with responsibility for public health care "increasingly . . . put on the international community."[41] The availability of medicines also declined during this period. A scarcity of water treatment chemicals resulted in a deterioration of drinking water quality in some cities. Despite these and other hardships, outbreaks of preventable disease and severe malnutrition did not appear in Yugoslavia. Infant mortality rates, after dropping continuously from 1971 to 1991, leveled off at the onset of the country's wars and may have even increased slightly.[42] Regional differences in the data were pronounced, however, with the highest infant mortality rates in Montenegro and Kosovo. Potential errors in reporting or inaccurate classification make the reliability of these figures uncertain.

Nonetheless, sanctions had many negative side effects on Yugoslav society and culture. They stimulated corruption, smuggling, and criminality and undermined the prospects for the emergence of a stronger civil society in Yugoslavia.[43] A vast network of black marketers emerged, much of it connected to and protected by the government. In the words of Sonja Licht, director of the Soros Foundation in Belgrade, "life under sanctions forced a significant portion of society to live on the fringes of legality. The black market became a way of life."[44] Ruling political elites and leaders of armed militia groups used their power to control smuggling operations and enriched themselves in the process. The result, according to Susan Woodward, was "a substantial redistribution of wealth that did not favor those who would oppose the Bosnian war."[45] The war and Belgrade's flawed economic policies also promoted criminality, but sanctions worsened the situation and created many additional opportunities for corruption and the enrichment of hard-line nationalists.

Sanctions impeded the efforts of peace and human rights groups in Serbia and undercut democratic reform movements. Especially in the early months of the sanctions, newsprint and communications equipment became scarce and expensive, and financial support from international organizations dried up.[46] The few independent media outlets and voices of opposition that remained in Belgrade were further isolated and more easily silenced. The economic hardships resulting from sanctions also accelerated the exodus from Serbia of middle-class professionals and students, precisely the groups most likely to support human rights and antiwar causes.[47] Their departure from Serbia weakened the prospects for creating a viable opposition to Milosevic's war policies. The isolation of intellectual, artistic, and academic elites also had negative consequences. The sanctions-imposed ban on educational, scientific, and cultural exchanges denied support to many of the most important critics of government policy and thereby further weakened the voices of domestic dissent.

The Milosevic regime used the hardships caused by sanctions to mobilize popular support and generate a rally 'round the flag effect. Sanctions became the convenient justification for every misfortune in Serbian society, a way of deflecting attention from Belgrade's own misguided war policies and economic mismanagement. Everything could be blamed on the Western powers and UN sanctions. Milosevic used the sanctions to appeal to the traditional Serbian sense of victimization and to rally support for his government. Hard-line nationalist opponents of Milosevic also used the sanctions to stir popular resentment and win support for their more extreme policies.

The impact of sanctions on internal political dynamics within Yugoslavia was counterproductive. Many of the democratic reform groups within Serbia were ambivalent about or opposed to the sanctions, questioning why such measures were imposed only against Serbia and not Croatia and challenging many of the assumptions underlying Western policy in the Balkans.[48] The sanctions weakened rather than helped the progressive forces opposed to Milosevic while strengthening the hand of criminals and extremists. As Woodward observed, sanctions may have increased the opposition to Milosevic's policies, but they strengthened hard-line nationalists, not middle-class democrats.[49]

Sanctions and Bargaining for Peace

As noted earlier, opinions on the impact and political utility of the sanctions against Yugoslavia are sharply divided. The official UN report asserted that the sanctions were "remarkably effective" and may well have been "the single most important reason for the government in Belgrade changing its policies and accepting a negotiated peace agreement."[50] Serbian scholar Milica Delevic similarly observed that "sanctions succeeded in making the Serb president Milosevic abandon the pan-Serb policy he had been pursuing."[51] Others took the opposite view. The SIPRI report concluded that sanctions failed to restrain Serb aggression in Bosnia.[52] Woodward argued that UN sanctions were fundamentally flawed and "did not achieve peace in Bosnia more quickly."[53] Sonja Licht wrote in 1993 that "sanctions did not help either to weaken Milosevic or end the war."[54] Our view is that although sanctions had negative side effects, on balance they made a positive contribution to the bargaining process that produced the Dayton peace accord. Although UN policy in Bosnia was flawed and inconsistent, the evidence suggests that sanctions were nonetheless effective as a bargaining instrument. They applied significant pressure on the Serbian government and were a dominant factor in the lengthy negotiating process that finally brought the war to an end in November 1995. The reversal of Bosnian Serb military fortunes in August and September 1995 had a decisive impact in shaping the final settlement, but sanctions also played a major role in the search for a diplomatic solution. According to chief U.S. negotiator Richard Holbrooke, economic sanctions were the "main bargaining chip with Milosevic."[55] Sanctions "were always a central issue" for Serb negotiators, he reported.[56] Former U.S. ambassador Warren Zimmerman also emphasized the importance of sanctions. Commenting on their imposition in 1992, Zimmerman wrote, "Milosevic's desire to get sanctions lifted would give a bargaining chip: Three years later that chip was to play an important role in Milosevic's decision to end the Bosnian war."[57] In the pages that follow, we review several key points during the negotiating process and examine how Western negotiators used sanctions to leverage Serbian policy.

According to David Owen, Milosevic's support for the Vance-Owen plan in the spring of 1993 was motivated by his desire to achieve a lifting of the "economic millstone" of sanctions. Intelligence reports showed that Milosevic was becoming very concerned about the rapidly deteriorating condition of the Serbian economy and was especially vulnerable in the area of financial sanctions.[58] Milosevic's price for backing the Vance-Owen plan was a commitment from Western leaders for a lifting of sanctions. Owen recounted a March 1993 meeting in Paris with French president François Mitterrand in which Milosevic specifically inquired about the lifting of sanctions in return for his support of the peace plan. "What he wanted was a bargain," reported Owen.[59] Delevic described Milosevic's support for the Vance-Owen plan as the "first serious attempt" by Belgrade to seek an end to the war and argued that this desire was motivated by the government's concern about the hemorrhaging of the Serbian economy caused by sanctions.[60]

Western officials were divided in the spring of 1993 about the best way of using the bargaining leverage provided by sanctions. Mitterrand favored a prompt lifting of sanctions in exchange for Milosevic's support of the Vance-Owen plan. Russia supported this approach as well. U.S. officials took a harder line. They argued for a tightening of sanctions to exert additional pressure on Milosevic to deliver the Bosnian Serbs. U.S. officials hoped that the threat of financial restrictions and stronger sanctions would ensure Milosevic's cooperation. When the Bosnian Serbs committed additional atrocities and intensified their military pressure against Srebrenica, the Security Council closed ranks behind the U.S. plan. The Council approved Resolution 820 in April 1993 and gave Milosevic nine days to attempt to change the minds of the recalcitrant Bosnian Serb leaders. These efforts failed, and the economic noose around Serbia tightened. Owen argued that the threat of stronger sanctions quickened Milosevic's resolve to gain Bosnian Serb support for the peace plan.[61] Even during the ill-fated assembly in Jahorina that rejected the peace plan, sanctions relief was a high priority. When a commission of the Bosnian Serb assembly drafted a set of conditions for accepting the Vance-Owen plan, the demand for lifting sanctions was the first item.[62]

The next potential turning point came in the summer of 1994, as Western negotiators attempted to win Serbian support for the Contact Group peace plan. Once again, Milosevic supported the plan and attempted to persuade his Bosnian Serb allies to agree. Western diplomats increased the pressure on Belgrade, however. Their objective was not only to gain Milosevic's signature on the Contact Group plan but to force Belgrade to isolate the Bosnian Serbs and cut off the flow of people and material crossing the Drina.[63] The stakes were higher, both in terms of the action demanded by the West and in the mounting damage to Serbia's economy from sanctions. Officials in Belgrade recognized that the recently instituted economic reform plan could not stave off the cumulative impact of sanctions. They knew that only a lifting of the UN embargo offered hope for economic recovery and stabilization. The priority for Milosevic remained lifting the sanctions, and he strongly backed the Contact Group plan and intensified pressure on the Bosnian Serbs.[64]

As noted earlier, when Belgrade placed an embargo on the Bosnian Serbs in August 1994 and invited UN monitors to verify its action, the Security Council responded by adopting Resolution 942, which imposed sanctions on Bosnian Serb territory, while approving Resolution 943, which suspended some of the sanctions on Yugoslavia. The actions taken in the latter resolution were minor, easing the restrictions on air and ferry service between Montenegro and Italy and suspending the ban on sporting and cultural events, but they were significant as a gesture of acknowledgment and support for Belgrade's actions. Milosevic's blockade of the Bosnian Serbs was politically risky at home and aroused anger and indignation among hard-line nationalists. The Security Council's decision to reciprocate Milosevic's concessions was an attempt to reward such behavior and encourage further compliance. By dangling the offer of sanctions suspension and offering a small concession in that direction, the Security Council hoped to reinforce Milosevic's efforts to gain Bosnian Serb agreement for a negotiated peace.

In the months prior to the Dayton negotiations in 1995, sanctions remained the principal form of leverage by which the major powers sought to extract concessions from Serbian authorities. European and U.S. negotiators continued to differ, however, on the conditions for easing sanctions. French and British officials, backed by Moscow, were prepared to offer a lifting of sanctions in May 1995 in return for Belgrade's recognition of Bosnia and new pressures on the Bosnian Serbs. The United States held out for stronger terms, arguing that sanctions should not be lifted until a final peace agreement was signed. U.S. officials were concerned that if Milosevic reneged on his pledges, it would be difficult to marshal the votes in the Security Council for a reimposition of sanctions.[65] According to Holbrooke, the decision to hold out for more concrete progress on ending the war "proved correct; had we not done so, we would have begun the [Dayton] negotiations with almost no bargaining chips."[66]

Sanctions and the Dayton Peace Accord

A crucial turning point in the Bosnian war was the August–September 1995 Croatian and Bosnian government military offensive that drove Serbian forces out of the Krajina and parts of western Bosnia. NATO warplanes joined the action against the Bosnian Serbs on 30 August and through 17 September flew more than 3,500 sorties in a campaign that forced the Bosnian Serbs to pull back their heavy weapons.[67] When the ground offensive and bombing campaign ended, the territory controlled by Bosnian Serbs had contracted from 70 percent to approximately 49 percent, in line with the percentage specified in the Contact Group peace plan. These dramatic Bosnian Serb reversals on the battlefield opened the door to the final negotiations in Dayton, Ohio, and were crucial in forcing a settlement of the war. Military defeat made the Bosnian Serbs more conciliatory at the bargaining table.[68]

Analysts have rightly observed that these military reversals were a crucial factor in persuading Bosnian Serb leaders to accept a negotiated solution.[69] Sanctions continued to exert a role, however. In the calculations of Milosevic, they retained paramount importance. When chief negotiator Holbrooke met with Milosevic soon after the NATO bombing campaign began, the Serbian leader did not raise the issue of NATO airstrikes until late in the meeting. Said Holbrooke, "I was struck by his lack of emotion on the subject, in contrast . . . to his passion on the subject of lifting the economic sanctions."[70]

In subsequent weeks, as the pieces fell into place for the conference at Dayton, the lifting of sanctions remained Milosevic's top priority.[71] During a major meeting in October to plan the Dayton conference, according to Holbrooke, the first agenda item for Milosevic was "a strong effort to get the sanctions lifted or suspended prior to Dayton."[72] According to Zimmerman, Milosevic's primary goal in the Dayton negotiations was to strengthen his position within Serbia "by doing what was necessary to get the economic embargo lifted and his own republic relieved of its pariah status."[73] On the first day of the Dayton negotiations, Holbrooke and U.S. secretary of state Warren Christopher met separately with the presidents of Croatia, Bosnia, and Serbia to set the framework for the bargaining process. As Holbrooke reported, "each president made his priority clear in these initial meetings . . . for Milosevic it was the sanctions."[74] A lifting of sanctions is what Milosevic wanted most, but Christopher and Holbrooke emphasized that this would only come with acceptance of a final peace agreement.[75]

As the bargaining process began at Dayton, U.S. officials offered a slight concession to further encourage Serbian cooperation. Negotiators agreed to suspend sanctions upon the initialing of a peace agreement, instead of waiting for its formal signing. This small change advanced the date of sanctions relief by approximately a month and gave Milosevic "more incentive to reach agreement."[76] The U.S. concession also smoothed over continuing differences within the Contact Group and was an important sign of bargaining flexibility. U.S. officials confirmed that they would indeed agree to the full lifting of sanctions in exchange for Belgrade's acceptance of the final peace agreement.[77] Once again sanctions were at the center of the diplomatic process.

The Contribution of Sanctions

On balance, it is probably safe to say that the UN sanctions against Yugoslavia were effective in applying pressure on Serbian officials and were key factors in the bargaining process that eventually brought the war in Bosnia to an end. The changes in the military balance of power in August and September 1995 were the immediate catalyst in bringing the parties to Dayton to forge a settlement, but the force of sanctions remained an important factor even in the final months. Sanctions created constant hardship that for more than three years applied pressure on Belgrade to pursue a negotiated peace. Although the assertion of the UN report, that sanctions were "the single most important reason" for Serbian acceptance of the peace settlement, is open to question, the study's conclusion, that sanctions "modified the behavior of the Serbian party," is valid. As Edward Luttwak argued in *Foreign Affairs,* sanctions "moderated the conduct of Belgrade's most immoderate leadership" and "induced whatever slight propensity has been shown to negotiate."[78] Admittedly, the workings of sanctions in this case were agonizingly slow. The support sanctions provided for the peace process was often too little and too late. But the fact remains that sanctions were the principal means by which negotiators sought to induce concessions from Belgrade.

A positive assessment of the bargaining influence of sanctions does not deny the flaws of the Dayton peace accord, or the many legitimate criticisms of the UN role in Bosnia, or the indecision and incoherence that often plagued U.S. and European policy during the conflict. A full consideration of these issues and the debate about whether earlier and more forceful UN or NATO military involvement would have been preferable to the slow workings of sanctions are beyond the purview of this book. The conclusion here is simply that, within the context of the tortured UN engagement in the Bosnian war, sanctions succeeded in establishing a bargaining framework and provided crucial leverage over Serbian decisionmakers in Belgrade. As emphasized throughout this volume, sanctions are only as effective as the overall policy they are designed to serve. Within the framework of the admittedly flawed and often contradictory framework of UN policy in Bosnia, sanctions were an effective means of bargaining leverage.

Kosovo: The Road Not Taken

When the UN Security Council lifted the sanctions and arms embargo against Yugoslavia following the signing of the Dayton peace accord, the United States maintained an outer wall of financial sanctions, barring Belgrade's participation in international financial institutions. The U.S. sanctions were intended to encourage Serbian cooperation with the

International Tribunal for Former Yugoslavia and to prevent Serbian repression and human rights violations in Kosovo. Despite the U.S. sanctions, though, the long-simmering conflict in Kosovo steadily intensified. By 1997, armed attacks by the Kosovo Liberation Army (KLA) and violent repression from Serbian security forces were on the rise. Once again the cauldron of Balkans conflict boiled over, this time in Kosovo.

In response to the mounting repression and violence in Kosovo, the Security Council voted on 31 March 1998 to adopt Resolution 1160 imposing an arms embargo on Yugoslavia. All countries were prohibited from selling or supplying arms or weapons-related material to Yugoslavia. Resolution 1160 established a new sanctions committee for Yugoslavia to monitor member state compliance with the resolution. In September 1998 the Council passed another resolution, 1199, which requested that states prevent the use of funds collected on their territory for violating the arms embargo. The United States and the European Union also imposed sanctions against Serbia in 1998, steadily tightening the pressure as the crisis intensified. By the spring of 1999, when NATO air attacks began, Serbia was subjected to an array of U.S./EU sanctions, including targeted financial sanctions and travel restrictions. The UN Security Council took no further action beyond the arms embargo, however. The Council chose not to broaden the sanctions, and European agencies did not apply the kind of intensive enforcement mechanisms that were successfully utilized during the Bosnia case. Although the UN's own report judged the earlier sanctions effective, the Security Council did not apply the lessons of Bosnia to the Kosovo crisis.

The decision to impose an arms embargo was curious in light of the controversies over the earlier embargo during the Bosnian war and the peculiar nature of the military capabilities on both sides of the Kosovo conflict. Serbian forces retained control over the resources of the Yugoslav People's Army and were heavily armed and largely self-sufficient militarily. An arms embargo would have little or no impact on their ability to repress civilians and wage war in Kosovo. The KLA was supplied from the large arsenal of the Albanian armed forces, which fell into civilian hands during the Albanian government crisis in early 1997 and which subsequently flowed across the border into Kosovo in large numbers. Attempting to police the arms embargo against the KLA would have required a huge, well-armed monitoring force, and even then substantial military supplies would have slipped through the region's rugged terrain. If the UN had tried to enforce the embargo, the practical effect would have been, as in Bosnia, to cement the substantial military advantage enjoyed by Serbian forces. Fortunately for the KLA, the UN took little action to ensure compliance. The decision to impose an arms embargo seemed to reflect a desire by the Security Council to do something, however modest, in response to the worsening crisis. It also reflected the minimum consensus that could be achieved within a divided Security Council in which some members opposed more assertive action against Serbia, whereas others were skeptical about applying sanctions in an "internal" dispute.

In a February 1999 report, the new Yugoslavia sanctions committee confirmed that little was being done to monitor and enforce the arms embargo. Although the Danube Commission, the European Union, and other regional organizations offered some assistance for sanctions implementation, the overall resources pledged were not sufficient for establishing the necessary comprehensive monitoring regime.[79] The committee also reported "serious violations of the arms embargo," pointing especially to "continuing military resupply and reinforcement of Kosovar Albanian armed groups."[80] The committee noted "dubious" fund-raising activities on behalf of the KLA in several countries, but it took no note of the blatant efforts in the United States and other countries to recruit soldiers and raise private military aid funds for the KLA. Without an effective means of enforcing the arms embargo and faced with an obvious lack of enthusiasm among the major powers for implementing more forceful sanctions, the sanctions committee was powerless to do anything about the lack of compliance with Resolution 1160.

The Western powers began to threaten the use of military force in the summer of 1998 and in March 1999 launched a seventy-eight-day, intensive NATO bombing campaign that drove Serbian forces out of Kosovo. NATO waged the bombing campaign without UN approval, and the Security Council was denied a role in attempting to resolve the Kosovo crisis. Officials in the United States showed an early preference for the use of military force, rather than attempting to gain Security Council support for stronger economic pressures. Whether sanctions would have been effective in the Kosovo crisis, or whether the results of sanctions would have been more or less satisfactory than the aftermath of the NATO bombing campaign, can never be known. Sanctions provided leverage in negotiating an end to the war in Bosnia, but they had little effect in efforts to address the crisis in Kosovo.

Notes

1. United Nations Security Council, *Letter Dated 24 September 1996 from the Chairman of the Security Council Committee Established Pursuant to Resolution 724 (1991) Concerning Yugoslavia Addressed to the President of the Security Council, Report of the Copenhagen Roundtable on United Nations Sanctions in the Case of the Former Yugoslavia, Held at Copenhagen on 24 and 25 June 1996,* S/1996/776, New York, 24 September 1996, par. 17.

2. Susan L. Woodward, *Balkan Tragedy: Chaos and Dissolution After the Cold War* (Washington, D.C.: Brookings Institution Press, 1995), 263.

3. Reneo Lukic and Allen Lynch, *Europe from the Balkans to the Urals: The Disintegration of Yugoslavia and the Soviet Union* (New York: SIPRI, Oxford University Press, 1996), 295.

4. Ibid., 246.

5. Ibid., 300.

6. United Nations Security Council, *Letter Dated 24 September 1996,* S/1996/776, 10.

7. Ibid., par. 58.

8. Warren Zimmerman, *Origins of a Catastrophe: Yugoslavia and Its Destroyers—America's Last Ambassador Tells What Happened and Why* (New York: Times Books, 1996), 231.

9. Richard Holbrooke, *To End a War* (New York: Random House, 1998), 88.

10. United Nations Security Council, *Letter Dated 24 September 1996,* S/1996/776, pars. 33 and 34.

11. United Nations Security Council, *Letter Dated 15 November 1996 from the Chairman of the Security Council Committee Established Pursuant to Resolution 724 (1991) Concerning Yugoslavia Addressed to the President of the Security Council,* S/1996/946, 15 November 1996, par. 14.

12. United Nations Security Council, *Letter Dated 24 September 1996,* S/1996/776, pars. 48 and 49.

13. United States, Department of State, *UN Sanctions Against Belgrade: Lessons Learned for Future Regimes,* paper prepared by the Interagency Task Force on Serbian Sanctions, Washington, D.C., June 1996, 11.

14. United Nations Security Council, *Letter Dated 24 September 1996,* S/1996/776, par. 78.

15. United States, Department of State, *UN Sanctions,* 11.

16. United Nations Security Council, *Letter Dated 24 September 1996,* S/1996/776, par. 80.

17. Woodward, *Balkan Tragedy,* 387.

18. United Nations Security Council, *Letter Dated 15 November 1996,* S/1996/946, par. 19.

19. Ibid.

20. David Owen, *Balkan Odyssey* (New York: Harcourt Brace and Company, 1995), 288.

21. Lukic and Lynch, *Europe from the Balkans to the Urals,* 301.

22. United Nations Security Council, *Letter Dated 15 November 1996,* S/1996/946, par. 25.

23. Owen, *Balkan Odyssey,* 288.

24. United Nations Security Council, *Letter Dated 15 November 1996,* S/1996/946, par. 26.

25. Stephen Engelberg, "Conflict in the Balkans: U.N. Steps Said to Dry Up Serbs' Cash," *New York Times,* 13 May 1993, A8.

26. United Nations Security Council, *Letter Dated 15 November 1996,* S/1996/946, pars. 22 and 23.

27. Ibid., par. 33.

28. Ibid., par. 7.

29. Ibid., par. 11.

30. Larry Minear, David Cortright, Julia Wagler, George A. Lopez, and Thomas G. Weiss, *Toward More Humane and Effective Sanctions Management: Enhancing the Capacity of the United Nations System,* Occasional Paper No. 31 (Providence, R.I.: Thomas J. Watson Institute for International Studies, 1998), 59.

31. United States, Department of State, *UN Sanctions,* 1.

32. Ibid.

33. Milica Delevic, "Economic Sanctions as a Foreign Policy Tool: The Case of Yugoslavia," *International Journal of Peace Studies* 3, no. 1 (January 1998): 79.

34. United States, Department of State, *UN Sanctions,* 1.

35. Ibid., 1–2.

36. Ibid., 3.

37. Delevic, "Economic Sanctions," 80.

38. United States, Department of State, *UN Sanctions,* 3.

39. Delevic, "Economic Sanctions," 82.

40. Statistics from these studies are presented in Thomas G. Weiss, David Cortright, George A. Lopez, and Larry Minear, eds., *Political Gain and Civilian Pain: Humanitarian Impacts of Economic Sanctions* (Lanham, Md.: Rowman and Littlefield, 1997); see especially chap. 5 and 164–182.

41. Mary Black, "Report," *British Medical Journal,* 30 October 1993, 1135.

42. Weiss et al., *Political Gain and Civilian Pain,* 173.

43. Delevic, "Economic Sanctions," 84.

44. Sonja Licht, "The Use of Sanctions in the Former Yugoslavia: Can They Assist in Conflict Resolution?" in David Cortright and George A. Lopez, eds., *Economic Sanctions: Panacea or Peacebuilding in a Post–Cold War World?* (Boulder, Colo.: Westview, 1995), 158.

45. Woodward, *Balkan Tragedy,* 294.

46. Licht, "The Use of Sanctions," 158.

47. Woodward, *Balkan Tragedy,* 294.

48. Licht, "The Use of Sanctions," 154–156.

49. Woodward, *Balkan Tragedy,* 386.

50. United Nations Security Council, *Letter Dated 24 September 1996,* S/1996/776, par. 1.

51. Delevic, "Economic Sanctions," 83.

52. Lukic and Lynch, *Europe from the Balkans to the Urals,* 300.

53. Woodward, *Balkan Tragedy,* 386.

54. Licht, "The Use of Sanctions," 158.

55. Holbrooke, *To End a War,* 4.

56. Ibid., 87.

57. Zimmerman, *Origins of a Catastrophe,* 213.

58. Owen, *Balkan Odyssey,* 134.

59. Ibid., 125.

60. Delevic, "Economic Sanctions," 82.

61. Owen, *Balkan Odyssey,* 151.

62. Ibid., 154.

63. Woodward, *Balkan Tragedy,* 362.

64. Zimmerman, *Origins of a Catastrophe,* 231; and Delevic, "Economic Sanctions," 82.

65. Owen, *Balkan Odyssey,* 320–321.

66. Holbrooke, *To End a War,* 88.

67. Richard H. Ullman, "The Wars in Yugoslavia and the International System After the Cold War," in Richard H. Ullman, ed., *The World and Yugoslavia's Wars* (New York: Council on Foreign Relations, 1996), 24.

68. Holbrooke, *To End a War,* 73.

69. See Dick A. Leurdijk, *The United Nations and NATO in Former Yugoslavia, 1991–1996: Limits to Diplomacy and Force* (The Hague: Netherlands Atlantic Commission, 1996).

70. Holbrooke, *To End a War,* 106.

71. Ibid., 169.

72. Ibid., 211.

73. Zimmerman, *Origins of a Catastrophe,* 234.

74. Holbrooke, *To End a War,* 236.

75. Ibid., 282.

76. Ibid., 236.

77. Milosevic demanded and won another minor sanctions concession during the Dayton talks. He proposed a "grain for fuel" deal to provide immediate supplies of heating oil and natural gas for Belgrade and other Serbian cities facing the approach of winter. Milosevic's request to sell grain to purchase fuel supplies was quickly supported by the members of the Contact Group, but U.S. officials balked at what they considered an unnecessarily large request. Serbian officials became increasingly adamant about the issue. As Holbrooke observed, "Every meeting with Milosevic . . . turned into an argument about sanctions." The issue prompted a two-hour meeting in the White House Situation Room, where the top officials of the U.S. government debated the amount of oil and natural gas Belgrade should receive during the winter. The arguments became so intense that at one point National Security Adviser Anthony Lake "actually banged his head on the oak table in frustration." Eventually U.S. officials agreed to grant the Serbian request. The incident is recounted in Holbrooke, *To End a War,* 250–259.

78. Edward M. Luttwak, "Toward Post-Heroic Warfare," *Foreign Affairs* 74, no. 3 (May–June 1995): 118.

79. United Nations Security Council, *Letter Dated 26 February 1999 from the Chairman of the Security Council Committee Established Pursuant to Security Council Resolution 1160 (1998) Addressed to the President of the Security Council,* S/1999/216, 4 March 1999, par. 11.

80. Ibid., par. 15.

5

Helping Haiti?*

When General Raoul Cedras overthrew democratically elected president Jean-Bertrand Aristide in September 1991, the Organization of American States (OAS) and then the United Nations imposed sanctions against Haiti. In October 1991 the OAS applied diplomatic and economic sanctions. In June 1993, the UN Security Council imposed a fuel and arms ban against Haiti, which led to the negotiation of the Governors Island agreement calling for the restoration of the elected government. When that agreement collapsed, the Security Council reimposed sanctions in October 1993 and called for a naval blockade of Haiti. In May 1994, the Security Council significantly expanded these measures, imposing travel restrictions, financial sanctions, and comprehensive trade sanctions, albeit with humanitarian exemptions. Before these measures could have much effect, however, the Security Council passed Resolution 940 authorizing the creation of a multinational force and the use of "all necessary means" to restore Aristide. Shortly after the U.S.-led troop intervention in September 1994, the military junta fled. Aristide returned to office, and on 15 October the Security Council agreed to lift all sanctions against Haiti.

In this chapter we examine the different phases of the international response to the crisis in Haiti, reviewing the porous sanctions initially applied by the OAS, assessing the impact of UN sanctions, and recounting the attempts to strengthen these measures and improve monitoring and enforcement. We consider the impact of UN sanctions on the bargaining process that led to the Governors Island agreement but also examine the flaws in that agreement that led to its unraveling. After discussing the humanitarian impact of sanctions in Haiti, we describe efforts by relief agencies to ameliorate these effects. In conclusion, we

* This chapter was coauthored by Jaleh Dashti-Gibson.

HAITI

International boundary
Departmental boundary
National capital
Departmental seat
Town, village
Main road
Secondary road
Airport
Airstrip

| 0 | 10 | 20 | 30 | 40 km |
| 0 | 5 | 10 | 15 | 20 | 25 mi |

DOMINICAN REPUBLIC

ATLANTIC OCEAN

CARIBBEAN SEA

Golfe de la Gonâve

Canal de la Tortue

Canal de Saint-Marc

Canal de la Gonâve

ÎLE DE LA TORTUE
ÎLE DE LA GONÂVE
ÎLE A VACHE
ÎLES CAYÉMITES
PRESQU'ÎLE DES BARADÈRES

Departments

NORD-OUEST
NORD
NORD-EST
ARTIBONITE
CENTRE
OUEST
SUD-EST
SUD
GRANDE-ANSE

Selected places

PORT-AU-PRINCE
Cap-Haïtien
Gonaïves
Hinche
Fort-Liberté
Port-de-Paix
Jacmel
Les Cayes
Jérémie

Môle St-Nicolas, Bombardopolis, Jean-Rabel, Baie de Henne, Grande Pointe, Cap Saint-Nicolas, Cap-à-Foux, Pointe Jean-Rabel, Palmiste, St Louis du Nord, Anse-à-Foleur, Le Borgne, Port-Margot, Plaine du Nord, Acul du Nord, Milot, Plaisance, Pilate, Gros-Morne, Terre-Neuve, Anse-Rouge, Bassin-Bleu, Limbé, Dondon, Grande Rivière du Nord, Quartier Morin, Limonade, Caracol, Phaëton, Trou-du-Nord, Sainte-Suzanne, Grand Bassin, Terrier-Rouge, Ferrier, Ouanaminthe, Dajabón, Fort-Liberté, Monte Cristi, Meneville

Saint-Raphaël, Saint Michel de l'Atalaye, Marmelade, Énnery, Bahon, Ranquitte, La Victoire, Cerca-Carvajal, Maïssade, Pignon, Mombin-Crochu, Vallières, Carice, Mont-Organisé, Perches, Thomassique, Cerca-la-Source

Dessalines, Petite-Rivière-de-l'Artibonite, Verrettes, La Chapelle, Saut-d'Eau, Mirebalais, Baptiste, Lascahobas, Belladère, Savanette, Thomonde

Grande-Saline, Pointe de Grande-Pierre, Baie de Grand-Pierre, Pointe de la Tortue, Saint-Marc, Anse-à-Galets, Pointe-à-Raquette, Pointe Ouest, Pointe de Montrouis, Pointe Fantasque, Arcahaie, Cabaret, Croix des Bouquets, Pétion-Ville, Kenscoff, Gressier, Carrefour, Léogâne, Grand-Goâve, Petit-Goâve, Trouin, La Vallée de Jacmel, Bainet, Côtes-de-fer, Marigot, Cayes-Jacmel, Gantheir, Ganthier, Fonds Parisien, Fonds-Verrettes, Belle-Anse, Bodarie, Thiotte, Grand-Gosier, Banane, Anse-à-Pitres, Pedernales, Jimani

Baie de Jacmel, Cap Raymond, Miragoâne, Petite Rivière de Nippes, Petit Trou de Nippes, Anse-à-Veau, L'Asile, Vieux Bourg d'Aquin, Aquin, Cavaillon, St Louis du Sud, Maniche, Torbeck, St Jean du Sud, Chantal, Camp-Perrin, Cavaillon, Barderes, Pestel, Corail, Roseaux, Trou Bonbon, Abricots, Moron, Chambellan, Dame-Marie, Anse d'Hainault, Les Irois, Tiburon, La Cahouane, Chardonnières, Les Anglais, Côteaux, Port-à-Piment, Roche-à-Bateau, Port-Salut

The boundaries and names shown on this map do not imply official endorsement or acceptance by the United Nations.

Map No. 3855 Rev. 1   UNITED NATIONS
October 1995 (Colour)

Department of Public Information
Cartographic Section

note that just as sanctions became more comprehensive and better enforced in 1994, they gave way to the use of military force.

Sanctions for Democracy

Haiti is the first country in which economic sanctions were used by the UN for the purpose of restoring a democratically elected government. In December 1990, Haiti held the first free and fair election in its nearly 200 years of history. An overwhelming 90 percent of the Haitian electorate turned out for the historic vote, electing Jean-Bertrand Aristide as president by a 67 percent majority.[1] For most Haitians, the election was a victory, but for the armed forces and the wealthy elite who had long controlled and exploited Haiti, the election represented a threat. As explained by Claudette Werleigh, former Haitian foreign minister:

> While the elections of 1990 inspired hope for Haiti's impoverished majority, fear of losing their privileges and power struck the nation's economic elite. For the first time they found it was not they who influenced the choice of the new government, nor the new president who had long advocated on behalf of the poor. The rich were exhorted by President Aristide to share their wealth and to pay their fair share of taxes. Even this call was met with fear by a class long accustomed to evading any fiscal responsibility.[2]

The military's reaction to Aristide's election was to overthrow the government and install handpicked successors in its place. The military junta instituted a reign of terror that took thousands of lives over the next three years.[3]

The response of the international community to the military takeover in Haiti can be described in four phases. The first phase began in October 1991 when the OAS imposed sanctions. Four months before the May 1991 coup in Haiti, the OAS had adopted the Santiago Commitment to Democracy as well as a resolution on representative democracy. The crisis in Haiti provided the first opportunity for the OAS to apply this commitment to democracy, and its response was swift.[4] At an emergency meeting of its Permanent Council on 30 September, the OAS, under U.S. insistence, condemned the coup and demanded the return of the legitimately elected government. The Permanent Council convened an ad hoc meeting of ministers of foreign affairs, which adopted a resolution on 3 October also condemning the disruption of the democratic process in Haiti. The resolution was the

---

HAITI, Security Council Resolutions

Resolution Number	Action
841	**16 June 1993** Imposed fuel and arms embargo Established sanctions committee
873	**13 October 1993** Reimposed the fuel and arms embargo
875	**16 October 1993** Called on member states to enforce the fuel and arms embargo with a naval blockade
917	**6 May 1994** Imposed comprehensive sanctions Imposed flight ban Froze the assets of the military junta and their supporters and families
940	**31 July 1994** Authorized the creation of a multinational force to oust coup leaders and restore Aristide
944	**29 September 1994** Moved to terminate sanctions upon Aristide's return to power

---

strongest ever adopted by the OAS. It declared that only the Aristide government would be recognized; that the OAS Inter-American Commission on Human Rights would protect human rights in Haiti; and that all states should suspend diplomatic, economic, financial, and commercial ties with Haiti.[5] One week later, on 10 October, the General Assembly of the United Nations (whose resolutions are not legally binding on UN member states) also strongly condemned the violent overthrow of the elected government and urged UN member states to uphold the measures of isolation called for by the OAS.

Despite a rhetorical commitment to the restoration of Haitian democracy, the OAS lacked the resources and political will to enforce trade sanctions or to make a concerted effort to restore Aristide to power. OAS member governments were inconsistent in their responses to the crisis, especially the United States, and this conveyed a message to members of the military junta that in time they might be accepted as the legitimate government of Haiti. Two early developments in particular contributed to this belief: (1) a Colombian tanker flying a Liberian flag delivered fuel to Haiti shortly after the coup and suffered no retaliation; and (2) several months after the coup, the Bush administration exempted U.S.-owned export assembly factories from sanctions so that U.S. businesses could maintain their operations in Haiti. The Bush administration's action was designed to help stem the flow of Haitian refugees to the United States, which was a dominant concern of U.S. policy throughout the crisis.[6] This weakening of sanctions highlighted the absence of an effective enforcement mechanism and the lack of political support within the United States and other key countries for more forceful measures. Indeed, U.S. policy suffered from a kind of schizophrenia. The Bush and Clinton administrations officially expressed support for the return of the elected president, but many U.S. policymakers were uncomfortable with Aristide's radicalism and his redistributive economic policies. The powerful chairman of the Senate Foreign Relations Committee, Senator Jesse Helms (R-N.C.), vilified the deposed president, and CIA officials circulated reports of Aristide's supposed mental instability. This ambivalence about Aristide contributed to Washington's erratic and inconsistent policies toward Haiti.

Sanctions and the Governors Island Agreement

The second phase of sanctions against Haiti was marked by the active involvement of the United Nations. The goal of UN efforts was to protect human rights and restore democracy. In the United States, the newly elected Clinton administration initially showed more concern than its predecessor about the Haiti crisis. It was spurred into action by increasing anxiety about the waves of desperate Haitian refugees heading toward U.S. shores. Anxious to respond to the Haitian refugee crisis and frustrated at the recalcitrance of the military junta, the United States began to take stronger action and to encourage the application of UN sanctions. In early June 1993, the United States froze the assets of members of the military junta and denied them entry visas to the United States. The freeze affected the cash accounts, real estate, and other property of eighty-three individuals and thirty-five institutions.[7] On 16 June 1993 the UN Security Council adopted Resolution 841, cutting off

the sale of fuel and arms to Haiti and establishing a sanctions committee to monitor implementation of the sanctions.[8] Although the United
States, France, Canada, and Argentina offered to help police the embargo, no provision was made at the time for a naval blockade or other
means of enforcement. In addition, it was not clear that the Dominican
Republic would comply with the UN sanctions despite its UN Charter
obligations to do so, leading to concerns about opportunities for smuggling across the Haitian-Dominican border.[9]

When the UN sanctions were imposed, they had an immediate
impact. They appeared to create a new willingness on the part of the
junta to negotiate Aristide's return. Prior to the passage of Resolution
841, coup leaders had been defiant.[10] The UN sanctions, particularly the
oil embargo, changed the political mood in Port-au-Prince. A *New York
Times* story reported that the armed forces were "extremely worried"
about the UN sanctions.[11] Important political groups in Haiti became
concerned about possible economic effects and were ready to begin
negotiations as UN officials urged. On 21 June, just five days after the
approval of Resolution 841 and two days before the sanctions were to
go into effect, Raoul Cedras agreed to meet UN representative Dante
Caputo. Previously the general had demanded a lifting of OAS sanctions as a precondition for talks. Now, under the pressure of UN sanctions, he dropped the conditions. A few days later formal negotiations
began on Governors Island in New York.

During this period, according to Robert Maguire and colleagues,
"sanctions became an effective lever for bringing the military to the
table." Unlike the previous OAS measures, these sanctions were
"worldwide, targeted, and enforced."[12] They had the potential to cause
real damage and exerted genuine pressure on the military regime.[13]
Elizabeth Gibbons also observed that the threat of economic sanctions
"appears to have brought the military . . . to the negotiating table."[14] To
this extent the imposition of sanctions was a success. Sanctions helped
to establish a bargaining framework and were effective in initiating a
diplomatic process for resolving the conflict. Within the bargaining
model analysis we have posited, this rates as a success. The fact that the
resulting Governors Island agreement was flawed and poorly enforced
does not deny the fact that sanctions played a decisive role in bringing
the military junta to the bargaining table.

Signed on 3 July 1993, the Governors Island agreement was negotiated through UN/OAS diplomats, in concert with the governments of
Canada, France, the United States, and Venezuela. The United States
applied a considerable amount of pressure on both the junta and

President Aristide to accept the agreement.[15] The accord had ten provisions, including the installation of a new prime minister, amnesty for coup leaders, international assistance for the transition, reform of the police force, the return of President Aristide, and the suspension of UN/OAS sanctions as soon as the new prime minister was approved and assumed his duties.[16] This last provision proved to be the undoing of the entire agreement. It meant that sanctions would be lifted before the departure of the coup leaders and the return of Aristide. The agreement had other flaws as well. No date was given for the departure of Cedras or his colleagues. The implementation timeline was too long, giving the military junta several months to depart and thus allowing them time to prepare countermeasures. The deployment of the UN force envisioned in the agreement, the United Nations Mission in Haiti (UNMIH), came too late in the process.[17]

One of the limitations of sanctions is that, although they can apply pressure for bargaining, they cannot guarantee success or a genuine commitment to change on the part of the targeted authorities. In the case of Haiti, as in other instances during the 1990s, targeted leaders gave the appearance of flexibility and displayed a willingness to negotiate, but they were not committed to compliance with the resulting agreement. The junta in Haiti succeeded in negotiating an agreement that gave them an extended lease on life. They used this time to intensify attacks against prodemocracy elements in Haitian civil society. They also became increasingly bold in violating the agreement and defying the tepid international efforts to implement it.

The woefully inadequate enforcement of the agreement was dramatically illustrated in the *Harlan County* incident. When the USS *Harlan County* arrived in Port-au-Prince with Canadian and U.S. military personnel on 11 October 1993, it was greeted by a small but boisterous crowd of gun-toting demonstrators who threatened the journalists and diplomats waiting on the docks. The ship was unable to dock, and the next day it left Haitian waters.[18] Without consulting with UN authorities, U.S. officials in Washington ordered the hasty retreat of the *Harlan County*.[19] The Clinton administration, still reeling from the deaths of eighteen U.S. soldiers in the streets of Mogadishu, Somalia, a week before, wanted to avoid any further risk to U.S. troops regardless of the diplomatic consequences. The ignominious departure of the *Harlan County* was sharply criticized within the United States, especially by members of the Congressional Black Caucus, who advocated a stronger U.S. role against the junta and were concerned that the incident would further embolden the military leaders in their obstruction of the

UN-negotiated agreement. They were also alarmed by the increase in government and paramilitary repression in Haiti at the time. Among the many victims of the junta's reign of terror was Justice Minister Guy Malary, who was gunned down on 14 October. Buried along with Malary were the last hopes for implementing the Governors Island agreement.

Starting Over

On 13 October 1993 the Security Council declared the situation in Haiti a threat to peace and security in the region and adopted Resolution 873 reimposing the oil and arms embargo. This marked the start of the third phase of sanctions. Three days later the Council passed Resolution 875, calling on member states to enforce the fuel and arms embargo with a naval blockade.[20] The United States responded by sending six warships to the region. Efforts continued into 1994 to reinstate the Governors Island agreement, but the military remained unyielding. The junta found new ways to adjust to sanctions pressure. It used the period between the lifting of sanctions in August and their reimposition in October to stockpile fuel supplies. It also rushed ahead with the construction of a new highway connecting Haiti and the Dominican Republic, allowing large vehicles to smuggle goods across the poorly monitored border crossings.[21] The sanctions still lacked effective enforcement mechanisms, despite the new provisions for a naval blockade.

The fourth phase of sanctions began on 6 May 1994, when the Security Council adopted Resolution 917, which imposed comprehensive sanctions against Haiti, including a flight ban, a freeze on the assets of the military junta and their supporters and families, and import and export bans. This imposition of stronger sanctions was largely the result of a new get-tough policy by the Clinton administration, which was under mounting domestic political pressure from African Americans and other political constituencies. High-visibility protests by members of the Congressional Black Caucus and a strong desire in Florida and other key states to halt the continuing flow of Haitian refugees into the United States quickened Washington's resolve to settle the Haiti crisis. In June, the United States halted all commercial flights between Haiti and the United States. With Canada joining the flight ban, 75 percent of all flights to and from Haiti were promptly canceled. By the end of July 1994, the last commercial flight departed Haiti, severing its link to the rest of the world. Washington also banned all financial transactions between Haiti and the United States, a measure that affected rich Haitians, who could no longer wire money back home.[22] It was only at this point that the White House canceled the Bush administration's sanctions exemption for U.S. assembly plants.[23]

These new, more potent measures, coming nearly three years after the beginning of the crisis, were not given much time to take effect. At the end of July, the United States pressured the Security Council into adopting Resolution 940, which authorized the creation of a multinational force and the use of "all necessary means" to oust the coup leaders from power and restore Aristide.[24] On 17 September, two days after warning Haiti's military leaders to step down, President Clinton dispatched a last-minute diplomatic mission to Haiti, including former president Jimmy Carter, former chairman of the Joint Chiefs of Staff Colin Powell, and Senator Sam Nunn (D-Ga.). With U.S. military planes already in the air on their way to Haiti, Carter announced an agreement with the de facto authorities. On 19 September, a 20,000-troop, U.S.-led multinational force landed in Haiti and began implementing the plan for restoring elected government.[25] Ten days later the Security Council responded with Resolution 944, moving to terminate all sanctions against Haiti on the day after Aristide returned to power. On 11 October the OAS suspended its sanctions against Haiti as well. Generals Cedras and Philippe Biamby departed Haiti for Panama on 13 October, and the military junta dissolved.[26] On 15 October 1994, Aristide returned to office, and the Council passed Resolution 948 confirming the lifting of sanctions.

Economic and Humanitarian Impacts

The effects of sanctions cannot be isolated from the impact of other causes of economic and social hardship in Haiti, including widespread corruption, bureaucratic mismanagement, political violence, and the long-term impoverishment and underdevelopment that made Haiti the poorest country in the Americas. Despite the difficulty of separating sanctions impacts from other sources of economic disruption, it is clear that the fuel embargo and comprehensive ban on Haitian exports led to a "significant deterioration" in the quality of life of ordinary Haitians.[27] Even the OAS sanctions, criticized as porous and ineffective, had a dramatic impact on Haitian jobs, with almost 30,000 positions disappearing in export industries shortly after the imposition of sanctions.[28] The

OAS embargo triggered a trend that eventually led to the elimination of 300,000 jobs in the formal employment sector by the time sanctions were lifted in 1994.[29]

Although humanitarian exemptions were included in the sanctions against Haiti, the fuel embargo and resulting increase in transportation costs meant that prices for food staples increased dramatically, placing them beyond the reach of the majority of Haitians. Prices for rice and corn, for example, increased by 137 percent and 185 percent, respectively, between 1991 and 1994.[30] The value of the Haitian gourde depreciated 200 percent against the dollar during this time.[31] Industrial and agricultural output dropped.[32] In order to cope with the economic hardships resulting from the coup and sanctions, many Haitians fled the cities for rural areas, or joined the informal service sector (food preparation, tailoring, transportation, black marketing) and reduced household expenditures by eating less and keeping their children home from school.[33]

Analysts disagree about the impact of sanctions on the nutritional status of Haitian children. Even before sanctions were imposed, Haiti suffered the highest rates of acute malnutrition in the Western Hemisphere. Gibbons, head of the UNICEF office in Haiti during the crisis, reported that malnutrition increased significantly between 1990 and 1994. According to Gibbons, health organizations working in Haiti estimated that the percentage of children suffering from at least some malnutrition increased from 27 percent in 1990 to 50 percent in 1994. Rates of acute malnutrition doubled. Rising maternal malnutrition also affected fetal growth and resulted in a higher percentage of low birth weight babies.[34] However, Sarah Zaidi saw little evidence of malnutrition during her research visits to Haiti. Citing figures from the Child Health Institute and a U.S. Agency for International Development (USAID) survey, Zaidi wrote that "it appears that sanctions had little impact on the nutritional status of Haitian children."[35]

Disagreement and controversy also surrounded the question of whether sanctions caused increased child mortality and declining public health. Before the crisis, one-third of the Haitian population had no access to medical care, and health conditions were among the worst in the world. The combination of sanctions and political terror resulting from the junta made matters worse. Many Haitians who had received at least some medical care previously were no longer able or willing to visit clinics or see health professionals. The sanctions and political crisis also led to a deterioration of the country's meager water supply and sanitation systems, increasing the risk of disease and illness.[36] The report of the UN Secretary-General of July 1994 found serious humanitarian problems, including "increasing incidence of certain illnesses, such as diarrhea, malaria, typhoid, acute respiratory infections, and measles." The same report also found "persistent malnutrition through the country."[37]

These impacts led to an increase in child mortality, although the extent of the rise is uncertain. In November 1993 a study team commissioned by the Harvard University School of Public Health published a highly controversial study, *Sanctions In Haiti: Crisis in Humanitarian Action,* alleging that up to 1,000 children a month were dying from the effects of sanctions.[38] A front-page article in the *New York Times* reported the study's findings and prompted a storm of criticism, including statements from the United Nations and the White House questioning the study's scientific methodology.[39] Two weeks later, physicians who had participated in the Harvard study team publicly distanced themselves from the report's findings and noted that other factors, including political repression, corruption, and economic mismanagement, contributed to the health conditions in Haiti.[40] The most reliable data on child mortality came from a *1994–95 Demographic and Health Survey,* funded by USAID. According to the study, as reported by Gibbons, the mortality of children ages one through five rose from 56 per thousand in 1987 to 61 per thousand in 1994.[41] This was a significant reversal of the long-term decrease in the rate of infant and child mortality in Haiti and indicated that thousands of children died prematurely during the country's political crisis.

Helping the Needy

To address the serious humanitarian suffering in Haiti, international relief organizations mounted a massive assistance campaign. UN agencies and the Pan American Health Organization (PAHO) played a leading role in this effort, with the United States providing the lion's share of the financing. U.S. support for humanitarian assistance in the last year of the crisis totaled $74 million.[42] Budgets for most of the UN agencies operating in Haiti increased dramatically. The budget for UNICEF jumped from $2 million annually to nearly $12 million.[43] Food aid was the top priority. By the summer of 1994, UN relief efforts were providing food to 940,000 people a day.[44] USAID-supported NGOs were feeding over a million Haitians a day, with the private agency CARE alone serving some 620,000.[45] A substantial portion of

Haiti's 6.5 million people thus received food aid from international agencies, truly a remarkable achievement.

Overall, the humanitarian assistance effort had a positive impact. Despite unremitting hostility from the military junta and enormous bureaucratic and mismanagement problems, international agencies succeeded in cushioning some of the most severe consequences of the sanctions.[46] According to Gibbons, who was at the heart of this humanitarian effort, "widespread famine was avoided, epidemics were contained, and the absolute minimum of social services were maintained for the vulnerable population. These were, and remain, important achievements."[47] Without this massive humanitarian effort, the social consequences of sanctions would have been far more severe.

Help or Harm?

The political impacts of sanctions within Haiti were difficult to ascertain. Many ordinary Haitians and leaders of the Lavalas movement that elected Aristide were strongly in favor of the sanctions.[48] Throughout the crisis President Aristide demanded from exile that the UN impose a "real, complete, and total" embargo to force the military leaders to leave.[49] Haitians knew that they would suffer most from the sanctions, but having been exploited for more than two centuries by what many considered a predatory state, they were prepared to bear the additional hardships of strict sanctions if this meant genuine democracy and development. In her interviews with Haitians, Zaidi found broad support for UN sanctions and a sense of encouragement from the international solidarity thus expressed.[50] People were willing to sacrifice if this meant a return of Aristide. Indeed, many Haitians wanted stronger and more effective sanctions, and they became progressively disappointed as the sanctions failed to produce results. Support for sanctions waned as Haitians observed the obvious lack of enthusiasm for more effective measures by the United States and other major powers.

Haitians also became disappointed when they witnessed the unintended, perverse impact of sanctions. As in the case of Yugoslavia, sanctions had negative side effects that weakened the already shaky foundations of civil society in Haiti. The greatest damage to Haitian society came at the hands of the military junta, which waged a systematic campaign to obliterate the forces of democracy. But sanctions also made the struggle for human rights more difficult. They reduced the population's capacity for political mobilization. Many people were too busy trying to avoid the repression and survive the sanctions to have time for political organizing. The military regime took advantage of shortages to seize greater control over the distribution of scarce goods, especially fuel. The sanctions led to the creation of a black market that enriched the armed forces and the allied paramilitary group, the Front for the Advancement and Progress of Haiti (FRAPH), which carried out a campaign of terror, rape, and murder against the population.[51] The sanctions had other negative effects as well. With the cutoff of foreign aid (upon which Haiti was heavily dependent), public officials and employees did not receive wages and were therefore forced to leave their posts in search of work. This resulted in a lack of personnel to perform state services. A similar deterioration of administrative capacity occurred in local government. The deterioration and weakening of state institutions affected even the postsanctions government.[52] The sanctions also gave the army an excuse to further restrict the population's access to information and deny freedom of assembly.[53]

Implementation and Monitoring

As with all sanctions imposed by the United Nations, implementation depended upon the cooperation and support of individual governments. In the case of Haiti, those efforts were piecemeal and lacked credibility. The United States and other major players communicated mixed messages that signaled uncertainty and confusion within the international community. Initially, the greatest problem was the regional nature of the sanctions. Only OAS member states agreed to implement sanctions, and the legal basis of that commitment was questionable, since the OAS Charter lacks enforcement provisions.[54] As a result, there was widespread circumvention of the sanctions among OAS members. Non-OAS states did not impose sanctions at all and carried on a lively trade with Haiti, as documented in a report by the U.S. General Accounting Office (GAO).[55] Although the United States had been the chief sponsor of the OAS sanctions, its blanket exemption to U.S. assembly plants revealed a lack of commitment to real enforcement.[56] U.S. measures to freeze financial assets and restrict travel were also very limited, leaving key supporters of the junta, such as the powerful Mev, Brandt, Acra, and Madsen families, exempt from sanctions.[57]

The role of the Dominican Republic in undermining sanctions enforcement was particularly large. It opposed sanctions from the beginning, ostensibly on humanitarian grounds, although economic and political factors played a much more important role. The governments and armed forces of the two countries have historically enjoyed close relations. The Dominican government not only ignored the many sanctions violations occurring along its 241-mile border with Haiti, but political leaders and business elites participated in and profited handsomely from the illicit trade. The freewheeling commercial traffic between the Dominican Republic and Haiti continued unabated until Venezuela threatened to cut the discounted rate for the petroleum it sold to Santo Domingo.

The sanctions imposed by the UN theoretically should have been more effective than OAS sanctions, since all members are legally bound to comply with Security Council resolutions. Little was done to monitor and enforce the UN sanctions, however, and the steps that were taken came too late to have much impact. Only when public opinion in the United States pressured the Clinton administration to take more decisive action did enforcement efforts improve.[58]

Two major attempts were made to strengthen cooperative enforcement. The first was the naval blockade, and the second was the Dominican Republic's agreement to patrol its border with Haiti. When the Security Council authorized a naval blockade in Resolution 875, U.S. warships were joined by three ships from Canada, and one each from Argentina, France, and the Netherlands.[59] The blockade had some impact in preventing shipping to and from Haiti, but the overall naval effort was quite modest, especially when compared to the blockade against Iraq (which involved ships from fifteen countries) or the Danube Patrol and Adriatic Sharp Guard employed against Yugoslavia (involving fourteen countries). The Haiti blockade also suffered a high-profile failure in May 1994 when a Bahamian vessel successfully evaded the blockade and docked off the small port of Jacmel in Haiti.[60] As David Malone observed, the naval blockade appeared to be a strong measure, but it was largely an act of desperation and improvisation by the Security Council in response to the failure of the Governors Island agreement.[61] It did not address the biggest problem of illicit trade, the flow of goods across the Dominican border.

When a *New York Times* reporter observed the Dominican border in November 1993, six heavy trucks passed a main crossing in fifteen minutes.[62] In May 1994 the U.S. ambassador to Haiti observed a similar scene of vibrant smuggling activity at the border, with traders merely pausing to wait for the observers to pass before resuming their operations.[63] Military and police forces on the Dominican side of the border worked to prevent Haitians from crossing the border rather than to stop smuggling.[64] Eventually, political pressure increased for a greater effort to halt the flow of illegal trade across the border. One proposal for getting the Dominican Republic to cooperate was to impose secondary sanctions if Santo Domingo did not take action to stop the smuggling.[65]

In May 1994 the situation changed as the Balaguer government of the Dominican Republic began to comply with the sanctions in response to U.S. pressure and to deflect international criticism surrounding suspected election fraud.[66] The Dominican government deployed 10,000 troops along the Haitian border, replaced all of the officers and soldiers who had been at the border for more than two months, and allowed the UN to provide technical support. All this was presumably intended to reduce the volume of sanctions violations, but trade continued at night at newly created and unsupervised crossing points. Werleigh's acid comment was: "The entire operation was *mise en scène*—pure theater."[67]

Nonetheless, U.S. officials took advantage of the Dominican Republic's apparent new willingness to cooperate by deploying an eighty-eight-member multinational observer force to help seal its border.[68] As part of the effort, the United States authorized $15 million and agreed to send six helicopters, eighteen military scouts, and several technical experts under a memorandum of understanding between it and the Dominican Republic.[69] This assistance mission was supposed to be ready for deployment in August but was delayed until mid-September 1994, only days before the U.S. military intervention. In the end, the enforcement support mission came too late and was never deployed.

Conclusion

The experience of sanctions against Haiti holds several important lessons for future sanctions episodes. In this case, as in several of the others examined, the initiative for sanctions came from the relevant regional organization. The OAS was the first to impose sanctions against Haiti, just as the Economic Community of West African States was first to enact sanctions against Liberia and Sierra Leone. In Latin America as in Africa, though, the regional organization lacked the legal authority and institutional capacity to enforce compliance with the sanctions. If regional organizations are to take the lead in imposing sanctions, they will need assistance in developing effective implementation mechanisms.

An important problem in Haiti was the communication of mixed messages to the military junta. The strong rhetoric of the sending countries indicated a commitment to the restoration of democracy, but the actions of the United States, the Security Council, and other major players suggested competing interests and uncertain purposes. The Bush administration's exemption of U.S. assembly factories shortly after the coup, the failure to target sanctions against the coup leaders immediately, and the lack of credible enforcement measures all sent signals to Haiti's military leaders that regional resolve to enforce sanctions was weak. Werleigh suggested that an early combination of economic and diplomatic measures to truly isolate the de facto government would have signaled the determination of the international community and could have been effective in bringing the military leaders to heel.[70] Others have suggested that against such a relatively weak adversary, the credible threat of the use of force would have been more effective than sanctions in getting the coup leaders to comply, although gaining Security Council support for such an action would have been extremely difficult.[71]

When sanctions were strengthened with the UN oil and arms embargo in June 1993, the coup leaders responded quickly in displaying a new willingness to negotiate an end to the crisis. This reaction indicated the potent bargaining leverage that sanctions could provide. But the resulting Governors Island agreement was deeply flawed, and the leverage gained through sanctions was squandered. The agreement's provision for lifting sanctions before the departure of the coup leaders was a crucial mistake, and the unwillingness of the United States to confront the armed thugs who disrupted the landing of the *Harlan County* sealed the fate of the agreement and signaled its final collapse. Using the opportunity provided by sanctions relief, coup leaders stockpiled strategic goods, especially fuel, and also intensified their reign of terror against Haitian civilians. The lesson here is obvious. When sanctions succeed in establishing a bargaining process, pressure should be maintained until the targeted authorities comply with the principal demands of UN negotiators. The case of Yugoslavia is also instructive in this regard. Serbian leaders sought to gain a lifting of sanctions prior to the signing of a peace agreement, a demand that some European officials were prepared to entertain. U.S. negotiators held out for a tougher position and insisted that sanctions would not be lifted until Belgrade accepted a final peace agreement. This strategy proved successful and helped to produce the Dayton peace accord.

The final point regarding Haiti, again similar to experiences in other cases, is the need for more systematic monitoring and enforcement efforts. No coherent effort was made to monitor the sanctions until very late. The naval blockade began only in October 1993, and cooperative efforts to close the Dominican border with Haiti came at the very end of the crisis, if at all. This experience reinforces the argument for quick and effective enforcement measures against states that violate sanctions. It also suggests the need for greater institutional capacity, both among regional organizations and within the UN Secretariat.

Notes

1. Claudette Werleigh, "The Use of Sanctions in Haiti," in David Cortright and George A. Lopez, eds., *Economic Sanctions: Panacea or Peacebuilding in a Post–Cold War World?* (Boulder, Colo.: Westview, 1995), 163.

2. Ibid., 164.

3. Sarah Zaidi, "Humanitarian Effects of the Coup and Sanctions in Haiti," in Thomas G. Weiss, David Cortright, George A. Lopez, and Larry Minear, eds., *Political Gain and Civilian Pain: Humanitarian Impacts of Economic Sanctions* (Lanham, Md.: Rowman and Littlefield, 1997), 199.

4. Elizabeth Gibbons, *Sanctions in Haiti: Human Rights and Democracy Under Assault,* Center for Strategic and International Studies, Washington Papers 177 (Westport, Conn: Praeger, 1999), 3.

5. Domingo E. Acevedo, "The Haitian Crisis and the OAS Response: A Test of Effectiveness in Promoting Democracy," in Lori Fisler Damrosch, ed., *Enforcing Restraint: Collective Intervention in Internal Conflicts* (New York: Council on Foreign Relations Press, 1993), 132. Humanitarian aid was exempted from the provisions of this resolution (OAS Resolution MRE/RES.1/91).

6. Zaidi, "Humanitarian Effects," 194–195.

7. U.S. officials acknowledged that some of those affected by the freeze probably moved their liquid assets offshore. Steven A. Holmes, "Haitian Rulers Are Target of New Sanctions by U.S.," *New York Times,* 5 June 1993, A2.

8. Zaidi, "Humanitarian Effects," 195.

9. Howard W. French, "U.N. Approves Ban on Shipments of Oil to Haitian Military," *New York Times,* 17 June 1993, A1.

10. David Malone, *Decision-Making in the UN Security Council: The Case of Haiti* (Oxford: Oxford University Press, 1998), 86.

11. Howard W. French, "UN Talks Bring Haiti Leaders and Aristide Together in New York," *New York Times,* 28 June 1993, A3.

12. Robert Maguire et al., *Haiti Held Hostage: International Responses to the Quest for Nationhood, 1986 to 1996,* Occasional Paper no. 23 (Providence, R.I.: Thomas J. Watson Institute for International Studies, 1996), 36.

13. Malone, *Decision-Making in the UN Security Council,* 95.

14. Gibbons, *Sanctions in Haiti,* 4–5.

15. Ian Martin, "Haiti: Mangled Multilateralism," *Foreign Policy* 95 (Summer 1994): 80. For a thorough account of the process involved in arriving at this agree-

ment and the events that followed, see Malone, *Decision-Making in the UN Security Council,* 86–92.

16. Gibbons, *Sanctions in Haiti,* 5.

17. Malone, *Decision-Making in the UN Security Council,* 88.

18. Martin, "Haiti," 72.

19. Malone, *Decision-Making in the UN Security Council,* 88.

20. This was only the fourth time the Security Council had authorized a naval blockade to enforce sanctions, the other instances being Rhodesia, Iraq, and Serbia. Paul Lewis, "Standoff in Haiti: U.N. Backs Use of Ships to Enforce Haiti Embargo," *New York Times,* 17 October 1993, A15.

21. Howard W. French, "New Haiti Road Could Be Anti-Embargo Lifeline," *New York Times,* 28 October 1993, A1.

22. Steven Greenhouse, "U.S. Bars Flights and Money Deals with the Haitians," *New York Times,* 11 June 1994, A1. By May 1994 the United States had targeted three categories of Haitians for sanctions, totaling more than 600 names: officers of the Haitian military and police and their families, individuals playing a role in the 1991 military coup and their families, and individuals (mainly business-people) employed by or representing the Haitian military and their families. Howard W. French, "U.S. Envoy to Haiti Sees Glaring Gap in Embargo," *New York Times,* 26 May 1994, A8.

23. Joanne Landy, "Suppose We Invade Haiti. Then What?" *New York Times,* 7 August 1994, D17.

24. John Stremlau, "Sharpening International Sanctions: Toward a Stronger Role for the United Nations," a report to the Carnegie Commission on Preventing Deadly Conflict, Carnegie Corporation of New York, November 1996, 31. Resolution 940 was groundbreaking in that (1) it was the first time the United States had obtained UN authorization for the use of force in its own hemisphere, and (2) it authorized force to remove one regime and install another within a member state. See Malone, *Decision-Making in the UN Security Council,* 110.

25. Maguire et al., *Haiti Held Hostage,* 40–41.

26. The credibility of the threat of force combined with an incentives package for the leaders of the military coup, including a comfortable exile in Panama, finally convinced the military junta to relinquish power. See Stremlau, "Sharpening International Sanctions," 32.

27. Gibbons, *Sanctions in Haiti,* 10.

28. Ibid.

29. Ibid., 11.

30. Ibid., 12.

31. Zaidi, "Humanitarian Effects in Haiti," 202.

32. Gibbons, *Sanctions in Haiti,* 13.

33. Ibid., 14–20.

34. Gibbons, *Sanctions in Haiti,* 23.

35. Zaidi, "Humanitarian Effects in Haiti," 203.

36. Gibbons, *Sanctions in Haiti,* 26–27.

37. United Nations Security Council, *Report of the Secretary-General on the Question of Haiti,* S/1994/871, 26 July 1994, par. 11.

38. Harvard University School of Public Health, *Sanctions in Haiti: Crisis in Humanitarian Action,* Program on Human Security, Working Papers Series (Cambridge, Mass.: Harvard University Center for Population and Development Studies, November 1993).

39. Howard W. French, "Study Says Sanctions Kill 1,000 Children a Month," *New York Times*, 9 November 1993, A1. Descriptions of the controversy and the debate about methodology can be found in Zaidi, "Humanitarian Effects in Haiti," 203–205; and Gibbons, *Sanctions in Haiti*, 59–61.

40. Howard W. French, "Embargo's Effect on Haiti Debated," *New York Times*, 24 November 1993, A 4.

41. Gibbons, *Sanctions in Haiti*, 61.

42. Zaidi, "Humanitarian Effects in Haiti," 206.

43. Ibid.

44. United Nations Security Council, *Report of the Secretary-General on the Question of Haiti*, S/1994/1012, New York, 26 August 1994, par. 9.

45. Gibbons, *Sanctions in Haiti*, 71.

46. Zaidi, "Humanitarian Effects in Haiti," 207.

47. Gibbons, *Sanctions in Haiti*, 72.

48. Werleigh, "The Use of Sanctions in Haiti," 162.

49. Quoted in Gibbons, *Sanctions in Haiti*, 50.

50. Zaidi, "Humanitarian Effects in Haiti," 201.

51. Gibbons, *Sanctions in Haiti*, 38–39.

52. Ibid., 28–31.

53. Ibid., 39–46.

54. Acevedo points out that the OAS Charter actually prohibits enforcement action and that Article 53 of the UN Charter prohibits regional enforcement efforts without Security Council authorization. See Acevedo, "The Haitian Crisis," 134, 136.

55. The GAO reported on the shipment of almost 1 million barrels of oil to Haiti from France, Colombia, Portugal, Senegal, and the Dutch Antilles. See United States General Accounting Office, *GAO Evidence Regarding Non-Compliance with the OAS Embargo*, GAO/NSIAD B-248828, Washington, D.C., GAO, 27 May 1992.

56. Werleigh, "The Use of Sanctions in Haiti," 164.

57. "Lean on the Dominican Republic," *New York Times*, 24 May 1994, A18.

58. Zaidi credits the Congressional Black Caucus, TransAfrica director Randall Robinson, and the Haitian diaspora with generating increased media coverage of the human rights abuses in Haiti and greater pressure on the White House. Zaidi, "Humanitarian Effects," 198.

59. Malone, *Decision-Making in the UN Security Council*, 93.

60. Douglas Jehl, "Bahamian Tug Evades Navy to Land in Haiti," *New York Times*, 25 May 1994, A3.

61. Malone, *Decision-Making in the UN Security Council*, 95.

62. Larry Rohter, "At Haiti-Dominican Border: Barrier or Loophole?" *New York Times*, 10 November 1993, A3.

63. French, "U.S. Envoy," A8.

64. Rohter, "At Haiti-Dominican Border," A3.

65. In a *New York Times* editorial, Congressman Ronald V. Dellums advocated denying the Dominican Republic some $22 million in foreign aid for 1994 and its $180 million sugar quota if it continued to violate the sanctions against Haiti. See Dellums, "Squeeze the Dominican Republic," *New York Times*, 24 July 1994, D15.

66. John Kifner, "Balaguer Says He'll Enforce Curbs on Haiti," *New York Times*, 30 May 1994, A4.

67. Werleigh, "The Use of Sanctions in Haiti," 165.

68. Eric Schmitt, "Legislators in U.S. Differ Over Haiti," *New York Times,* 1 September 1994, A10.

69. Eric Schmitt, "Pentagon Worries About Cost of Aid Missions," *New York Times,* 5 August 1994, A6; Larry Rohter, "Last Flight Out of Haiti Strands Some," *New York Times,* 31 July 1994, A10.

70. Werleigh, "The Use of Sanctions in Haiti," 170.

71. Malone, *Decision-Making in the UN Security Council,* 172.

6

Taming Terrorism: Sanctions Against Libya, Sudan, and Afghanistan*

United Nations sanctions against Libya and Sudan had many similarities but also significant differences. The cases were similar not only in the geographic proximity and cultural similarities of the two North African states but also in the nature of the issue being addressed: support for international terrorism. These two cases stand out as the first major attempt by the United Nations to respond to specific acts of terrorism and to the problem of international terrorism in general. The cases differ significantly, however, in the nature and extent of the actions taken by the Security Council. In the Libya case the UN imposed forceful but selective sanctions and maintained these restrictions for more than seven years. In the Sudan case, by contrast, the Council imposed only diplomatic measures. It voted for but did not impose broader aviation sanctions and took no action to apply more forceful measures to tame Sudanese support for terrorist activities. In the pages that follow we examine the cases of Libya and Sudan, as well as the November 1999 sanctions imposed against the Taliban regime in Afghanistan, to analyze the differing ways in which the Security Council responded to the challenge of terrorism.

Sanctions Against Libya

The UN sanctions against the Libyan Arab Jamahiriya represented the first time that organization had used sanctions as a means of combating international terrorism. On the surface the sanctions were intended to bring two indicted Libyan suspects to trial for involvement in the bombing of civilian airliners, but the sanctions also served as a deterrent

---

* This chapter was coauthored by Jaleh Dashti-Gibson and Richard W. Conroy.

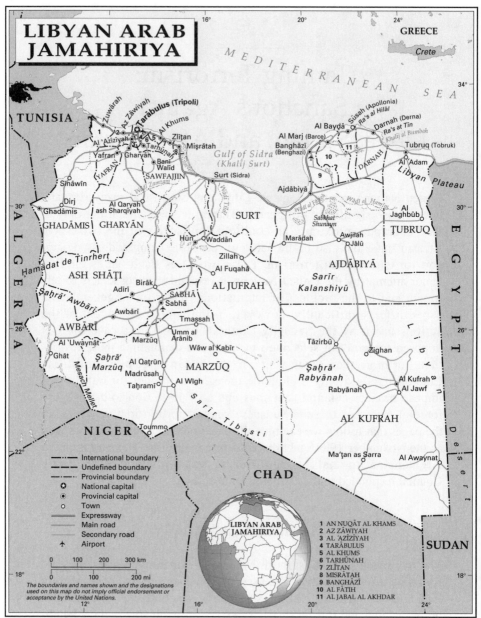

LIBYAN ARAB JAMAHIRIYA

GREECE
Crete

MEDITERRANEAN SEA

TUNISIA

Zuwārah
Az Zāwiyah
Ţarābulus (Tripoli)
Al Khums
Al 'Azīzīyah
Zlīţan
Yafran
Tarhūnah
Mişrātah
Gharyān
Bani Walīd
Gulf of Sidra (Khalīj Surt)
Sīnāwin
SAWFAJJIN
Surt (Sidra)

Al Baydā
Sūsah (Apollonia)
Ra's al Hilāl
Al Marj (Barce)
Darnah (Derna)
Ra's at Tīn
Khalīj al Bumbah
Banghāzī (Benghazi)
Tubruq (Tobruk)
DARNAH
Al 'Adam
Libyan Plateau

Ajdābiyā

Dirj
Ghadāmis
Al Qaryah ash Sharqīyah
GHADĀMIS
GHARYĀN
SURT
Sabkhat Shunayn
Al Jaghbūb
ŢUBRUQ

Hūn
Waddān
Marādah
Awjilah
Jālū

Hamādat de Tinrhert
Zillah
ASH SHĀŢI
Birāk
Al Fuqahā
AJDĀBIYĀ
Adīrī
Sarīr Kalanshiyū

Şahrā' Awbārī
SABHĀ
AL JUFRAH
Awbārī
Sabhā

AWBĀRĪ
Tmassah
Al 'Uwaynāt
Marzūq
Umm al Arānib
Wāw al Kabīr
Tāzirbū
Zighan
Ghāt
Şahrā' Marzūq
Al Qaţrūn
Madrūsah
Al Wīgh
MARZŪQ
Şahrā' Rabyānah
Rabyānah
Al Kufrah
Al Jawf
Taḥramī

Sarīr Tibasti

NIGER
Toummo

AL KUFRAH

Libyan Desert

CHAD

Ma'tan as Sarra
Al Awaynat

SUDAN

Legend

- –·–·– International boundary
- – – – Undefined boundary
- ······· Provincial boundary
- ✪ National capital
- ◉ Provincial capital
- ○ Town
- ═══ Expressway
- ─── Main road
- ─── Secondary road
- ✈ Airport

0 100 200 300 km
0 100 200 mi

The boundaries and names shown and the designations used on this map do not imply official endorsement or acceptance by the United Nations.

LIBYAN ARAB JAMAHIRIYA

1 AN NUQĀT AL KHAMS
2 AZ ZĀWIYAH
3 AL 'AZĪZĪYAH
4 ŢARĀBULUS
5 AL KHUMS
6 TARHŪNAH
7 ZLĪTAN
8 MIŞRĀTAH
9 BANGHĀZĪ
10 AL FĀTIH
11 AL JABAL AL AKHDAR

Map No. 3787 Rev 1 United Nations
April 1994

Department of Public Information
Cartographic Section

against future acts of terrorism and as a means of encouraging the Libyan regime to end its suspected harboring and support of terrorist organizations. Both policy objectives were partially achieved, although it is impossible to know how much sanctions helped to determine these developments.

The sanctions against Libya were targeted against aviation and armaments. As such, they were early examples of the use of selective sanctions. In this case the targeting was appropriately tailored to the offense, the bombing of airliners. The sanctions had only modest impacts on Libya's economy, but the pressure was sufficient to cause serious inconvenience. The Tripoli government attempted to use the sanctions to rally public support, stirring up anti-Western sentiment and blaming the country's ills on external pressure. But the regime resented the diplomatic isolation and economic hardships resulting from sanctions and placed great importance on obtaining relief from these measures.

Initially imposed in March 1992, the sanctions remained in force for more than seven years, making them second only to those against Iraq as the longest sanctions episode of the 1990s. The evidence suggests that the sanctions were initially very effective in establishing a bargaining framework. Libya responded to the threat of sanctions by offering to surrender the two suspects to an international tribunal. The major Western powers refused this offer, however, insisting on a trial in the United States, Great Britain, or France. It took more than six years before a diplomatic solution emerged. The final settlement was, ironically, very similar to the original offer proposed by Tripoli, although Libya also made some concessions. The Western powers accepted a compromise in part because of growing pressure against the Libya sanctions within the Arab League and the Organization of African Unity (OAU). This case thus illustrated a reverse bargaining dynamic: neighboring states and regional organizations applying pressure on the permanent members of the Security Council to adopt more flexible diplomacy or face an end to sanctions compliance. The message seemed to work and led to a successful negotiation that finally resolved the crisis in April 1999.

The Origins of the Crisis

During the 1980s the United States and other Western governments became concerned about Libyan involvement in terrorist activity. In 1981, 1982, and 1986 Washington imposed progressively stronger uni-

---

LIBYA, Security Council Resolutions

Resolution Number	Action
748	**31 March 1992** Imposed aviation sanctions Banned the supply of weapons Required reductions in personnel at Libyan diplomatic/consular missions abroad Restricted travel of Libyan nationals suspected of terrorist activity Created sanctions committee
883	**11 November 1993** Imposed additional sanctions Froze Libyan government assets abroad Tightened the aviation sanctions Banned the import of some oil-transporting equipment
1192	**27 August 1998** Suspended sanctions upon receipt of the Secretary-General's report that the two suspects had arrived in the Netherlands for the proposed trial Threatened additional sanctions if Libya did not accept the offer

---

lateral sanctions against Libya. In 1986 the Reagan administration launched air strikes against Tripoli and other cities, targeting a residence of Libyan leader Muammar Qaddafi and killing his adopted daughter. Concerns about Libyan terrorist activities intensified greatly in December 1988, when Pan Am Flight 103 exploded in the air over Lockerbie, Scotland, killing 259 passengers and crew on the plane and eleven people on the ground. Less than one year later, on 19 September 1989, French UTA Flight 772 exploded in the air over Niger, killing all passengers and crew. Investigations into the crashes found evidence that both bombings were the work of Libyan intelligence agents. In October 1991, a French judge issued a warrant for the arrest of four Libyans for the UTA bombing, including Qaddafi's brother-in-law. Shortly thereafter, the United States and Britain indicted two Libyan security officials, Abdel Basset al-Megrahi (a high-level intelligence official) and

Al-Amin Khalifa Fhimah (ex-manager of the Libyan Arab Airlines office in Malta) for the Lockerbie bombing.

In January 1992 the Security Council passed Resolution 731 condemning the bombings and deploring Libya's lack of cooperation with the criminal investigations. Within the United States, the family members of the Pan Am Flight 103 victims became a visible and influential interest group, demanding that the suspects be brought to justice. In both the United States and Great Britain, domestic political pressure mounted for tougher action against Libya and the imposition of UN sanctions. In an attempt to avoid sanctions, Qaddafi offered in February 1992 to turn over the UTA suspects to a French court and the Lockerbie suspects to an international tribunal. Washington and London insisted that the Lockerbie trials had to be in U.S. or British courts. A month later Qaddafi made another last-minute attempt to stave off sanctions by announcing that the suspects would be turned over to the Arab League. Again the offer was deemed inadequate, and the Security Council rejected it. The Libyan offers to extradite the suspects were a direct result of the threat of sanctions, another sign of the potential impact sanctions can have as inducements to bargaining.

On 31 March 1992, the Council determined that the government of Libya had failed to comply with its demand and voted to adopt Resolution 748 under Chapter VII of the UN Charter, imposing mandatory sanctions against Libya. The resolution imposed aviation sanctions, banned the supply of weapons, required reductions in personnel at Libyan diplomatic and consular missions abroad, and restricted the travel of known Libyan nationals suspected of terrorist activity. Resolution 748 also called on Libya to cooperate with criminal investigators, cease all support for terrorist activities, and compensate the families of the Pan Am and UTA victims. Targeting the entire Libyan aviation industry, Resolution 748 banned all flights to and from Libya by requiring that states refuse landing, takeoff, and overflight rights for Libyan-bound aircraft and close Libyan Arab Airlines offices. It prohibited the supply of aircraft parts, maintenance, engineering, and airworthiness certification for Libyan aircraft. Also banned were the payment of insurance claims and the provision of flight insurance. Resolution 748 established a sanctions committee with the standard mandate to seek information from states regarding the implementation of these measures, report on violations, and consider requests for humanitarian exemptions and special assistance under Article 50.

In the months after sanctions were imposed, Libya again tried to settle the dispute. In June 1992 the government offered to try the two suspects in a court monitored by either the Arab League or the United Nations. This was the first time that Tripoli suggested a UN-supervised trial. In announcing the offer, the secretary-general of Libya's General People's Congress publicly rejected terrorism and called for improved relations with Western countries. The United States and Great Britain dismissed the Libyan offer, however, and the Qaddafi regime refused to make any further concessions. The result was a diplomatic stalemate and mounting Western pressure for stronger sanctions.

On 11 November 1993, the Security Council adopted Resolution 883, which froze some Libyan government assets abroad, tightened the aviation sanctions, and banned the import of some oil-transporting equipment. The resolution prohibited the sale, acceptance, or endorsement by other airlines of Libyan Arab Airline tickets; banned the sale of equipment and services to maintain or construct aviation infrastructure such as airfields; and proscribed the supply of training services to aviation personnel. This tightening of sanctions was primarily intended to have a psychological impact. The United States wanted the Security Council to follow its lead and impose an oil boycott, but Europeans resisted because they depended heavily on imports of Libyan oil, consuming 90 percent of Libya's oil exports.[1] Although the European powers wanted to do something to demonstrate their concern, they were not willing to incur high costs.

Political support for tougher sanctions against Libya was weak in Europe and other regions. Many countries viewed the dispute as a concern mainly for France, Great Britain, and the United States, over an issue that did not have the urgency of such crises as the war in Bosnia or the continuing confrontation with Iraq. Because of this limited political support, the sanctions remained narrowly focused. Indeed, many countries were willing to cooperate with the sanctions precisely because they were selective and targeted. The aviation sanctions also had a symbolic aspect. Because the Security Council was responding to terrorist attacks against international aviation, the sanctions denied Libya the benefits of participation in international aviation. Since Libya's support for terrorism involved weapons, the sanctions aimed at restricting Libyan access to arms. In terms of operational goals, the flight ban sought to isolate Libya from the rest of the international community, reduce its ability to make trouble for others, and impose modest economic hardships on the country.[2]

Despite the stronger sanctions, Libya still refused to hand over the suspects, and a long period of stalemate descended over the Libyan crisis. For several years after the passage of Resolution 883, Tripoli offered no new gestures of partial compliance, and no major attempts were made to negotiate a solution to the dispute. In the United States, meanwhile, attitudes hardened. In the U.S. Congress pressure mounted to impose even tougher sanctions. In July 1996 Congress passed the Iran and Libya Sanctions Act (ILSA), which imposed secondary sanctions on companies that continued to do business with Libya. This controversial legislation had little noticeable impact on Libya, which already faced near-total U.S. sanctions, but it created tensions between the United States and its major European allies, which considered ILSA a violation of international trade rules and resented being dictated to by the U.S. Congress.

Within Libya as well, some political hardening developed. Western sources reported several instances of political unrest within Libya, although it is unclear how much these were motivated by economic or psychological dissatisfaction arising from sanctions.[3] According to *The Middle East,* an attempted coup against Qaddafi by military officers in October 1993 was the result of the Lockerbie affair. The apparent leader of the coup attempt, Qaddafi's hard-line second-in-command, Major Abdul Salam al Jalloud, was related to one of the Lockerbie suspects.[4] Qaddafi crushed this rebellion by ordering his air force to bomb the rebels' barracks outside the town of Misurata. Qaddafi faced a domestic political dilemma in offering to hand over the Lockerbie suspects, since one of the accused terrorists, Abdel Basset al-Megrahi, was a prominent member of the powerful Megrahi tribe, whose support the government needed to maintain power. Pressure from this important domestic political faction militated against compromise and made Qaddafi reluctant to comply with UN demands.

The Economic Impact of Sanctions

Sanctions appear to have had a modest economic impact, although the Libyan government claimed the opposite. A 1997 Libyan report to the UN listed over $2 billion in aviation-related losses allegedly caused by sanctions and another $2.5 billion in damages to Libya's overburdened road network.[5] But a French news source cited a 1998 Libyan government figure of $378 million lost in Libya's aviation sector.[6] Only one company, Royal Dutch Shell, stopped doing business in Libya because of the new travel difficulties.[7] Libya suffered shortages of aviation spare parts due to the sanctions, but these were not sufficiently severe to shut down domestic flights, which the sanctions still allowed.[8] An August 1993 report indicated that Libya was still conducting domestic flights to

Benghazi, although the flights were nowhere near capacity because many Libyans feared that the lack of spare parts had degraded flight safety.[9] Libyan Arab Airlines carried 638,627 passengers with a fleet of twenty-eight aircraft as late as 1996, or more than 1,700 passengers per day, according to the Arab Air Carriers Organization.[10] A lack of comparative presanctions data on Libya's domestic aviation makes it difficult to assess how much Libya's domestic aviation declined after 1992.

Libyan, UN, and independent reports indicated an increased burden on Libyan roads, resulting in an increase in traffic accidents. In 1997, Libya reported 3,050 road accident deaths, with 12,515 seriously injured.[11] At present, no data exist to determine how these numbers compare with either presanctions Libyan road accidents or with road accidents in states with similar driving populations, mileage, and road conditions.

Libya also claimed damage to other sectors of its economy. A 1998 UN fact-finding team reported that the aviation sanctions damaged Libya's agricultural sector by making it more difficult to import agricultural goods, conduct aerial crop dusting, and deliver veterinary supplies.[12] Libya claimed that its agricultural sector lost $248 million in crop production and over $5 billion in livestock production, but these numbers have not been independently verified.[13] Data from the Food and Agricultural Organization (FAO) do not support Libya's claims. A comparative analysis of FAO statistics for 1991 (before sanctions) and 1997 shows no evidence of major losses in crop and livestock production.[14] Libyan agricultural yields suffered small to moderate losses in some commodities (dates, olives, groundnuts, wheat, and chickens) but made modest gains in others (barley, citrus, eggs). Notwithstanding Libyan claims to the contrary, the impact of the sanctions on the agricultural sector appears to have been modest.

The aviation embargo may have indirectly complemented and reinforced the arms embargo. Both sets of sanctions proscribed overlapping activities pertaining to training, provision of parts, and engineering. The aviation ban complicated the travel of military advisers, mechanics, and radar technicians that the arms embargo already banned. *Jane's Intelligence Review* reported that the Libyan Air Force's cumulative flying time was a paltry eighty-five hours in 1994.[15] The U.S. Central Intelligence Agency credited UN sanctions generally for slowing Libya's chemical weapons and ballistic missile programs.[16] The sanctions also had the positive economic impact of causing Libya to reduce its military spending.[17]

The impacts of the UN sanctions on Libya's oil sector are more difficult to assess. Part of the challenge lies in differentiating the impact of the more limited measures imposed by the UN Security Council from the comprehensive oil embargo adopted by the United States. Libya has proven reserves of 30 billion barrels of oil, as much as Norway and Britain combined and more than Nigeria and Indonesia. The sanctions adversely affected Libya's ability to refine and load petroleum by prohibiting trade in oil-related equipment. U.S. sanctions deprived Libya of the licenses it needed for refining processes, which in turn reduced the availability of petroleum for domestic consumption.[18] Nonetheless, Libya was able to maintain steady levels of crude oil production in spite of sanctions, pumping 1.39 million barrels a day in 1998, according to the International Energy Agency.[19] But exploration and maintenance activities lagged.[20] The World Bank estimated that sanctions cost Libya as much as $18 billion in lost revenue, primarily resulting from underinvestment in the oil industry, which may have been the most significant economic impact of sanctions.[21] The falling price of oil and economic mismanagement—factors that had nothing to do with the sanctions—also had an impact.[22] The price of oil fell by almost half between 1990 and 1999. Because of this, Libya's oil revenues dropped from $22 billion in 1980 to $6 billion in 1998.[23]

Financial sanctions were imposed on Libyan government assets in Resolution 883, following months of debate and political jockeying in the Security Council. Libya had ample time prior to the actual freezing of assets to move its financial resources to sheltered locations, depositing much of them beyond reach in Morocco, Egypt, and Switzerland. In the months before the imposition of financial sanctions, Libya moved an estimated $6.5 billion to sheltered havens in the developing world.[24] These assets were safely beyond the reach of treasury officials in the United States and other countries, but their financial utility to Libya was limited. Since oil is traded in dollars on the world market, and most major financial transactions are cleared through banking centers in the West, Libya was unable to put its sheltered assets to much use. The United States and a few other countries managed to seize some Libyan assets. As of January 1998, the net amount of blocked Libyan assets in the United States totaled $966.1 million.[25] Other countries were much less aggressive in freezing Libyan assets and allowed Libyan-owned companies to operate freely in the real estate, banking, and oil industries. In 1994, the U.S. Treasury reported 103 financial institutions in forty countries that were part of Libya's worldwide network of banking industries.[26] Given these problems, it is probably safe to assume that the financial sanctions against Libya had only limited impacts.

The Humanitarian Impact of Sanctions

Given the modest economic effects of UN sanctions against Libya, it is hard to find evidence of substantial humanitarian impacts. In reports submitted to the Secretary-General of the UN, Libya claimed that the sanctions were having a serious humanitarian impact, increasing the rate of deaths among infants and women and decreasing the vaccination rate.[27] But during the period of UN sanctions, infant mortality rates in Libya continued to decline. From 1987 to 1992, the infant mortality rate per 1,000 live births was 36.9, whereas from 1992 to 1996, the rate was 24.4. Vaccination rates in Libya also remained very high. In 1995, 91.3 percent of children between twelve and twenty-three months were vaccinated (total for all vaccines).[28] This rate was higher than the vaccination rate in Egypt. Libya may have experienced some slight decrease in the significant rates of public health improvement registered in previous years, but the overall impact of sanctions was very limited.

The sanctions may have had other humanitarian consequences. As noted, Libya reported a huge increase in traffic fatalities resulting from greater use of roads. Libya also claimed to the UN fact-finding mission that many ill patients died waiting for permission to be airlifted out of Libya or en route overland for treatment. These claims have not been independently verified. Resolution 748 permitted medical evacuation flights conducted by preapproved aviation companies, as well as aircraft maintenance by five European companies for the medical evacuation aircraft. In addition to its 1996 and 1997 reports, the sanctions committee approved a total of 175 medical evacuation flights between 1995 and 1997. Libyan authorities also reported an 11 percent increase in unemployment and an overall rise in poverty as a result of sanctions. According to the Office of the UN High Commissioner for Refugees in Tripoli, the air embargo created hardships for some 7,000 registered refugees in Libya and increased the cost of refugee repatriation.[29]

Sanctions Enforcement

The flight ban against Libya was remarkably effective, virtually eliminating all but a few symbolic flights. The only ways to reach Libya were by flights to neighboring states followed by overland travel or ferry service from Malta. The only exceptions to the nearly universal cooperation with the air ban were Muslim pilgrimage flights to Saudi Arabia. The original travel ban as specified in Resolution 748 allowed flights for the hajj (the Muslim pilgrimage to Mecca) on EgyptAir, under very restricted conditions, but some additional unauthorized flights also took place. The Security Council issued mild verbal reprimands for such flights,[30] but otherwise looked the other way so as not to offend Muslim sensibilities.[31]

The restrictions against providing aviation services and spare parts were less well enforced, according to an extensive study published in *U.S. News and World Report*. U.S. officials charged that European countries were not enforcing the sanctions vigorously and were using loopholes in Resolutions 748 and 883 to carry on business as usual.[32] Several European companies openly supplied aircraft parts and services to Libya, arguing that the sanctions did not apply to preexisting contracts.[33] These violations included the 1994 sale of two aircraft engines by a Dutch company, with the Dutch government's approval.[34] European companies based in Switzerland, the Netherlands, Malta, and France also provided aircraft to Libyan oil companies.[35] Other reports included the sale of embargoed aircraft parts through Malta.

Less evidence is available about the enforcement of the arms embargo. The overall level of weapons imports declined significantly during the 1990s, due not only to sanctions but also to Libya's drop in oil revenues resulting from lower world oil prices. Press reports identified a number of arms violations, but it is difficult to determine the extent or significance of such incidents. In 1993, private Egyptian firms sold Libya spare parts for tanks and Mig-23 aircraft. Egyptian technicians were also present at the Tarhuna center, where Libya was working to develop an upgraded SCUD missile.[36] In September 1996, an Iranian ship was discovered carrying arms and explosives to Libya in apparent violation of UN sanctions.[37] Despite these violations, Libyan military capabilities were constrained by the sanctions.

The sanctions committee for Resolution 748 played only a limited role in monitoring and enforcing sanctions. As usual, the committee's mandate included examining states' reports on their implementation of sanctions, receiving and considering reports of violations, and recommending remedial actions. In practice, the sanctions committee interpreted its role passively. It merely accepted reports from the limited number of member states that bothered to reply to the committee's requests for such reports. When it received evidence of violations, it took up these matters privately with the states concerned. The burden of enforcement and investigation was left to member states, many of which failed to report on compliance measures. The committee received reports about flights that violated Resolution 748, but it received no information about the provision of prohibited aviation parts and services, even though these violations were public knowledge.[38]

Sanctions and the Political Settlement

After years of diplomatic stalemate, the Libya dispute moved toward settlement in 1998. The spark for change came from an unexpected quarter: rising discontent with the sanctions from neighboring Arab states and regional organizations. Many Arab and North African states were concerned about reports, however exaggerated, of the economic and humanitarian costs of the sanctions. They also resented what they perceived as U.S. and British intransigence in rejecting what seemed to be reasonable Libyan offers to settle the dispute. The concern of the Arab states may have been motivated as well by the backlash against the Iraq sanctions that developed in these countries. In September 1997, the Arab League voted to relax enforcement of the air embargo by allowing more medical evacuation flights out of Libya. The decision was merely a threat to take such action, in the hope that this would spur negotiations—the league did not actually carry out the threat.[39] More important was the announcement by the OAU in June 1998 that it would openly defy the flight ban and other sanctions if a settlement of the dispute was not reached by September of that year.[40]

The decision by the OAU jolted U.S. and British leaders and prompted a flurry of diplomatic activity. On 24 August 1998, just a week before the threatened OAU deadline, the United States and Great Britain unveiled a new proposal for resolving the crisis. They offered to hold the trial of the two Libyan suspects under Scottish law in a court in the Netherlands. The next day, the Arab League, Egypt, Sudan, and South African president Nelson Mandela expressed support for the U.S.-British proposal. Two days later the Security Council unanimously approved the new plan and adopted Resolution 1192 offering to suspend sanctions upon receipt of the Secretary-General's report that the two suspects had arrived in the Netherlands for the proposed trial. The Council also threatened additional sanctions if Libya did not accept the offer. Qaddafi promptly announced his acceptance of the proposal "in principle," and the end of Libya's sanctions ordeal seemed in sight.

Diplomatic wrangling over the fine print in the agreement took several more months, however. Even though Libya accepted Resolution 1192 in theory, it balked over some of the conditions in the U.S.-British proposal. Libya asserted that the two suspects should serve their prison terms in Libya if convicted.[41] U.S. and British officials termed this condition unacceptable. Secretary-General Kofi Annan and Mandela interceded to preserve the August agreement, and in March 1999 Mandela announced a final resolution. Three weeks later, on 5 April 1999, the two Libyan suspects were delivered from Libya to The Hague for trial. The Secretary-General promptly presented his required report to the Security Council, and on 8 April sanctions were suspended. After more than seven years, Libya obtained relief from UN sanctions.

When the Security Council suspended sanctions, Annan was asked if the sanctions regime was primarily responsible for Libya finally agreeing to hand over the suspects. He responded by saying:

> I prefer to think it played a role. Of course they have lived with it for seven years, and I think apart from living with the sanctions for seven years, no country likes to be treated as an outcast and outside the society of nations, which, to some extent, when one is branded and sanctions are imposed, one is marked by that kind of thing. And I think Libya wanted to get back to the international community. Libya wanted to get on with its economic and social development. And Libya wanted to be able to deal freely with its neighbours and with the rest of the world.[42]

Clearly, UN sanctions were a major irritant to the Libyan government. Finding a way to lift sanctions was one of the Qaddafi regime's highest priorities.[43] Although the government played the nationalist card and attempted to mobilize a rally 'round the flag effect at home, it made numerous attempts to find a face-saving solution to avoid or end sanctions. It did so in the face of considerable domestic political pressures against any such compromise. Although the sanctions did not cause major economic disruption, they were a significant inconvenience. They impeded Libya's aspirations to earn a larger international role commensurate with its great oil wealth. The psychological impact of the isolation Libya endured is not measurable but undoubtedly had an impact as well. The combination of these factors created sufficient pressure to induce Qaddafi to negotiate a settlement.

The Libya dispute could have ended years earlier if the Western powers had been more flexible in their diplomacy and had been willing to accept the kind of settlement that was finally negotiated in 1999. The threat of sanctions was highly effective in early 1992 in encouraging the Libyan government to turn over the suspected terrorists. Offers made at that time by the Qaddafi regime admittedly did not meet all of the conditions established by the Western powers, but they represented political movement on the part of the government and could have formed the basis for a negotiated agreement. Instead, the United States and its Western allies adopted a take it or leave it approach, and the dispute dragged on needlessly for years. Arab and African states became increasingly impatient with this hard-line policy and in 1997 began to apply pressure on the Western states for greater diplomatic flexibility. Faced with the prospect of a complete erosion of the sanctions, the United States and Great Britain responded with a creative new proposal that satisfied their demands for a trial under British or French law while also partially meeting Libya's proposal for a trial under international auspices. The settlement resulted from a unique form of double pressure: the weight of sanctions on Libya and the threat to Western powers from Arab and African states to cease cooperation with the sanctions. In the end both the Libyan government and the Western powers compromised.

In addition to helping resolve the dispute over the two suspected terrorists, the imposition of sanctions may have had a positive effect in restraining Libyan government support for international terrorism. In some respects, this was by far the most significant result of the sanctions. Since the Security Council imposed sanctions in 1992, there have been no allegations of Libyan terrorist attacks on international aviation. Although Libya continued to support and host Palestinian extremist groups, including Abu Nidal's organization, its active involvement in terrorist activities declined significantly.[44] The U.S. State Department's 1996 report on global terrorism stated flatly: "Terrorism by Libya has been sharply reduced by UN sanctions."[45] This was an extraordinary assertion. It suggested that the UN sanctions achieved a significant success in acting as a deterrent against future terrorist activities. If the State Department claim is true, sanctions were effective in altering Libyan government policy and prevented Libyan support for further acts of aviation terrorism. If the relationship between UN sanctions and the decline of Libyan support for terrorism can be documented, this would provide powerful evidence of the effectiveness of these sanctions in the struggle against international terrorism.

Conclusion

On balance, UN sanctions can be rated a partial success. The limited sanctions on travel, oil equipment, and finance did not have major economic impacts, but they were sufficiently burdensome to encourage the search for a negotiated settlement of the dispute. The Libya sanctions thus provide an example of the potential effectiveness of selective sanctions for achieving very specific diplomatic objectives. By themselves sanctions did not resolve the dispute, but they provided a crucial bargaining framework around which a final settlement could be reached.

More important, sanctions encouraged the Libyan government to reduce its involvement in the underworld of terrorist violence and served as an effective deterrent against the government's support for international terrorism. The Libya case thus demonstrated the effectiveness of sanctions both as a catalyst for diplomacy and as a deterrent against international criminality. Success could have come earlier if the Western powers had shown more diplomatic flexibility and if the offers from Libya had been more forthcoming. Ironically, it was the OAU threat to withdraw from sanctions cooperation that in the end induced the necessary compromises on both sides.

Sanctions Against Sudan

The Sudan and Libya cases were in some respects quite similar. In both cases, sanctions were imposed to halt the targeted country's support for international terrorism and to obtain the release of suspects wanted in connection with terrorist incidents; the United States took the lead in mobilizing international pressure against what it considered pariah states and attempted to obtain UN sanctions in support of its own unilateral sanctions; and the Security Council resisted calls for broad trade restrictions and instead imposed more limited, targeted sanctions. In the case of Sudan the measures consisted only of diplomatic sanctions. More far-reaching travel sanctions were provisionally approved by the Security Council but were never implemented, due in part to a UN preassessment report on the likely humanitarian impact of such measures, as well as Egypt's reluctance to support stronger sanctions.

In response to an assassination attempt on the life of Egyptian president Hosni Mubarak in Addis Ababa, Ethiopia, on 26 June 1995, the Security Council adopted Resolution 1044 on 31 January 1996. It condemned the "terrorist assassination attempt" and called upon the government of Sudan to comply within sixty days with the requests of the OAU to extradite to Ethiopia for prosecution the three suspects wanted in connection with the attempt and to cease assisting terrorist activities and giving shelter to terrorists. Although the Sudanese government contended that two of the suspects were not in Sudan and that the identity of the third suspect was not known, the Security Council determined that Sudan had not complied with Resolution 1044.[46] The Council also determined that Sudan's noncompliance constituted a threat to international peace and security. On 26 April 1996, acting under Chapter VII of the UN Charter, the Security Council adopted Resolution 1054

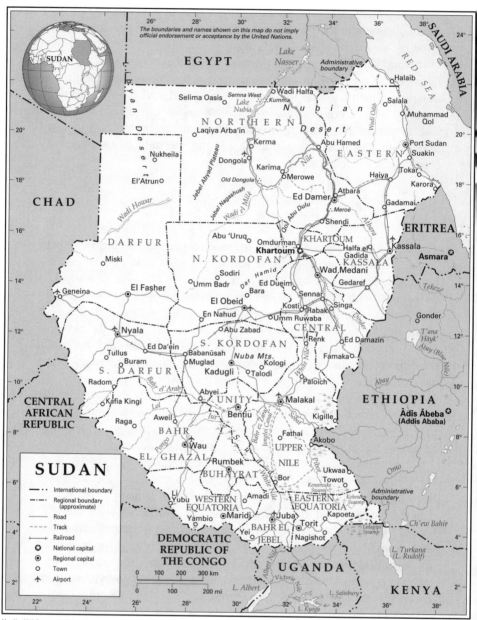

SUDAN

Map No. 3707 Rev. 4   UNITED NATIONS
February 1999

Department of Public Information
Cartographic Section

imposing diplomatic sanctions on Sudan. Resolution 1054 called on member states to significantly reduce the number of staff at diplomatic missions and consular posts, restrict the movement of those that remained, and restrict entry into their territory of Sudanese government officials and military personnel. In addition, Resolution 1054 required that international institutions and regional organizations refrain from convening any conferences in Sudan.

Unlike most cases of UN sanctions, the Security Council did not establish a sanctions committee in this instance. States were requested to notify the Secretary-General directly of the steps taken to implement Resolution 1054. As of December 1998, sixty-six replies had been received from member states.[47] With no sanctions committee, states received even less guidance than usual on how to interpret the requirements of the resolution. The result was very uneven implementation of the diplomatic restrictions. Egypt, Great Britain, and the United States complied fully, expelling diplomats and restricting the movement of remaining Sudanese officials within their territories, but other states complied only partially or not at all.[48]

When Sudan failed to respond to Resolution 1054 and took no action to turn over the suspected terrorists, the Security Council took steps to increase the pressure on the government in Khartoum. On 16 August 1996, the Security Council adopted Resolution 1070 imposing travel sanctions against Sudan. Resolution 1070 required all states to deny any Sudanese aircraft permission to take off from, land in, or fly over their territories and applied to any aircraft registered in Sudan or owned, leased, operated, or substantially owned or controlled by the government or public authorities of Sudan. These measures were not immediately required of member states, however. Resolution 1070 called for a separate Security Council decision within ninety days to determine a date for its entry into force, pending the Secretary-General's report on Sudanese compliance with Resolution 1054. The aviation ban never went into effect, in part because some regional states, including Egypt, opposed such measures for political reasons. Stronger economic measures were also ruled out because of their potential humanitarian effects on a country already suffering from extreme poverty. Egypt feared that it would suffer significantly from such sanctions[49] and was concerned that Sudan would retaliate by reducing the flow of water along the Nile and expel the hundreds of thousands of Egyptians working in Sudan.[50] Egypt also opposed an arms embargo against Sudan out of fear that such a measure would threaten the unity

---

SUDAN, Security Council Resolutions

Resolution Number	Action
1054	**26 April 1996** Imposed diplomatic sanctions Called on member states to reduce the number of staff at diplomatic missions and consular posts and restrict the movement of those that remained Restricted entry into their territory of Sudanese government officials and military personnel Required international institutions and regional organizations to refrain from convening any conferences in Sudan
1070	**16 August 1996** Imposed travel sanctions requiring all states to deny Sudanese aircraft permission to take off from, land in, or overfly their territories Called for a separate Security Council decision within ninety days to determine a date for entry into force Aviation ban never went into effect

---

of Sudan in light of its ongoing civil war between the government and southern rebels demanding greater autonomy.

The Preassessment Report

As the Security Council considered whether to proceed with the threatened imposition of aviation sanctions in the fall of 1996, it decided to send an assessment team to Sudan to investigate the potential humanitarian impact of such measures. The resulting UN report of 20 February 1997 concluded that the proposed aviation sanctions could have serious negative consequences.[51] According to the report, an aviation ban would hinder the evacuation of critically ill patients for treatment abroad.[52] The report also concluded that a flight ban would restrict the import of refrigerated vaccines and might have a serious impact on immunization programs, the domestic distribution of drugs, and food production.[53] Also, the flight ban could compromise Sudan's cooperation with Operation Lifeline Sudan,[54] a vital humanitarian relief operation that had been established a few years before to stem the threat of famine in the south. If the government in Khartoum responded to the flight ban by halting its cooperation with Operation Lifeline and denying it access to the country, the humanitarian consequences would be dire.

The report's relatively gloomy conclusions reinforced the Council's reluctance to impose stronger sanctions. Apart from its role in discouraging further sanctions against Sudan, the preassessment report was significant for the precedent it established in Security Council policy. Instead of responding to humanitarian concerns only after sanctions are imposed, the Council attempted to anticipate such consequences by assessing likely impacts before the imposition of sanctions. Humanitarian officials and experts had been advocating preassessment as a potentially effective tool for preventing some of the most glaring humanitarian consequences of sanctions. The Sudan case illustrated that such assessments were possible and that they could help the Council determine the potential impact of sanctions. A similar assessment report was commissioned in the case of Sierra Leone in 1998. These developments reflect growing support in the UN system for more systematic attempts to preassess potential impacts whenever sanctions are being considered.

Policy Impacts

To outward appearances, the government in Khartoum remained defiant in the face of increasing international isolation. It consistently maintained its lack of involvement in the assassination attempt on Mubarak, and it never turned over any suspects wanted in connection with the 1995 incident. After the Security Council adopted Resolution 1054 in April 1996, however, Khartoum made an initial gesture to give the appearance of complying with the demand that it stop harboring terrorists. The Sudanese government sent a letter to the Security Council at the end of May 1996 indicating that it had asked Usama bin Laden, a major financial supporter of Islamic radical groups, to leave the country.[55] Bin Laden subsequently left Sudan and set up operations in Afghanistan. In November 1999 bin Laden again found himself at the center of controversy when the Security Council imposed financial and aviation sanctions against Afghanistan to force his extradition to stand trial for the terrorist bombings against U.S. embassies in Africa in August 1998.

The specter of sanctions may have furthered a split between the powerful Islamic National Front of Sudan and the country's military leaders, who did not want to be under international sanctions after the experience of Libya and Iraq. Such a split may have led the front to purge hundreds of army officers from key posts and replace them with front loyalists.[56] Internal dissatisfaction with the regime increased after the spiraling inflation of 1996, and the prolonged war with southern Christian and animist rebels took a severe toll on the economy.[57] This mounting discontent prompted the government to make gestures of conciliation, appointing members of the opposition to minor cabinet posts in March 1998 and eventually allowing opposition groups to organize legally in January 1999. It is unclear how much these measures resulted from outside pressure, however, as opposed to increasing internal dissatisfaction brought on by years of domestic strife and economic troubles.

Conclusion

The purposes of the sanctions against Sudan closely paralleled those against Libya. In both cases the goal was to extradite suspected terrorists and deter further support for international terrorism. In the Libya case, the Security Council imposed selective but forceful measures, and after a long period of diplomatic stalemate, a negotiated solution was reached that permitted the extradition of the suspected terrorists. In addition, sanctions persuaded Libya to reduce its support for international terrorism.

In the case of Sudan, the government continued to deny any knowledge of the terrorist suspects, and there was no indication of a change in Khartoum's policy of hosting and supporting terrorist organizations. The Security Council chose not to impose stronger sanctions because of political and humanitarian considerations, and the controversy over alleged involvement in the 1995 assassination attempt against President Mubarak remained unresolved. The most significant feature of the Sudan case was the humanitarian preassessment report of February 1997. This was the first example of such a report, but it is unlikely to be the last. The policy of conducting a preassessment report was repeated in Sierra Leone and may serve as a precedent for future sanctions episodes.

Isolating the Taliban

In October 1999 the Security Council again used sanctions as a means of combating international terrorism when it approved Resolution 1267 imposing aviation and financial sanctions against the Taliban regime in Afghanistan. Their purpose was to convince the Taliban regime to end its support for international terrorists, and to turn over to "appropriate authorities" Usama bin Laden, who had been indicted in the United States for his involvement in the August 1998 bombings of U.S. embassies in Africa that killed 224 people.[58] The sanctions were also a response to violations of international humanitarian law and human rights, especially discrimination against women and girls, and the sharp rise in the production of opium in Afghanistan. Approved on 15 October 1999, the sanctions went into effect a month later on 14 November. Resolution 1267 created a sanctions committee to monitor and report on compliance by member states and to designate the aircraft and financial assets to be sanctioned.

The Security Council's action against Afghanistan was another example of the trend away from general trade sanctions toward the use of more selective, targeted measures. As in the case of Libya, the sanctions were specifically focused on the aviation sector. The Council denied permission for any aircraft to take off from or land in Taliban-controlled territory, which represented approximately 90 percent of the country, and banned flights of any aircraft owned, leased, or operated by or on behalf of the Taliban regime. The Council also froze all overseas funds and financial resources controlled by the Taliban and banned the use of such funds for the benefit of the Taliban. The United States had previously imposed sanctions against Afghanistan in July, freezing an estimated $500,000 in assets held in the United States by the state-owned Afghan airline. The aviation sanctions exempted flights for religious obligations such as observance of the hajj. An exemption was also provided for the payment of air traffic control and overflight fees to Afghanistan's aeronautical authority from the International Air Transport Association. This provision was added so that international airliners would not have to divert their flight paths to avoid Afghan airspace, but it had the effect of allowing the Taliban to continue collecting funds from international air carriers.

The sanctions against Afghanistan were designed to apply pressure on the Taliban leadership, but their impact was likely to be extremely limited. The aviation sanctions affected only the official Ariana Afghan

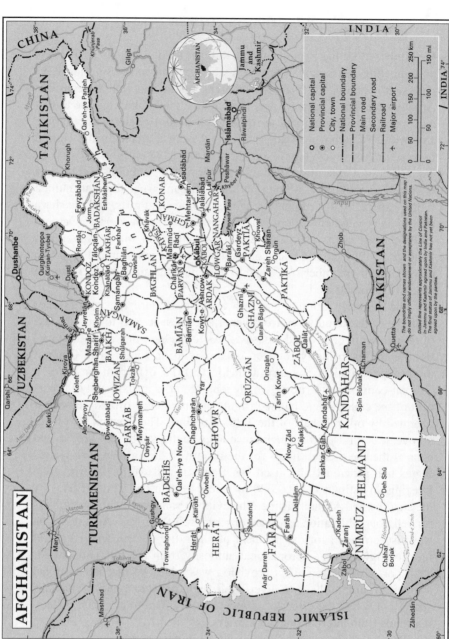

AFGHANISTAN

Map No. 3958 UNITED NATIONS
October 1996 (Colour)

Department of Public Information
Cartographic Section

Legend

- ⊙ National capital
- ◉ Provincial capital
- ○ City, town
- ---·- National boundary
- ---··- Provincial boundary
- ——— Main road
- ——— Secondary road
- ——— Railroad
- ✦ Major airport

The boundaries and names shown and the designations used on this map do not imply official endorsement or acceptance by the United Nations.

Dotted line represents approximately the Line of Control in Jammu and Kashmir agreed upon by India and Pakistan. The final status of Jammu and Kashmir has not yet been agreed upon by the parties.

0   50   100   150   200   250 km

0   50   100   150 mi

CHINA

TAJIKISTAN

UZBEKISTAN

TURKMENISTAN

ISLAMIC REPUBLIC OF IRAN

PAKISTAN

INDIA

Jammu and Kashmir

BADAKHSHĀN

TAKHĀR

KONDOZ

BALKH

JOWZJĀN

FĀRYĀB

BĀDGHĪS

HERĀT

GHOWR

SAMANGĀN

BAGHLĀN

BĀMIĀN

PARVĀN

KĀPĪSĀ

KONAR

NANGARHĀR

LOWGAR

KĀBOL

WARDAK

LOGHMĀN

PAKTĪĀ

KHOWST

GHAZNĪ

ORŪZGĀN

ZĀBOL

KANDAHĀR

HELMAND

NĪMRŪZ

FARĀH

PAKTĪKĀ

Dushanbe

Islāmābād

Rāwalpindi

Peshāwar

Khyber Pass

Mardān

Asadābād

Mehtarlām

Jalālābād

Lal'pūr

Peywār Pass

Gardēz

Khowst

Sharan

Orgūn

Zareh Sharan

Barakī

Kābol

Mahmūd-e Rāqī

Chārīkār

Baghlān

Kondoz

Tāloqān

Rostāq

Jorm

Feyzābād

Eshkāshem

Qal'eh-ye Panjeh

Khorugh

Gilgit

Khunjerab Pass

Qal'eh-ye Panjeh

Khāvak

Farkhar

Dowshī

Khānābād

Kholm

Mazār-e Sharīf

Sheberghān

Shibirghān

Andkhvoy

Dowlatābād

Meymaneh

Qeysār

Qal'eh-ye Now

Owbeh

Chaghcharān

Dowlatābād

Kerki

Kelefī

Kiroya

Qarshī

Keleft

Towraghondī

Gushgy

Herāt

Karokh

Anār Darreh

Shindand

Farāh

Delārām

Zābol

Zaranj

Chāhār Borjak

Deh Shū

Kadesh

Now Zād

Kajakī

Lashkar Gāh

Kandahār

Spīn Būldak

Chaman

Qalāt

Tarīn Kowt

Orūzgān

Qarah Bāgh

Ghaznī

Ghazni

Baraki

Mashhad

Zāhedān

Quetta

Zhob

Mehtarlām

Mary

Kerki

Jeyretān

Samangān

Shulgarah

Tokzār

Yar

Nayak

Bāmiān

Ashrow

Kowt-e Ashrow

Āybak

Airlines, which flew but a single flight a day to the United Arab Emirates.[59] The financial sanctions also had limited impact since Taliban leaders claimed to have no funds abroad.[60] Some members of the Security Council, including Russia and the United States, urged the imposition of an arms embargo on the Taliban, which could have had a significant impact on the Taliban and would have restrained its continuing military operations against the remnants of the former regime, still recognized by the UN as the official government of Afghanistan. The Council chose not to take this action, however, in part because the task of stemming the flow of weapons into Afghanistan, largely across the Pakistani border, was deemed infeasible. Major states were unwilling to take the extensive measures that would be required to reduce arms trafficking along the Afghan-Pakistani border. The military coup in Pakistan in October 1999 made the challenge of cutting off Pakistani support for the Taliban even more difficult, since the previous government of Nawaz Sharif had begun to distance itself from the Taliban, while the new military regime in Islamabad was viewed favorably by the Taliban.

The Security Council imposed only limited measures in part to avoid exacerbating already severe humanitarian conditions in the country. During more than twenty years of war and civil strife, Afghanistan suffered massive social and economic dislocations, dropping to near the bottom of the United Nations Development Programme (UNDP) human development index. Out of a population of 15 million people, more than 6 million were driven from their homes (5 million as refugees, and 1 million as internally displaced persons).[61] In 1999 alone, more than 230,000 were displaced by the regime's various military campaigns.[62] The Taliban has generally cooperated with UN relief agencies operating in the country, which include UNICEF, the World Food Program, and the Food and Agricultural Organization, but UN officials have struggled to convince the regime to permit women to work for the relief agencies, and to give women and girls access to education, employment, and medical care.[63] When UN sanctions were imposed, the Taliban spokesman in New York claimed that the travel and financial restrictions would add misery to the long-suffering people of Afghanistan and would only hurt Afghan traders and middle-class citizens who use the Afghan airline. Given the selective nature of the sanctions, however, it is extremely unlikely that these measures would add to the burdens of the people of Afghanistan.

To date the political effects of the UN sanctions have been minimal. The initial reaction of the Taliban leadership to sanctions reflected an attempt to rally the population and gave no indication of a willingness

AFGHANISTAN, Security Council Resolution

Resolution
Number   Action

1267   **15 October 1999**
            Created sanctions committee
            Imposed aviation and financial sanctions against
            Taliban regime

to bargain or compromise. In the days before the sanctions went into effect in November 1999, Taliban activists organized public rallies against the United States and the United Nations in Kabul and other cities, in a classic example of the rally 'round the flag effect. The top Taliban leader, Mohammad Omar, vowed that the regime would never force bin Laden to leave Afghanistan or turn him over to international authorities. The only slight sign of flexibility from the regime was an offer to convene a panel of Islamic scholars from Afghanistan and Saudi Arabia to examine the bin Laden case and perhaps find a way to meet the request of the international community.[64] This offer was rejected by the United States and other countries as inadequate, and in the initial period after imposition of the sanctions no progress was made on negotiating a solution to the dispute. Meanwhile Afghanistan remained a pariah state internationally, with only Pakistan, Saudi Arabia, and the United Arab Emirates recognizing the Taliban regime. The country faced the prospect of a prolonged period of economic and diplomatic isolation. Whether these pressures would be sufficient to stimulate a bargaining framework, end the regime's support for terrorism, or improve its human rights practices remained to be seen.

Notes

1. Political Risk Services, "Libya," *International Country Risk Guide: Middle East and Africa* (May 1995).
2. Gideon Rose, "Libya," in Richard Haass, ed., *Economic Sanctions and American Diplomacy* (New York: Council on Foreign Relations, 1998), 136.
3. Associated Press, "Libya May Be Facing an Islamic Rebellion: Fighting Reported Outside Tripoli," *Chicago Tribune*, 27 September 1995, 8; "Anti-

Government Demonstrations," *Africa Review World of Information—The Africa Review* (March 1998).

4. "Libya: Call My Bluff," *The Middle East,* no. 231 (February 1994): 19 (2).

5. United Nations Security Council, *Letter Dated 27 May 1997 from the Permanent Representative of the Libyan Arab Jamahiriya to the United Nations Addressed to the Secretary-General,* S/1997/404, New York, 27 May 1997, 9.

6. "Libyan Air Sector Says It Has Lost 378 Million Dollars Since Embargo," *Agence France Presse,* 2 February 1998.

7. Rose, "Libya," 141.

8. "Libya Aviation Sector Suffers from Lack of Spare Parts," *BBC Summary of World Broadcasts,* 24 December 1992.

9. Stephen Sackur, "Libya Lies Back and Thinks of Oil," *Reuters Textline Observer,* 29 August 1993.

10. Arab Air Carriers Organization, "Airline Profile, 1996," Beirut, Lebanon.

11. United Nations Security Council, *Letter Dated 27 May 1997,* S/1997/404, 3.

12. United Nations Security Council, *Letter Dated 15 January 1998 from the Secretary-General Addressed to the President of the Security Council,* S/1998/201, New York, 6 March 1998, 3–4.

13. United Nations Security Council, *Letter Dated 27 May 1997,* S/1997/404, New York, 27 May 1997, 5.

14. Libyan agricultural commodities identified in Central Intelligence Agency, *1997 World Factbook* (Dulles, Va.: Brassey's Incorporated for Central Intelligence Agency, November 1997). Food And Agricultural Organization, Online Databases: FAOSTAT, www.fao.org/waicent/faoinfo/agricult/guides/resource/data.htm. Libyan figures in United Nations Security Council, *Letter Dated 27 May 1997,* S/1997/404, list production, not yields. Production figures are misleading because they hide crop area planted and can inflate losses. Lower production figures could result from a decision to plant fewer hectares or from poor yields.

15. Robert Waller, "The Libyan Threat to the Mediterranean," *Jane's Intelligence Review* 8 (1 May 1996): 226.

16. United States, Central Intelligence Agency, *Report of Proliferation-Related Acquisition in 1997* (Langley, Va.: Central Intelligence Agency, 1998).

17. "Libya Urged to Help Bring Lockerbie Saga to an End," *Mideast Mirror* 12, no. 217 (10 November 1998).

18. Judith Gurney, *Libya: The Political Economy of Oil* (Oxford: Oxford University Press for the Oxford Institute for Energy Studies, 1996), 220–221.

19. "Ban Lifted, Libya Is Set to Retool Oil Works," *New York Times,* 11 April 1999, A17.

20. Colin Barraclough, "Qaddafi Still Defiant After 25 Years as Ruler," *Christian Science Monitor,* 15 September 1994, 8.

21. *Economist,* "Libya and the Bombed Airliners," 13 March 1999, 56.

22. *Economist,* "Libya and Lockerbie: Deadlock Broken," 10 April 1999, 44.

23. Minh T. Vo, "Libya Plans for Future Without UN Embargo," *Christian Science Monitor,* 17 March 1999, 6.

24. "OGJ Newsletter," *Oil and Gas Journal* 91, no. 47 (22 November 1993): 2.

25. United States, Department of the Treasury, Office of Foreign Assets Control, *Terrorist Assets Report* (Washington, D.C.: Department of the Treasury, January 1998), 5.

26. Edward T. Pound, "Sanctions: The Pluses and Minuses. World Leaders Love Them. But Do They Work?" *U.S. News & World Report* 117, no. 17 (31

October 1994): 58. This article elaborates on the many difficulties involved in effective enforcement of financial sanctions against Libya.

27. United Nations Security Council, *Letter Dated 27 May 1997*, S/1997/404.

28. League of Arab States, *Arab Libyan Maternal and Child Health Survey,* 1996. Pan Arab Project for Child Development.

29. United Nations Security Council, *Letter Dated 15 January 1998*, S/1998/201.

30. See United Nations Security Council, *Statement by the President of the Security Council,* S/PRST/1997/2, 29 January 1997; United Nations Security Council, *Statement by the President of the Security Council,* S/PRST/1997/18, 4 April 1997; United Nations Security Council, *Statement by the President of the Security Council,* S/PRST/1997/27, 20 May 1997.

31. "UN Unsure How to Respond to Iraqi, Libyan Violations of Flight Ban," *Chicago Tribune,* 11 April 1997, 24.

32. "USA/UK Question Dutch on Libyan Deal," *Flight International,* 26 October 1994.

33. According to an official in the UN Secretariat, the aviation restrictions did in fact apply to preexisting contracts, although press reports claimed that these arrangements were exempt. Alan George, "Swiss Terminate Libyan Contracts," *Jane's Intelligence Review* (3 December 1996): 13; "USA/UK Question Dutch on Libyan Deal."

34. "USA/UK Question Dutch on Libyan Deal."

35. George, "Swiss Terminate Libyan Contracts," 13.

36. "Libya-Egypt Major Breach of Arms Embargo," *Intelligence Newsletter,* 1 December 1994.

37. "Ban-busting Iran Arms Ship Said Heading for Libya," *Reuters World Service,* 2 September 1996.

38. Richard W. Conroy, interview with UN Secretariat official, 10 November 1998.

39. Farhan Haq, "Libya-U.N.: Britain Attacks Arab League Decision on Libya," *InterPress Service,* 23 September 1997.

40. For the OAU noncompliance threat, see Organization of African Unity, Assembly of Heads of State and Government, "The Crisis Between the Great Socialist People's Libyan Arab Jamahiriya and the United States of America and the United Kingdom," 8–10 June 1998, AHG/DEC.127 XXXIV. The Arab League and Organization of the Islamic Conference endorsed the Libyan proposal to extradite the two suspects to the Netherlands for trial by a Scottish court and criticized the sanctions but did not threaten to terminate Arab or Islamic compliance with sanctions. See United Nations Security Council, *Letter From the Permanent Observer of the League of Arab States,* S/1998/895, 29 September 1998; and United Nations, *Letter from the Permanent Representative of Qatar,* S/1998/926, 7 October 1998.

41. In this respect, Resolution 748 is vague, as is the preceding Resolution 731. Resolution 748 does not explicitly request the extradition of the two suspects but refers to conditions in three Security Council documents (S/23306, S/23308, and S/23309) that Libya must meet before sanctions end.

42. United Nations, "Transcript of Press Conference by Secretary-General Kofi Annan at Headquarters, 5 April," SG/SM/6944, 5 April 1999, 3–4.

43. John M. Goshko, "U.N. Council Refuses to Order Libya to Turn Over Bombing Suspects," *Washington Post,* 27 February 1999, A13.

44. This record of Libyan restraint in response to UN sanctions should be contrasted with Libya's response to the U.S. bombing attacks of the 1980s, which were

followed by the bombings of Pan Am Flight 103 and UTA Flight 772 within three years.

45. United States, Department of State, *Patterns of Global Terrorism 1996*, Publication 10535 (Washington, D.C.: Government Printing Office, 1996).

46. United Nations Security Council, *Report of the Secretary-General Pursuant to Security Council Resolution 1070*, S/1996/940, 14 November 1996.

47. United Nations, *Informal Background Paper Prepared by the Department of Political Affairs, United Nations Secretariat for the Symposium on Targeted Sanctions*, 7 December 1998, 15.

48. Ian Black, "Britain Expels Three Sudanese Diplomats," *Guardian*, 21 May 1996, 2; "Egypt Expels Three Sudanese in Line with Sanctions," *Reuters World Service*, 10 June 1996.

49. Ian Black, "Sudan Faces UN Sanctions," *Guardian*, 29 March 1996, 12.

50. James Bone, "UN Votes to Impose Sanctions on Sudan," *Times*, 27 April 1996.

51. United Nations, Department of Humanitarian Affairs, *Note from the Department of Humanitarian Affairs Concerning the Possible Humanitarian Impact of the International Flight Ban Decided in Security Council Resolution 1070 (1996)* (New York: Department of Humanitarian Affairs, 20 February 1997).

52. Ibid., 2.

53. Ibid., 4–7.

54. Ibid., 16.

55. United Nations Security Council, *Report of the Secretary-General Pursuant to Security Council Resolution 1070*, S/1996/940.

56. Joyce Hackel, "An Islamic Revolution Falters," *Christian Science Monitor*, 29 March 1996.

57. Ibid.

58. United Nations Security Council, *Security Council Resolution 1267 (1999)*, S/RES/1267 (1999), 15 October 1999, par. 2.

59. Christopher Wren, "UN Official Says Taliban Resisting Opening Supply Route for Refugees," *New York Times*, 4 November 1999.

60. Barbara Crossette, "U.S. Steps Up Pressure on Taliban to Deliver Osama bin Laden," *New York Times*, 19 October 1999.

61. United Nations, Department of Humanitarian Affairs, *Report of the DHA Mission to Afghanistan*, 15 May 1997, 9.

62. Wren, "UN Official Says Taliban Resisting."

63. United Nations, *Report of the DHA Mission to Afghanistan*.

64. Crossette, "U.S. Steps Up Pressure."

7

Cambodia:
Isolating the Khmer Rouge

After two decades of war and repression, the Paris accords of October 1991 brought the hope of peace to the killing fields of Cambodia. The United Nations mounted one of the largest missions in its history in a partially successful effort to restore constitutional order to this once tranquil land. The UN tried to end the violence and human rights abuses that had engulfed Cambodia after 1970, when this "sideshow" of the Vietnam War exploded in war and revolutionary fanaticism, leading to the deaths of more than 1 million people at the hands of the Khmer Rouge.[1] The negotiations leading to the Paris accords were managed by and resulted from unprecedented cooperation among the five permanent members of the Security Council. The UN mission in Cambodia was one of the first examples of the new UN activism that emerged in the aftermath of the Cold War. Cambodia, one of the countries that suffered most during the military conflicts of the Cold War era, was thus an early beneficiary of the cooperative internationalism that emerged in the early 1990s.

The UN-brokered Paris accords provided for a comprehensive settlement of Cambodia's political and military turmoil. They called for a monitored cease-fire, the demobilization and cantonment of military forces, the release of prisoners, the repatriation of refugees and displaced persons, and a major program of international reconstruction assistance. The accords also authorized the UN to organize and conduct free and fair elections and to assist in administering Cambodia until an elected government could take charge.[2] The plan was extraordinarily ambitious. The UN mission, the United Nations Transitional Authority in Cambodia (UNTAC), numbered more than 15,000 peacekeepers and 6,000 civilian workers and cost $1.7 billion during its eighteen months of operation in Cambodia.[3] Although plagued by inefficiencies and corruption, the UN mission nonetheless achieved its major objectives of reducing the level of armed conflict, restoring some semblance of social order, and initiating a democratic political process.

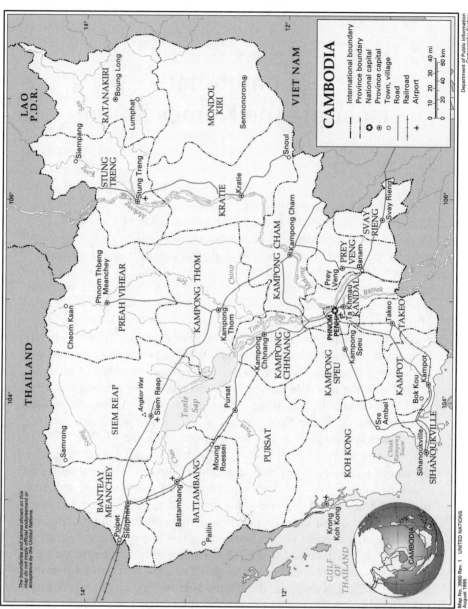

The boundaries and names shown on this map do not imply official endorsement or acceptance by the United Nations.

CAMBODIA

⌁·⌁·⌁	International boundary
─·─·─	Province boundary
⊛	National capital
⊙	Province capital
○	Town, village
──	Road
───	Railroad
✦	Airport

0 10 20 30 40 mi
0 20 40 60 km

LAO P.D.R.

THAILAND

VIET NAM

RATANAKIRI
Boung Long
Lumphat
Siempang
STUNG TRENG
Stung Treng
MONDOL KIRI
Senmonorom
Snoul
Kratie
KRATIE
Cheom Ksan
Phnom Thbeng Meanchey
PREAH VIHEAR
KAMPONG THOM
Kampong Thom
KAMPONG CHAM
Kampong Cham
Prey Veng
PREY VENG
Banam
Ta Khmau
SVAY RIENG
Svay Rieng
KANDAL
PHNOM PENH
Samrong
SIEM REAP
Angkor Wat
Siem Reap
Tonle Sap
BANTEAY MEANCHEY
Poipet
Sisophon
Battambang
Pailin
BATTAMBANG
Moung Roessei
Pursat
PURSAT
KAMPONG CHHNANG
Kampong Chhnang
KAMPONG SPEU
Kampong Speu
Takeo
TAKEO
KAMPOT
Bok Kou
Kampot
Sre Ambel
KOH KONG
Krong Koh Kong
Sihanoukville
SIHANOUKVILLE
Chhak Kampong Saom
GULF OF THAILAND
Mekong
Sen
Chinit
Stung
Sangker
Chas
Pursat
Sreng
Kong
Bassak
Tonle Sap
CAMBODIA

Map No. 3860 Rev. 1   UNITED NATIONS
August 1995

Department of Public Information
Cartographic Section

Sanctions played only a minor part in this story, but they were important in demonstrating the UN's resolve to continue the peace process despite noncooperation and resistance from the Khmer Rouge. By imposing sanctions against areas of Cambodia controlled by the Khmer Rouge, the Security Council signaled its determination to pursue the UN mission and refused to yield to the rebel group's brutal methods. Sanctions helped to isolate and weaken the Khmer Rouge and contributed to the steady erosion of support that ultimately led to its demise.

Imposing Sanctions

The Paris accords were predicated on the cooperation of all Cambodian factions. The two main parties, the United National Front for an Independent, Neutral, Peaceful, and Cooperative Cambodia (FUNCIN-PEC) and the Cambodian People's Party (CPP), cooperated with the UN mission to some extent, although the CPP used its control of the state of Cambodia to undermine its political opponents. But the Khmer Rouge and its political arm, the Party of Democratic Kampuchea (PDK), obstructed and resisted the peace process at every turn. PDK forces not only refused to disarm but launched renewed military attacks from their redoubt in the western and northern regions of Cambodia adjacent to Thailand. The Khmer Rouge controlled only about 10 percent of Cambodia's territory, but its armed forces of approximately 10,000 fighters allowed it to wreak considerable havoc. Although the other major factions also violated the Paris accords, especially in the period prior to the May 1993 election, the greatest threat to the peace process came from the Khmer Rouge.[4] Despite the loss of Chinese economic and military support, which Beijing withdrew as part of the Paris accords, the Khmer Rouge acquired money to continue its political and military operations by pillaging Cambodia's mineral and forest resources.[5] With the help of the Thai army and private Thai companies, the PDK earned an estimated $20 million a month exploiting Cambodia's valuable lumber and gem resources.[6] UNTAC feared that the income earned from these operations would facilitate continued PDK noncooperation and allow it to maintain its military strength.[7]

The armed resistance of the PDK forced the UN to alter its mission. UNTAC stopped attempting to implement all aspects of the comprehensive plan spelled out in the Paris accords. Instead, it focused on creating a politically viable Cambodian government among the factions willing

CAMBODIA, Security Council Resolutions

Resolution Number	Action
766	**21 July 1992** Specified that international financial assistance for reconstruction would go only to factions supporting the Paris accords
783	**13 October 1992** Demanded compliance with the Paris accords (again) Confirmed that elections would proceed regardless of PDK obstruction
792	**30 November 1992** Imposed sanctions on PDK-controlled areas of Cambodia Imposed oil embargo Supported moratorium on log exports, previously adopted by Cambodia's Supreme National Council (SNC), to go into effect 1 January 1993 Urged the SNC to embargo the export of minerals and gems

to cooperate with the UN mission, while progressively isolating the Khmer Rouge.[8] A series of Security Council resolutions confirmed the gradual shift in mission. In July 1992 the Council adopted Resolution 766 condemning violations of the Paris accords and specifying that international financial assistance for reconstruction would go only to factions supporting the peace plan. The Council thereby cut off the Khmer Rouge from the substantial economic aid that flowed into the country after 1991. In October 1992 the Security Council adopted Resolution 783, again demanding compliance with the Paris accords and confirming that the elections would proceed regardless of PDK obstruction.

As PDK violations continued, the Security Council began to consider the imposition of sanctions. The Paris accords lacked any specific provisions for enforcement of the peace plan. Faced with the PDK's resistance, the UN was forced to decide between continuing what Secretary-General Boutros Boutros-Ghali called "patient diplomacy" or applying coercive pressure on the Khmer Rouge. As PDK obstruction intensified in the summer and fall of 1992, support for the sanctions approach increased. Australia issued a paper in September 1992 urging the Security Council to set a deadline for sanctions if the PDK continued to impede the peace process. France also strongly advocated sanctions against the Khmer Rouge, and Indonesia joined France as cochairs of the Paris peace conference in advocating sanctions. The Secretary-General recommended against such action, however, urging the continuation of quiet diplomacy.[9] Japan was also skeptical about the feasibility of sanctions.[10] China was reluctant to approve sanctions, but it did not stand in the way of Council action. The major Western powers and most members on the Security Council were impatient with the fruitless attempts to gain PDK cooperation and favored sanctions.

In November 1992 the Security Council adopted Resolution 792 imposing sanctions on the PDK-controlled areas of Cambodia. The goal of the sanctions was to reduce the Khmer Rouge's petroleum supplies and its sources of export revenue, thereby weakening the rebel group and facilitating implementation of the Paris accords. Resolution 792 imposed an oil embargo on Khmer Rouge territory and supported a moratorium on the export of logs that had been adopted by Cambodia's Supreme National Council (SNC), a transitional authority representing the major political parties cooperating with the UN mission. The ban on logging exports was scheduled to go into effect on 1 January 1993. Resolution 792 also urged the SNC to impose an embargo on the export of minerals and gems. These measures were designed to cut off the economic lifeblood of the Khmer Rouge, thereby diminishing the threat it posed to the people of Cambodia and the peace process. Although the sanctions lacked effective enforcement and were vitiated by widespread violations along the Thai-Cambodian border, they helped to isolate the Khmer Rouge and contributed to the steady decline in the PDK's fortunes. The most important factor in the isolation of the Khmer Rouge was the cutoff of aid and political support from China, but the UN sanctions complemented this process.

The SNC cooperated with UN officials in applying sanctions, voting in September 1992 to set a December deadline for imposing a moratorium on the export of timber. This measure was approved ostensibly to preserve Cambodia's natural resources, but it also had the effect of isolating and sanctioning the PDK. The environmental consequences of the Khmer Rouge's extensive logging operations were indeed severe. Reporters described the area around Pailin, the unofficial Khmer Rouge capital, as a moonscape, with trees completely cleared and thousands of tons of topsoil scraped away in the search for gems. Resolution 792 supported the export ban not only as a resource conservation measure but as an essential step in the process of isolating the Khmer Rouge.

Soon after the ban on logging exports went into effect, the SNC and UNTAC took steps to tighten economic restrictions. In January 1993, UN officials developed a proposal to implement the Security Council's recommendation for a ban on the export of minerals and gems. The participating political parties helped to draft the plan, and the Supreme National Council approved it on 10 February 1993. At that same meeting the SNC also approved an UNTAC proposal to tighten the embargo on timber exports by agreeing to impose a ceiling on the export of sawn lumber. UN officials subsequently established a quota for lumber exports that reduced the volume of approved timber shipments by 30 percent from 1991 levels.[11]

Attempting to Enforce the Sanctions

Resolution 792 did not establish a sanctions committee, which meant there was no focal point for ensuring implementation of the sanctions. As a result, much of the responsibility for monitoring compliance fell to UNTAC, adding another task to UNTAC's already long list of responsibilities. The Paris accords established a series of UN-staffed checkpoints throughout the country and on the borders. Originally, the checkpoints were intended to verify the withdrawal from Cambodia of foreign forces and the cessation of external military assistance. After the imposition of Resolution 792, they were given the additional task of monitoring the oil embargo and the moratorium on the export of timber, minerals, and gems.[12] UNTAC developed procedures permitting a "controlled volume" of petroleum products to enter Cambodia from Thailand for distribution to the parties fulfilling their responsibilities under the Paris accords. Monitored shipments through other borders were also permitted. Internal movements of oil products were administered by the state of Cambodia, which was closely associated with the CPP. To deter violations of the oil embargo, UNTAC established monitoring stations and mobile checkpoints on all roads leading to the PDK-controlled zone.[13]

Effective enforcement of the sanctions depended primarily on the cooperation of neighboring states. At the end of December 1992, Laos, Vietnam, and Thailand announced that they would impose a complete ban on the import of Cambodian logs beginning 1 January 1993. Laos and Vietnam generally cooperated with the sanctions, but not Thailand. Although Bangkok announced its support for the sanctions and took some steps to implement the oil embargo and logging ban, the Thai armed forces permitted large-scale smuggling operations to continue along their border with Cambodia.

The Thai government had not supported sanctions when they were initially imposed. In a November 1992 letter circulated to the Security Council, Bangkok expressed its preference for patient diplomacy as the best means of getting the peace process back on track.[14] Thailand suggested that the Council's "specific measures" were not realistic and called for consultations with neighboring states in accordance with Article 50 of the UN Charter. The head of the Thai National Security Council demanded a large cash payment to cover the costs associated with attempting to monitor the border. Indeed, Thailand was heavily dependent on trade with the Khmer Rouge–controlled areas of Cambodia. One report estimated that 70,000 Thai jobs depended on logging and mining operations in Cambodia.[15]

Bangkok also insisted on a strict interpretation of the Paris accords, which stipulated that border checkpoints were to be established along the Cambodian side of the border.[16] This position effectively undermined any prospect for effective border control, since the areas in question were within the PDK zone of Cambodia and beyond UN authority. Despite numerous press reports of open violations of the lumber ban and UN sanctions, officials in Bangkok refused to permit UN monitoring along the border. The Secretary-General attempted to gain the cooperation of Thai officials but was consistently rebuffed.[17]

It was not realistic to expect cooperation in sanctions enforcement from Thailand. Thai military leaders had major economic interests in the extensive logging and mining concessions in Cambodia and reportedly took part in Khmer Rouge logging and gem-mining operations.[18] In July 1992, before the imposition of sanctions, the *Far Eastern Economic Review* estimated the value of Thai-Cambodian border trade at $300 million annually.[19] The Thai military provided military, economic, and political backing for the Khmer Rouge. In 1993 U.S. assistant secretary of state Winston Lord testified before the Senate Foreign Relations Committee that "Thailand is the major supporter of the Khmer Rouge."[20]

Given the lack of UN enforcement capability and the cozy relationship between the Thai military and Khmer Rouge, efforts to circumvent the UN sanctions and export bans were widespread. Secretary-General Boutros-Ghali reported "numerous and large-scale violations."[21] Illegal trading was particularly prevalent across the Thai border. News reports documented a steady flow of truck traffic even as Thai officials claimed to have stopped shipments. Soon after the ban on timber exports took effect on 1 January 1993, logging trucks were backed up for miles in early attempts to beat the ban.[22] One reporter observed 132 trucks lined up at the border. At the same time, Thai army commander Wimol Wongwanich claimed that "not a single log has come in."[23]

Despite widespread violations, the sanctions nonetheless had some impact in restricting the flow of oil to the Khmer Rouge and slowed the volume of trade in timber, minerals, and gems. According to a report from Oxfam America, the oil embargo was sufficiently successful to disable some gem-mining operations.[24] The ban on logging exports also had some effect in reducing the level of shipments. Although Thailand was highly skeptical of sanctions, it nonetheless established border checkpoints, which in some cases slowed or halted cross-border trade. One reporter interviewed Thai workers in Cambodia who were shocked by the severity of the government's enforcement of the ban.[25] UNTAC observers reported a steady decline in the number of violations and the quantity of logs exported. In January 1993, forty-six violations were reported, but this number fell to eleven and five in February and March, respectively. The volume of timber traded also fell from 48,094 cubic meters in January to 2,345 cubic meters in March.[26] These figures must be treated with caution, however, for UNTAC officials lacked access to the Thai-Cambodian border and therefore could not monitor the principal routes of prohibited commerce.

Standing Firm

As sanctions pressures tightened and the UN electoral effort began to show success, Khmer Rouge forces responded with a wave of terror and military attacks directed principally at Vietnamese-speaking villagers. More than 100 people were killed in the weeks leading up to the May 1993 elections. The Khmer Rouge also directed its wrath at the United Nations. PDK units attacked UNTAC units and fired on UN helicopters. Thirteen UNTAC peacekeepers and civilian workers were killed in these attacks.[27] Most of the fatalities occurred in the weeks leading up to the elections. To its credit, the United Nations refused to capitulate to this campaign of intimidation and terror. Just as it refused to allow Khmer Rouge obstruction to derail the overall peace process, so the UN held its ground during the election campaign despite the escalating toll of death and destruction. It responded to the attacks on its forces and to the growing PDK terror within the country by intensifying its efforts to isolate and contain the Khmer Rouge and by continuing its missions to conduct free and fair elections.

The firm UN stance in Cambodia contrasted sharply with later UN experiences in Haiti and Angola. In Haiti the advance elements of a UN mission, approaching Port-au-Prince aboard the USS *Harlan County,* were bullied by a small band of armed vigilantes waiting at the docks and turned tail without even attempting to carry out their mission. Sanctions against the military junta were lifted prematurely, and the peace process negotiated at Governors Island collapsed. In Angola the UN responded pusillanimously to frequent violations of the peace process by the National Union for the Total Independence of Angola (UNITA), threatening but not imposing more coercive measures and maintaining a preference for quiet diplomacy even as UNITA openly violated the Lusaka Protocol and built up one of the largest armies in Africa. When UNITA reportedly shot down two UN airplanes in 1999, the UN withdrew its observer mission entirely. Admittedly, many differences can be found among these three cases. The UN faced a much larger and more heavily armed adversary in Angola than in Cambodia, and it had large forces on the ground in Cambodia, compared to none in Haiti and a small observer mission in Angola. Nonetheless, the fact remains that a firm stance in Cambodia enabled the UN to fulfill its mission, whereas weakness and hesitance brought failure in Haiti and Angola.

Despite the limitations of the UN mission and the allegations of corruption and mismanagement leveled against UNTAC officials, the United Nations achieved many of its objectives in Cambodia. A ceasefire was effectively monitored by international forces, Cambodian military units were partially demobilized (except for those of the Khmer Rouge), and the level of fighting decreased. More than 360,000 displaced persons were able to return to their homes. Most important, the UN organized an electoral process in which 4.6 million voters were registered, and 90 percent of those eligible went to the polls. The enthusiastic public participation in the May 1993 balloting, despite attempted Khmer Rouge intimidation, was "a ringing endorsement" of the peace process, according to William Shawcross, and a "serious rebuff" to the Khmer Rouge.[28] Although the elections produced a shaky and often tense political relationship between FUNCINPEC and CPP, the May 1993 vote established a precedent for more democratic government.

Perhaps most important, the success of the UN mission and the imposition of sanctions helped to isolate and weaken the Khmer Rouge and contributed to its demise a few years later. The PDK utterly failed in its attempts to sabotage the elections and the peace process. As the new Cambodian government took control, defections from the Khmer Rouge increased, and support for the rebel movement diminished. The lack of political, economic, and diplomatic support, both internally and internationally, ultimately doomed the PDK and led to its collapse.

Sanctions also figured into the larger strategy of progressively isolating the Khmer Rouge. Although their economic impact was minimal, their diplomatic function was significant. They served as a vehicle for mobilizing the international community to tighten the political and economic noose around the Khmer Rouge. The UN strategy of pressing ahead with the Paris accords despite PDK resistance effectively forced the Khmer Rouge to opt out of the peace process and thereby further isolate itself. As former U.S. diplomat Frederick Brown observed, the UN strategy was successful at "backing the Khmer Rouge into a corner bit by bit."[29] By the late 1990s, the Khmer Rouge had disintegrated. Sanctions and the UN mission ultimately succeeded in helping to set the country on the path to a less violent, more democratic future.

Notes

1. The reference is to William Shawcross's classic account of Cambodia's descent into chaos. See William Shawcross, *Sideshow: Kissinger, Nixon, and the Destruction of Cambodia* (New York: Simon and Schuster, 1987).

2. United Nations, *The United Nations and Cambodia 1991–1995*, United Nations Blue Book Series, vol. 2 (New York: United Nations Department of Public Information, 1995), 9.

3. Ibid., 54.

4. Ibid., 21.

5. Richard Ehrlich, "Cambodia: Whittling Rainforests into Weapons of War," *InterPress Service*, 16 January 1993.

6. William Shawcross, *Cambodia's New Deal: A Report* (Washington, D.C.: Carnegie Endowment for International Peace, 1994), 17.

7. United Nations, *United Nations and Cambodia*, 35.

8. Shawcross, *Cambodia's New Deal*, 15.

9. United Nations Security Council, *Report of the Secretary-General on the Implementation of Security Council Resolution 783 (1992) on the Cambodia Peace Process*, S/24800, New York, 15 November 1992, par. 24; see also Peter James Spielmann, "UN Chief Recommends Against Sanctioning Khmer Rouge," *Associated Press*, 20 November 1992.

10. "Envoy Says Sanctions Against Khmer Rouge Won't Work," *Japan Economic Newswire*, 18 September 1992.

11. United Nations Security Council, *Fourth Progress Report of the Secretary-General on UNTAC*, S/25719, 3 May 1993, par. 101.

12. United Nations Security Council, *Third Progress Report of the Secretary-General on UNTAC*, S/25154, 25 January 1993, par. 55.

13. Ibid.

14. United Nations Security Council, *Letter Dated 30 November 1992 from Thailand Outlining the Position of the Royal Thai Government with Regard to Security Council Resolution 792 (1992)*, S/24873, 30 November 1992, par. 3.

15. "Thailand, Not Khmer Rouge the Loser from UN Sanctions," *Japan Economic Newswire*, 3 December 1992.

16. United Nations Security Council, *Letter Dated 30 November 1992 from Thailand*, S/24873, par. 5.

17. United Nations Security Council, *Fourth Progress Report*, S/25719, par. 102.

18. United Nations, *United Nations and Cambodia*, 35.

19. *Far Eastern Economic Review*, 30 July 1992, cited in Oxfam America, "Cambodia: Still Waiting for Peace; A Report on Thai-Cambodia Collaboration Since the Signing of the Paris Peace Accords," February 1995, 10.

20. Quoted in ibid., 10.

21. United Nations Security Council, *Report of the Secretary-General on the Implementation of Security Council Resolution 792 (1992)*, S/25289, 13 February 1993, par. 22.

22. Oxfam America, "Cambodia: Still Waiting for Peace," 11.

23. *Reuters Newswire*, 4 January 1993, "Logs Still Trucked Across Cambodia Border Despite Sanctions," quoted in ibid., 11.

24. Oxfam America, "Cambodia: Still Waiting for Peace," 12.

25. Tan Lian Choo, "Thai Traders Feeling Impact of UN Sanctions," *Straits Times*, 12 February 1993, 17.

26. United Nations Security Council, *Fourth Progress Report*, par. 98.

27. United Nations Security Council, *Report of the Secretary-General in Pursuance of Paragraph 6 of Security Council Resolution 810 (1993) on Preparations for the Election for the Constituent Assembly in Cambodia*, S/25784, 15 May 1993, par. 13.

28. Shawcross, *Cambodia's New Deal*, 21.

29. Quoted in Lucia Mouat, "An Uncooperative Khmer Rouge Prompts Delicate UN Diplomacy," *Christian Science Monitor*, 19 November 1992, 6.

8

Angola's Agony*

In 1991 the long postindependence civil war between the government of Angola and the National Union for the Total Independence of Angola (UNITA) seemed finally to be coming to an end. In the Accordos de Paz signed in May of that year, the two sides pledged to end their conflict and hold UN-monitored elections. The Luanda regime, dominated by the Popular Movement for the Liberation of Angola (MPLA), pledged to accept UNITA forces into a unified Angolan Armed Forces. For its part, UNITA agreed to demobilize most of its fighting units. Both sides agreed to accept the deployment in Angola of the United Nations Verification Mission (UNAVEM II) and to respect its judgment on the validity of the scheduled elections. Balloting took place in late September 1992 in an election judged by UN officials as generally free and fair. MPLA won a decisive victory in legislative elections. In the crucial presidential vote, the acting head of state and MPLA leader Jose Eduardo Dos Santos won 49 percent of the vote, whereas UNITA leader Jonas Savimbi won nearly 41 percent.

What should have been the end of the story turned out to be the beginning of a terrible new chapter in Angola's agonizing history of armed conflict. UNITA refused to participate in the required presidential runoff election and rejected the ballot results. The country was soon plunged into another, more savage paroxysm of war and violence. The United Nations, already deeply committed to finding a peaceful solution for the country, found itself bogged down in a frustrating, largely fruitless attempt to end the fighting and bring about a negotiated settlement. The Security Council imposed sanctions in 1993, helped to negotiate a new peace agreement (the Lusaka Protocol) in 1994, sent a new verification mission in 1995, and imposed stronger sanctions in 1997

---

* This chapter was coauthored by Richard W. Conroy.

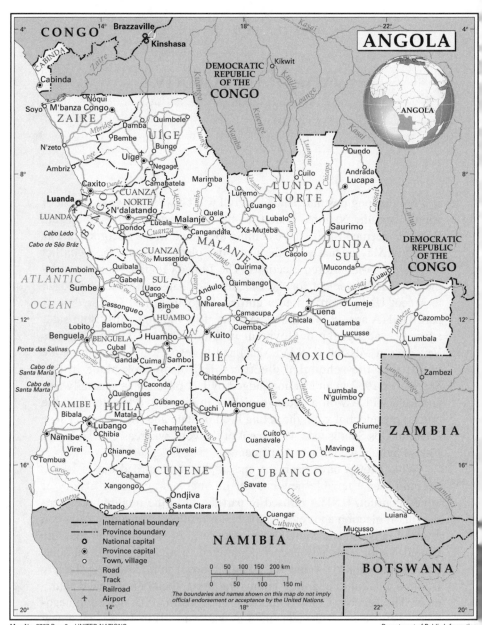

ANGOLA

CONGO — Brazzaville — Kinshasa

CABINDA — Cabinda

DEMOCRATIC REPUBLIC OF THE CONGO — Kikwit

Soyo — Nóqui — M'banza Congo — ZAIRE — Quimbele

N'zeto — Damba — UIGE — Bungo — Bembe — Uige — Negage

Ambriz — Camabatela — Marimba — Dundo

Caxito — CUANZA NORTE — Luremo — LUNDA NORTE — Andrada Lucapa — Cuilo

Luanda — N'dalatando — Quela — Cuango — Lubalo

LUANDA — Dondo — Lucala — Malanje — MALANJE — Cangandala — Xá-Muteba — Saurimo

Cabo Ledo — Cabo de São Bráz — CUANZA Mussende — Quirima — Cacolo — LUNDA SUL — Muconda

DEMOCRATIC REPUBLIC OF THE CONGO

Porto Amboim — Quibala — SUL — Andulo — Quimbango — Luau

ATLANTIC OCEAN — Sumbe — Gabela — Uaco Cungo — Nharea — Camacupa — Lumeje — Cazombo

Cassongue — Bimbe — HUAMBO — Cuemba — Luena — Chicala — Luatamba — Lumbala

Lobito — Balombo — Kuito — Lucusse

Benguela — BENGUELA — Huambo — MOXICO

Ponta das Salinas — Cubal — Ganda — Cuima — Sambo — BIÉ — Zambezi

Cabo de Santa Maria — Caconda — Chitembo — Lumbala N'guimbo

Cabo de Santa Marta — Quilengues — Cubango — Cuchi — Menongue — Chiume

NAMIBE — HUÍLA — Matala — Techamutete — Cuíto Cuanavale — ZAMBIA

Bibala — Lubango — Chibia — Mavinga

Namibe — Virei — Chiange — Cuvelai — CUANDO

Tombua — Cahama — CUNENE — CUBANGO — Savate

Xangongo — Ondjiva — Santa Clara — Cuangar — Luiana

Chitado — Mucusso

NAMIBIA

BOTSWANA

- ◉ International boundary
- ⋅—⋅— Province boundary
- ◌ National capital
- ◉ Province capital
- ○ Town, village
- — Road
- — Track
- — Railroad
- ✛ Airport

0 50 100 150 200 km
0 50 100 150 mi

The boundaries and names shown on this map do not imply official endorsement or acceptance by the United Nations.

Map No. 3727 Rev. 2   UNITED NATIONS
October 1997 (Colour)

Department of Public Information
Cartographic Section

and 1998 as fighting flared up again. At the end of the decade, despite years of UN sanctions and concerted diplomatic efforts, war continued to rage, hundreds of thousands lay dead, devastation was more extensive than ever, and the conflict was no closer to resolution than it had been seven years before.

In the late 1990s the war in Angola became entangled in a widening web of conflict encompassing the Democratic Republic of Congo and much of central Africa. The MPLA government of Angola supported the regional effort that helped to oust former Zairean dictator Mobutu Sese Seko, who had been one of the chief patrons of UNITA, and instead provided support for the new regime of Laurent Kabila. Meanwhile, UNITA and several African governments backed the rebels in eastern Congo who were fighting Kabila's regime. This regionalization of the conflict complicated the task of resolving the Angola crisis and made the UN peace mission all the more difficult.

Sanctions have played little or no role in the ongoing Angola tragedy. Sanctions contributed in a limited fashion to establishing a bargaining framework in 1993, exerting some pressure on UNITA to comply with UN demands, but their impact was very limited. As with the overall UN policy in Angola, sanctions were hampered by the Security Council's reluctance to take stronger, more assertive measures toward UNITA. Through most of the decade, little effort was made to monitor and enforce the sanctions, leading to pervasive violations of the arms embargo and sanctions on the diamond industry and financial transactions. Hopeful efforts were under way at the end of the decade to enforce the stronger sanctions imposed in 1997 and 1998, but whether tighter implementation efforts would be possible and, if so, whether they would be sufficient to help resolve the crisis remained highly uncertain.

War and Sanctions

Angola has experienced almost constant fighting since 1961, when its war for independence began, punctuated by brief periods of relative peace in 1992 and 1994–1998 monitored by UN peacekeepers.[1] Angola's wars since 1975 have cost an estimated 1.5 million lives. The worst suffering occurred in the 1990s, when in 1993 it was dubbed the "world's worst war." During the 1970s and 1980s Angola was a Cold War battleground. UNITA received assistance from South Africa and the United States, whereas the Soviet Union and Cuba provided arms and thousands of troops to help the nominally Marxist MPLA regime in Luanda. Whether the Angolan principals ever took these Cold War ideologies seriously is questionable. Ideology served mainly as a label to

ANGOLA, Security Council Resolutions

Resolution Number	Action
864	**15 September 1993** Imposed arms embargo on UNITA Imposed petroleum embargo except through ports of entry designated by the Angolan government Created sanctions committee
890	**15 December 1993** Threatened stronger sanctions, upon the Secretary-General's future recommendations, but gave no deadline or timetable for action
1075	**11 October 1996** Threatened additional sanctions against UNITA for its failure to comply with the Lusaka Protocol
1087	**11 December 1996** Authorized the gradual withdrawal of UNAVEM III but made no mention of the threat of additional sanctions made in Resolution 1075
1127	**28 August 1997** Imposed travel sanctions banning travel of senior UNITA officials and prohibiting flights to and from UNITA-held territory Imposed diplomatic sanctions closing UNITA diplomatic offices Suspended the sanctions twice, hoping UNITA would document its disarmament efforts Finally imposed the stronger sanctions in October 1997
1173	**12 June 1998** Froze UNITA financial assets Banned all financial transactions with UNITA Imposed an embargo on diamond imports not certified by the Angolan government Banned any form of travel to UNITA-controlled territories

attract foreign support.[2] Rebel leader Jonas Savimbi was never the democrat that U.S. and South African Cold Warriors portrayed him to be, as evidenced by his repression of internal dissent within UNITA and his preference for war over losing an election.

The continuation and intensification of the conflict after the end of the Cold War suggested that both factions have remarkably similar agendas: to appropriate Angola's vast wealth for themselves.[3] For both the MPLA government and the UNITA rebels headed by Savimbi, the war has become "commerce by other means," a process for enriching those who control the nation's wealth. Angola is richly endowed with oil and diamonds. It has the world's fifth-largest deposits of oil, which constitute 90 percent of the government's export earnings.[4] Government forces control most of these oil resources, which are used to finance the war and huge imports of arms. The government has mortgaged an estimated five to seven years' worth of oil revenue to purchase weapons.[5] Angola also produces 15 percent of the world's diamonds, with more than 70 percent of these diamonds of gem quality.[6] UNITA controls more than 75 percent of Angola's $700 million to $1 billion in annual diamond revenues.[7] It is a key player in the global diamond business, controlling almost one-sixth of the world's diamond production.[8] The economic stakes in Angola's oil and diamond riches are so high that leaders of both sides have no incentive to end the war and have rebuffed repeated attempts to resolve the conflict.

When UNITA renounced the UN-supervised elections and resumed military attacks on government forces, the Security Council adopted Resolution 864 in September 1993, imposing an arms and petroleum embargo. Resolution 864 banned the sale of arms and weapons-related material to UNITA and prohibited the sale of petroleum and petroleum products, except through ports of entry designated by the Angolan government. The resolution called upon UNITA to sign an effective cease-fire and to implement the Accordos de Paz, also known as the Bicesse agreement, which it had signed in May 1991. Resolution 864 also created a sanctions committee with the standard mandate. The resolution established a deadline of 1 November 1993, after which additional sanctions would be imposed if the Secretary-General reported that UNITA was violating the cease-fire or failing to implement the accords. The additional sanctions threatened in the resolution included unspecified "trade measures" and travel restrictions against UNITA.

In response to the sanctions and the threat of additional measures, UNITA declared a unilateral cessation of hostilities (although not a formal cease-fire) and called for immediate negotiations. UNITA's prompt response to the Security Council's actions indicated a serious concern about the potential impact of sanctions. It illustrated the bargaining impact of sanctions and the effect such measures could have in encouraging negotiations. But UNITA's reply was disingenuous and made no reference to the Bicesse agreement or the 1992 electoral results. UNITA subsequently proclaimed its "acceptance" of the elections but described the balloting as "fraudulent." The rebel movement was willing to enter negotiations and make promises of compliance as a way of avoiding sanctions pressure, but it had no real intention of accepting the elections or dismantling its armed forces. The initial sanctions and threat of tougher measures to follow succeeded in bringing the parties to the bargaining table, but they could not force the two sides, especially UNITA, to make the concessions necessary to resolve the dispute. As the November 1993 deadline approached, therefore, the Security Council faced a crucial decision. Should it carry out the threat to impose additional sanctions or allow more time for talks to succeed?

The Council chose the latter option. Although negotiations between UNITA and the government had not yet produced any results and the rebels had stepped up their military attacks, the Security Council decided to delay the imposition of stronger sanctions. After postponing a decision in November, the Council met in December to consider Secretary-General Boutros Boutros-Ghali's recommendations. He reported that fighting was continuing, that UNITA still refused to unconditionally accept the Bicesse agreement, and that UNITA was trying to use the peace talks to change the agreement. Despite this, he recommended postponing the imposition of additional sanctions, claiming that the cease-fire was working and that the peace talks were making progress.[9] Two days later, on 15 December 1993, the Security Council adopted Resolution 890. The resolution again threatened tougher sanctions, upon the Secretary-General's future recommendation, but gave no deadline or timetable for action. In effect, the threat of additional sanctions was suspended, despite the lack of any real compliance by UNITA.

Meanwhile, a savage civil war raged within Angola. UNITA's rejection of the election results and its renewal of armed attacks prompted an all-out military response from the government and the outbreak of a horrendous killing spree: 300,000 people (3 percent of the Angolan population) died as a result of the intensified fighting in 1993 and 1994. As many as 1,000 people died every day, making this the bloodiest war in the world at the time.[10] While public attention in the United States and Europe focused on conflicts in Bosnia, Somalia, and Haiti, the people of Angola died in appalling numbers. As UN diplomats labored to negotiate an end to the conflict, UNITA's military position steadily weakened. When costs and casualties on both sides began to mount, the pace of negotiations quickened, leading to the Lusaka Protocol, which was signed by the two parties in November 1994. At the time of the signing, UNITA was under the most intense military pressure it had faced from Angolan government forces.

The thirty-seven-page Lusaka Protocol established a cease-fire in situ between the government and UNITA, to be monitored by the UN. It required UNITA to provide updated information on the location, numbers, and types of its weapons and called for most UNITA forces to be demobilized and reintegrated into society and for the remaining UNITA forces to be integrated into the government's armed forces. It pledged both parties to complete the electoral process that was suspended in 1992. The protocol also formally established the Troika of Observers (the United States, Portugal, and Russia) and a joint commission to monitor the implementation of the agreement. The Lusaka Protocol was important for establishing a framework for settling the conflict, but like the previous Accordos de Paz, it was more frequently violated than implemented and as of this writing remains largely a paper agreement.

Sanctions had little or no influence on the negotiation of the Lusaka Protocol. They may have helped to get talks under way a year before, but it was the tide of battle, not economic coercion, that dictated the pace of the negotiations and the content of the final agreement. The arms embargo established in Resolution 864 was not effectively enforced, and the stronger sanctions that were threatened as part of that resolution were never imposed. UNITA forces enjoyed relatively unimpeded access to petroleum and weapons supplies. They also found it easy to manipulate UN diplomats with empty promises of compliance. Sanctions were but a minor footnote in a bloody conflict determined primarily by the force of arms.

The UN mounted three different peacekeeping operations in Angola during the period when sanctions were in force. When the UN first imposed sanctions, the second UN Verification Mission in Angola (UNAVEM II) was still in Angola. It monitored the demobilization of combatants, the integration of UNITA forces into the army, and the conduct of the 1992 elections. Given Angola's size, UNAVEM II was grossly underfunded and understaffed, which made it much easier for UNITA to conceal its preparations for war while pretending to disarm. In February 1995 the Security Council created UNAVEM III, with a force of 7,000 monitors, to verify the implementation of the Lusaka Protocol. It reported on disarmament efforts and the extension of government authority throughout Angola. Although much larger than UNAVEM II, it still faced daunting challenges in attempting to monitor the agreement. When the Security Council renewed sanctions against UNITA in August 1997, UNAVEM III's initial mandate had expired, and it was replaced by the much smaller UN Observer Mission in Angola (MONUA). As fighting escalated in 1998 and 1999 and after UNITA shot down two UN aircraft, the Security Council withdrew MONUA in March 1999.

Toward Renewed War and Stronger Sanctions

For a brief time after the signing of the Lusaka Protocol, UNITA cooperated with the peace process, and relative quiet settled over Angola's troubled landscape. But UNITA never really accepted a settlement that required it to admit defeat, both militarily and politically, and it soon resumed its previous pattern of violations and armed attacks. The government responded in kind, and the conflict began to flare up again. In November 1996 the Security Council adopted Resolution 1075, threatening additional sanctions against UNITA for its failure to comply with the Lusaka Protocol, particularly its failure to demobilize military forces. UNITA responded to this threat of renewed sanctions by announcing that it had disbanded its military component. UNAVEM III reported that UNITA had indeed demobilized over 68,000 troops, although independent analysts challenged these assertions.[11] Alioune Blondin Beye, the UN's special representative in Angola, reported that the disarmament tasks specified by the Security Council had largely been implemented and that another war in Angola was unlikely.[12] In fact, however, UNAVEM III and MONUA also sent reports to the Security Council detailing UNITA violations of the Lusaka Protocol. UN monitors noted that UNITA was maintaining contact with demobilized soldiers and that the weapons turned into UN demobilization centers were of older, inferior quality. Nonetheless, Blondin Beye's optimistic reports eased the sanctions threat. In December 1996, the Security Council adopted Resolution 1087, authorizing the gradual withdrawal of UNAVEM III but making no mention of the threat of additional sanctions made in Resolution 1075. The peace process moved to the next step, the extension of Angolan state administration throughout the country, even though the demobilization phase was far from complete.

The events of late 1996 and early 1997 repeated the experience of 1993 and 1994. In 1996 as in 1993, the Security Council threatened stronger sanctions but then postponed additional coercive measures in the hope that diplomatic efforts could prevent renewed warfare. In each instance the Security Council threatened to impose additional sanctions unless the Secretary-General or the UN's special representative reported that UNITA had complied with Security Council demands or met the timetable of the peace process. UNITA usually responded with a last-minute gesture of compliance—an ambiguous announcement that it had disarmed, a carefully worded statement that sounded compliant but failed to match the terms of Security Council demands, or an actual gesture of compliance that it later reversed. The Secretary-General, or his special representative to Angola, then certified UNITA's partial compliance with Security Council demands and recommended an extension of previous deadlines. As a result of these dynamics, the perception developed that the UN repeatedly let UNITA violate the Bicesse agreement.[13] The Security Council hoped that the limited progress on implementing the Lusaka Protocol would lead to a peaceful resolution of the conflict, but in fact UNITA refused to accept a political settlement, and the two sides steadily drifted toward renewed war. Neither diplomatic soft gloves nor the sanctions stick resulted in UNITA compliance.

As military hostilities increased and the evidence of UNITA's refusal to demobilize became increasingly clear in 1997, pressure mounted on the Security Council to take more forceful action. In August the Council adopted Resolution 1127, imposing travel and diplomatic sanctions on UNITA. The resolution demanded that UNITA provide information on the strength of its armed forces and condemned "any attempts by UNITA to rebuild its military strength."[14] The Council postponed implementation of the sanctions, giving UNITA a month to take "concrete and irreversible" steps toward compliance with the Lusaka Protocol and UN resolutions. After suspending the sanctions twice, in the vain hope that UNITA would document its disarmament efforts, the Council finally imposed stronger sanctions in October 1997. Resolution 1127 banned the travel of senior UNITA officials, closed UNITA diplomatic offices, and prohibited flights to and from territory held by UNITA. The delay in imposing sanctions accomplished nothing on the diplomatic front and gave UNITA two additional months to prepare its response to the sanctions. The delay also gave the rebels time to prepare for the looming military showdown with government forces and the renewal of open warfare.

Once again UN officials were slow in responding to UNITA violations. International officials and UN diplomats hoped that they could sustain the "momentum" of the peace process by glossing over UNITA's violations and that the hoped-for success in negotiations would render such violations irrelevant. Paul Hare, the U.S. ambassador to Angola from 1993 to 1998, commented on this strategy of wishful thinking:

> As I look at it over time, various things, which in retrospect may have been fools' dreams, at the time seemed to be steps forward in the process. In the case of UNITA's final statement that its forces had in fact been demilitarized, no one is a total fool and believed that absolutely. But there was a drive . . . to get that statement and move on.[15]

Special Representative Blondin Beye staunchly advocated patient diplomacy with Savimbi, lest UNITA hard-liners be provoked. What Blondin Beye saw as patience, Savimbi and UNITA leaders interpreted as a signal that the UN would tolerate UNITA's violations. The Security Council's hesitation once more reinforced UNITA's propensity to believe that it could violate the Lusaka Protocol and Security Council demands with impunity.

As the fighting escalated in 1998 and UNITA violations continued, the Security Council responded more forcefully with a new round of sanctions. The tenor of Security Council policy on Angola began to change toward a firmer approach. Member states were increasingly frustrated by UNITA's deceits and the rising level of violence and were determined to take tougher action in an attempt to forestall another cycle of war. On 12 June 1998 the Council adopted Resolution 1173, imposing the strongest sanctions measures yet against UNITA. It demanded that UNITA accept the extension of Angolan government authority called for in the Lusaka Protocol, cease its military buildup and comply with demobilization commitments, and halt attacks against UN personnel. The sanctions included a freeze on UNITA financial assets, a ban on financial transactions with UNITA, an embargo on the import of diamonds not certified by the Angolan government, and a ban on any form of travel to territories controlled by UNITA. The measures went into effect immediately and have remained in force to the present.

The tougher sanctions in Resolution 1173 were no more successful at ending the war than the limited measures imposed earlier. Fighting between UNITA and government forces escalated further and continued through 1999, as negotiators failed to find a diplomatic solution. UNITA responded to the Security Council's more forceful measures by turning its wrath on UN officials. In January 1999 UNITA suspended all contacts with the Troika of Observers and reportedly shot down two UN aircraft. The UN in turn accelerated the withdrawal of MONUA. With each side increasingly determined to pursue a military solution, international negotiators were powerless to prevent renewed carnage. The combined pressures of government military action and tougher UN sanctions did not reverse UNITA advances on the battlefield or encourage Savimbi to accept a negotiated solution.

Humanitarian Costs

The military and political crisis in Angola created one of the worst humanitarian tragedies in the world. According to UNICEF's 1999 report, *Progress of Nations*, children were at greater risk in Angola than anywhere else on earth.[16] From 1997 to 1998, Angola dropped four places in the United Nations Development Programme's human development index, from 156 to 160. Infant mortality increased from 132 to 170 per 1,000 live births, and mortality for children under five rose to 292 per 1,000.[17] UNICEF estimated that 40 percent of Angola's children were underweight and that more than half did not attend school.[18]

Food shortages and starvation claimed a growing number of lives as the war intensified in 1998 and 1999. According to the Angola government, 200 people were dying daily from starvation.[19] Critical food shortages developed in the cities of Malanje, Cuito, and Huambo, all under siege by UNITA forces. Food deliveries by road or air became extremely hazardous and dwindled to a trickle. In Malanje, half the children under five were reported malnourished, and one in four persons was starving.[20] In Huambo, a World Food Programme (WFP) survey found 17 percent of the population malnourished.[21]

The number of displaced persons in Angola also rose sharply. By the summer of 1999 the number of internally displaced persons was estimated at 1.7 million, a significant proportion of the country's approximately 12.6 million people.[22] More than 1 million people were forced to flee in 1999 alone.[23] In beleaguered Huambo, nearly half the previous population of 750,000 people died or fled as a result of the war. Displaced populations had to rely on international relief agencies such as WFP, which did not receive the financial support needed to purchase adequate supplies and faced mounting security dangers in attempting to deliver assistance.

The appalling humanitarian miseries of Angola resulted primarily from war, not sanctions. The brutal nature of the military struggle and the sieges of Malanje, Huambo, and other civilian population centers were the principal cause of the country's agony. Sanctions, particularly the oil embargo, may have contributed in a limited way to these hardships, through price increases and some shortages of fuel, but the social impact of these measures was minor. The Security Council imposed more selective and targeted sanctions precisely because of its concern for avoiding any actions that would exacerbate already disastrous humanitarian conditions. To this extent the Council succeeded. The sanctions were neither sufficiently broad nor comprehensive to cause serious humanitarian hardships. However, because the sanctions were so limited and were imposed so hesitantly (at least prior to 1998), they had no impact on the course of the war and thus contributed little to the prospects for a long-term political solution.

Sanctions Evasion

Sanctions were not effective in disrupting UNITA's extensive international networks of diamond trading and arms supply. They failed in large part because they were not enforced. The resolutions adopted by the Security Council reflected a strengthening of diplomatic, economic, and financial restrictions on UNITA, but in the field very few of these measures were actually implemented. The attempt to apply sanctions on UNITA was undermined by the lack of effective government authority in many of the border areas surrounding the rebel movement's territory, by the chaotic and desperate conditions caused by nearly continuous warfare and the resulting flood of refugees, and by the pervasiveness of corruption and criminality in the region (often involving government officials). Weapons traffickers and mercenaries openly flouted the arms embargo, and UNITA's financial assets continued to swell despite financial sanctions. The major powers did little to enforce the sanctions, and little or no support was given to neighboring states to assist them in carrying out the Security Council's mandates.

UNITA proved clever and resourceful in adjusting to sanctions and finding alternative means of commerce. It also found ways to circumvent travel restrictions and benefited from large-scale truck traffic across the Zambian border.[24] When the Angolan army helped topple pro-UNITA governments in Zaire and Congo-Brazzaville in 1997, UNITA recovered from this loss of arms supply by finding alternative sources of weapons and new routes to ship them. The arms embargo failed to prevent UNITA from becoming one of the best equipped fighting forces in Africa, with an army of 70,000 men, Ukrainian tanks, and twelve combat aircraft.[25] UNITA also employed mercenaries and military trainers from several countries. In January 1999 UNITA displayed its new military prowess with battle tactics that overwhelmed government forces and nearly seized Cuito.[26]

With a few exceptions (Zaire from 1993 to 1997, Uganda, and Zambia), most of UNITA's arms purchases came from independent dealers using private air and sea transport.[27] Pilots and ship captains concealed their shipments by falsifying flight plans, cargo manifests, and bills of lading.[28] Officials in neighboring Zambia and even in the Angolan armed forces permitted and profited from these dealings.[29] Former officials of the South African apartheid government and arms dealers from African and Middle Eastern countries as well as Europe and North America arranged weapons deliveries and mercenary support for UNITA.[30] Private air transport came from companies in the former USSR and Africa, with many of the transport pilots being Russian or Ukrainian. Sanctions caused some inconvenience and additional costs for UNITA, but they did not prevent the flow of weapons to the rebel movement.

UNITA's massive investment portfolio and generous diamond income enabled it to absorb the higher prices it had to pay for arms. It managed to circumvent the diamond-trading sanctions by stockpiling a huge number of gems before it handed over two key diamond-trading centers, Cuango and Lundas, to the government in 1997 and 1998. This caused UNITA's diamond revenues to dip temporarily before the UN imposed the diamond sanctions.[31] When the Security Council imposed Resolution 1173, UNITA released these diamonds onto the market, which threatened to cause global diamond prices to collapse. In response, DeBeers, the largest diamond firm in the world, bought huge numbers of illicit UNITA diamonds to stabilize the market.[32]

UNITA also responded to sanctions by completely reorganizing its diamond-trading network. Instead of sending diamonds directly to Antwerp or through contacts in Kinshasa, Brazzaville, Togo, or Ivory Coast, UNITA began to ship its diamonds through other ports in Africa and then on to minor diamond-trading centers like Tel Aviv and Moscow.[33] Smuggled UNITA diamonds were then once again exported without the requirement of an Angolan government certificate of origin.

In addition, Ivory Coast, Zambia, and numerous private diamond-trading companies provided false certificates of origin.[34] The Angolan government's parastatal diamond company, Endiama, estimated that only 10 percent of Angola's diamonds were exported legally, making it difficult to trace illegal sales by private dealers or government officials.

UNITA easily circumvented diplomatic and travel sanctions, often through legal methods. After Resolution 1127 was passed, UNITA offices were reopened under different names. UNITA missions suddenly transformed themselves into policy-lobbying organizations or cultural and trade associations. Diplomatic sanctions were hampered by the fact that many UNITA officials had citizenship or permanent resident status in Western countries, giving them the right to travel freely in those states. UNITA officials continued to operate in several European countries, even arranging all-expenses-paid trips for journalists to meet UNITA officials in Angola.[35] Ivory Coast violated the travel sanctions by providing UNITA officials with passports, allowing them to move freely and even reside in European countries.[36]

Strengthening Enforcement

The UN sanctions committee in New York was powerless to prevent the massive violations that vitiated the impact of Resolutions 864, 1127, and 1173. The committee had no means of ensuring enforcement of the sanctions, and it had no independent means of monitoring the flow of illegal trade. For several years the Security Council benefited from the UN verification missions, UNAVEM II and III and MONUA, but these forces were reduced and then later withdrawn. Although the inspectors' missions did not include sanctions monitoring, they used their disarmament mandate to accurately report UNITA's rearmament effort, arms imports, and flights into UNITA territory. Gradual force reductions, leading to the eventual termination of MONUA in 1999, greatly downgraded the UN's sanctions monitoring abilities.

After the adoption of stronger sanctions in 1997 and 1998, the Security Council began to pay greater attention to improving the enforcement of these measures. The sanctions committee met more frequently in 1998, and the committee chair, Kenyan ambassador Njuguna Mahugu, took the initiative of meeting with African regional leaders to discuss strengthening the implementation of sanctions. In January 1999 Secretary-General Kofi Annan issued recommendations for improving the effectiveness of sanctions. He called upon member states to improve their border monitoring and to provide better information to the sanctions committee on violations. The Secretary-General also suggested commissioning an experts group to study ways of tracing and preventing sanctions violations.[37] In February 1999, the sanctions committee recommended that states pass legislation to criminalize sanctions violations, urged states to enlist the help of private companies to obtain information on sanctions violations, and encouraged financial institutions to trace UNITA's assets and financial flows.[38] In May 1999 the committee acted upon the Secretary-General's January recommendations by appointing two expert panels, one to trace UNITA's sources of oil and money (including revenues from illicit diamond trading) and the other to investigate UNITA's arms supplies.[39]

The key to better enforcement, officials recognized, was a more determined monitoring effort at regional airports and seaports. Though this would not eliminate all violations and would still allow cross-border truck traffic, it would block much of UNITA's supply of weapons and fuel. An effective monitoring effort would require the deployment of civilian monitors and sanctions assistance missions throughout the region, equipped with a communications and data network. Diamond sanctions were enforceable in theory, but in practice the task proved very difficult. The gem trade is dominated by one company, DeBeers, and 80 percent of all trading takes place in one city, Antwerp. Diamonds must meet exacting standards of quality inspection and can be traced, even to the specific mine from which they were extracted. Angolan diamonds are very distinctive, among the best in the world, and few countries have sufficient quality gems to match Angolan diamonds. To take advantage of these factors and effectively monitor the diamond trade, however, would require unprecedented transparency in and international intrusion into the diamond business. It would also require a high degree of cooperation from private selling companies and governments that profit from the lucrative trade.

In 1999, the new chairman of the Angola sanctions committee, Canadian ambassador Robert Fowler, launched a determined effort to mobilize support for tighter enforcement of the diamond sanctions and greater international cooperation in isolating UNITA. Fowler traveled extensively in southern Africa and Europe, meeting with government officials, arms trade experts, and diamond industry officials to discuss ways of improving the effectiveness of the sanctions. Fowler's mission was a groundbreaking effort that gave new vitality to the Angola sanctions committee and offered a model for how other sanctions committees could meet the challenge of sanctions implementation. It recommended a number of steps for improving sanctions monitoring and enforcement, among them that UN customs inspectors be stationed at various sites in Africa and Ukraine to monitor the arms embargo and that trained inspectors be assigned to the world's major diamond-trading centers. The Fowler report also recommended enlisting the aid of national intelligence agencies and Interpol to enforce sanctions and establishing liaisons with international diamond companies.[40]

The report cited the constructive role of nonstate actors in sanctions enforcement. After the downing of the two UN aircraft in January 1999, the UN enlisted the International Civil Aviation Organization (ICAO) to help investigate the incidents. The UN also asked the International Telecommunications Union and the International Telecommunications Satellite Organization to make recommendations on possible telecommunications sanctions (Resolution 1221). Human Rights Watch published two separate reports on violations of the arms embargo,[41] and the British organization Global Witness released a report on UNITA's diamond income and diamond-trading network.[42] Largely as a result of the Global Witness report, the European Parliament set up a committee to investigate illicit trafficking in UNITA diamonds.[43] In the case of Angola as in other examples, nongovernmental organizations (NGOs) played an important role in raising awareness of sanctions violations, especially illicit arms trafficking, and mobilizing public concern for more effective measures against human rights abuse.

Conclusion

UN sanctions on UNITA must be rated a failure. They did not prevent the renewed outbreak of war or impede UNITA's ability to build up its military power. The political impact of sanctions was limited to last-minute, token gestures of compliance by UNITA to ward off stronger sanctions. The sanctions helped to establish an initial bargaining framework in 1993, but they could not bring adherence to the Lusaka Protocol or prevent repeated violations of that agreement. The failings of the Angola sanctions resulted from several factors. As noted earlier, the widening regional war in central Africa, involving both the government and UNITA, made the task of resolving the Angola crisis more difficult. UNITA proved extremely resistant to compromise and peaceful suasion and very resourceful at circumventing sanctions. The Security Council's reluctance to take a firmer stance until late 1997 encouraged Savimbi's tendency to be intransigent and made it easier for UNITA to violate previous peace commitments. The almost complete lack of enforcement efforts undermined the credibility of the entire sanctions enterprise.

As noted, the Security Council began to adopt a tougher line in 1998. Under the leadership of Ambassadors Mahugu of Kenya and Fowler of Canada, the Angola sanctions committee took a more proactive approach to implementation and in the process established a model for how a sanctions committee might operate in the future. Rather than simply issuing perfunctory reports with no recommendations for improvement, the Angola committee developed far-reaching yet practical proposals for improving the implementation of sanctions. Whether this more activist approach to sanctions will be successful in fulfilling UN objectives in Angola remains to be seen. Much depends on the commitment of key states and private actors to take the necessary steps toward implementation. Ultimately, peace in Angola will hinge on the willingness of the antagonists themselves to accept a political rather than military solution.

Notes

1. Some Angolans divide the fighting into separate wars according to the issues at stake or peace agreements between wars: the war for independence, from 1961 to 1975; the Cold War fighting, from 1975 to 1991; the "third war," from late 1992 to 1994; and the "fourth war," from 1998 to the present time.

2. For example, rebel leader Jonas Savimbi professed both Maoism to attract Chinese support during the 1970s and liberal democracy to attract U.S. support during the 1980s.

3. See Chris McGreal, "Profits Fuel Angola's War," *Manchester Guardian Weekly*, 14 July 1999, 3.

4. Al J. Venter, "Winds of War Set to Blow Across Angola," *Jane's Intelligence Review* 10 (1 October 1998).

5. Human Rights Watch, *Between War and Peace: Arms Trade and Human Rights Abuses Since the Lusaka Protocol* (Washington, D.C.: Human Rights Watch, February 1996), 13.

6. Most diamond-exporting states have only 5 to 10 percent of their diamonds rated as gem quality. The higher proportion of gemstones among Angola's diamonds is directly relevant to sanctions monitoring, as noted below.

7. Global Witness, *A Rough Trade: The Role of Companies and Government in the Angolan Conflict* (London: Global Witness, December 1998), 4–5, 16.

8. Patrick Smith, "Cursed for Their Mineral Wealth: Business in War Zones," *Financial Mail* (South Africa), 14 August 1998.

9. United Nations Security Council, *Report of the Secretary-General on the Situation in Angola*, S/26872, 13 December 1993.

10. Human Rights Watch, *Between War and Peace.*

11. Human Rights Watch, *Angola Unravels: The Rise and Fall of the Lusaka Peace Process* (New York: Human Rights Watch, September 1999).

12. *Angola Peace Monitor* 3, 30 November 1996, 1–4. This same issue of *APM* contained journalistic accounts of UNITA arms imports that contradicted Blondin Beye's upbeat reporting on UNITA compliance.

13. Mercedes Sayagues, "No War, No Peace, No Solution for Angola," *Johannesburg Mail and Guardian,* 3 July 1998; "Angola: Quo Vadis United Nations?" *Africa News,* 6 September 1998.

14. United Nations Security Council, *Security Council Resolution 1127,* S/RES/1127, 28 August 1997, par. 7.

15. "Disarming Rebels Conned UN: They Handed in Old Weapons and Hid the Good Ones," *Vancouver Sun,* 13 February 1999, 7.

16. Cited in United Nations Security Council, *Letter Dated 28 July 1999 from the Chairman of the Security Council Committee Established Pursuant to Resolution 864 (1993) Concerning the Situation in Angola, Addressed to the President of the Security Council,* S/1999/829, 28 July 1999, par. 22.

17. "Social Indicators Plummet," *Angola Peace Monitor* 5, 28 July 1999, 3.

18. Cited in ibid.

19. Manuel Muanza, "Starvation: Angola's Hidden War," *Agence France Presse,* 29 July 1999.

20. Manuel Muanza, "Northern Angolan City Declared a 'Humanitarian Disaster Area,'" *Agence France Presse,* 5 August 1999.

21. As reported by Suzanne Daly, "Hunger Ravages Angolans in Renewed Civil War," *New York Times,* 26 July 1999, A1.

22. See European Commission, "Statement by the President of the European Union on Angola, July 1999." Newspaper reports put the number of internally displaced persons at up to 2 million; see also Muanza, "Northern Angolan City Declared."

23. United Nations Administrative Committee on Coordination/Subcommittee on Nutrition, *Refugee Nutrition Information System—Angola,* New York, 4 August 1999.

24. "Zambian Aid for Angolan Rebels," *Africa News,* 9 April 1999.

25. Patrick Smith, "Cursed for Their Mineral Wealth"; Tom Fennell and Stefan Lovgren, "The Diamond War," *MacLeans,* 22 March 1999, 18; Helmoed-Romer Heitman, "UNITA Forces Developing an Air Capability," *Jane's Defense Weekly* 31 (14 April 1999).

26. Christine Gordon, "Angola: UNITA Launches New Offensive," *Jane's Intelligence Review* (1 February 1999): 7.

27. Human Rights Watch, *Between War and Peace,* 15.

28. Mark Honigsbaum and Antony Barnett, "U.K. Firms in African Arms Riddle: Mystery of Cargo Planes and Lethal Trade That Is Fueling a Continent's Murderous Civil Wars," *Observer,* 31 January 1999, 9.

29. An expert at the South African Institute for Security Studies reported that UNITA was even getting supplies from planes delivering weapons to the Angolan armed forces. He noted that in some cases, planes landed and divided their bulk cargoes between UNITA and the Angolan army. Suzanne Daly, "Hunger Ravages Angolans," 1.

30. "Serious Allegations of UNITA Arms Imports Raise Doubts on UNITA's Motives," *Angola Peace Monitor* 3, 30 November 1996, 3; Al J. Venter, "Winds of War Set to Blow Across Angola," 37–45.

31. Global Witness, *A Rough Trade,* 12.

32. Dan Atkinson, "Angola Rebels Provoke Crisis in Diamond Trade," *Guardian,* 3 August 1998, 1.

33. "Uncertainty over Gem Trade," *Africa Energy and Mining* 247 (3 March 1999); Francois Misser, "How UNITA Beats UN Gems Embargo," *African Business* (May 1999).

34. "Diamonds: No Way to Stifle UNITA," *Africa Energy and Mining* 235 (9 September 1998).

35. David Leppard and Chris Hastings, "Angolan Rebels Flout Ban on London Offices," *London Times,* 16 August 1998.

36. Global Witness, *Angola Sanctions: Recent Developments* (London: Global Witness, 22 April 1999).

37. United Nations Security Council, *Report of the Secretary-General on the United Nations Observer Mission in Angola,* S/1999/49, 17 January 1999, 3.

38. United Nations Security Council, *Letter from the Chairman of the Sanctions Committee Concerning the Situation in Angola,* S/1999/147, 12 February 1999, 4.

39. United Nations Security Council, *Letter from the Chairman of the Security Council Committee Concerning the Situation in Angola,* S/1999/509, 4 May 1999.

40. United Nations Security Council, *Letter from the Chairman of the Security Council Committee Concerning the Situation in Angola,* S/1999/644, 4 June 1999.

41. Human Rights Watch, *Between War and Peace;* Human Rights Watch, *Arms Trade and Violations of the Laws of War Since the 1992 Elections* (Washington, D.C.: Human Rights Watch, November 1994).

42. Global Witness, *A Rough Trade.*

43. "Uncertainty over Gem Trade," *Africa Energy and Mining.*

9

Sierra Leone:
The Failure of Regional and
International Sanctions*

In Sierra Leone as in Angola, sanctions were imposed in the midst of a savage civil war against an armed rebel movement that refused to accept the results of a democratic election. In May 1997 disgruntled army officers calling themselves the Armed Forces Revolutionary Council (AFRC) overthrew the newly elected government of Ahmed Kabbah and established a military junta headed by Major Johnny Paul Koromah. In August 1997 the Economic Community of West African States (ECOWAS) responded to the coup by imposing comprehensive economic sanctions. In October 1997 the UN Security Council followed suit with Resolution 1132 imposing an oil and arms embargo on Sierra Leone and travel sanctions on members of the AFRC junta. ECOWAS also sent its military arm, the Economic Community of West African States Military Observer Group (ECOMOG), and a force of 14,000 troops (mostly from Nigeria) to remove the junta, which was driven from Freetown in February 1998. The Security Council lifted sanctions on the government but reimposed an arms embargo and travel sanctions on former members of the junta and on the Revolutionary United Front (RUF), the rebel group that had fought the government for over seven years and that continued to resist the extension of government control over rebel-held territory. In October 1998 the RUF launched a major military offensive, seizing control of two-thirds of the country and gaining representation in the government in the Lomé agreement of July 1999. As in the case of Angola, sanctions were ineffective in constraining the military power of the rebels and played little or no role in attempts to negotiate a just settlement of the conflict.

In this chapter we describe the sanctions imposed by ECOWAS and the UN and their relation to the shifting tide of battle and outside mili-

---

* This chapter was coauthored by Richard W. Conroy.

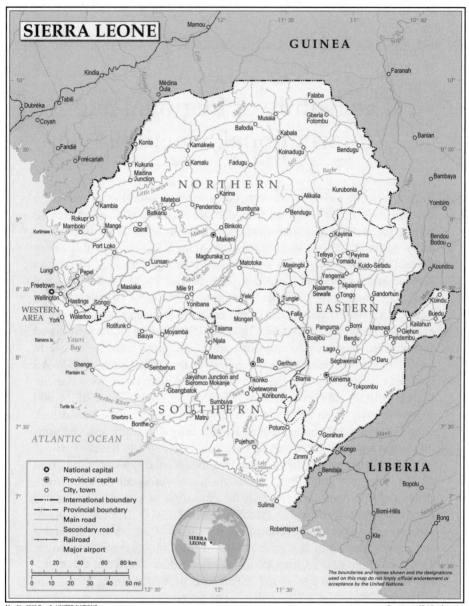

SIERRA LEONE

GUINEA

LIBERIA

ATLANTIC OCEAN

NORTHERN

EASTERN

SOUTHERN

WESTERN AREA

Mamou

Kindia
Médina Oula
Dubréka
Tabili
Coyah
Faranah
Falaba
Musaia
Gberia Fotombu
Bafodia
Kabala
Banian
Fandié
Konta
Kamakwie
Koinadugu
Bendugu
Forécariah
Kukuna
Kamalu
Fadugu
Bambaya
Madina Junction
Karina
Alikalia
Kurubonla
Yombiro
Kambia
Mateboi
Pendembu
Bumbuna
Bendugu
Rokupr
Batkanu
Mambolo
Mange
Gbinti
Binkolo
Kayima
Bendou Bodou
Kortimaw I.
Port Loko
Makeni
Koundou
Lungi
Lunsar
Magburaka
Matotoka
Masingbi
Tefeya
Yomadu
Peyima
Kuido-Sefadu
Pepel
Yengema
Freetown
Masiaka
Mile 91
Yele
Njaiama-Sewafe
Njaiama
Tongo
Gandorhun
Koindu
Wellington
Yonibana
Tungie
Hastings
Songo
Falla
Buedu
Waterloo
Mongeri
Panguma
Bomi
Manowa
Kailahun
York
Rotifunk
Taiama
Boajibu
Bendu
Giehun
Pendembu
Banana Is.
Bauya
Moyamba
Njala
Lago
Yawri Bay
Mano
Bo
Gerihun
Segbwema
Daru
Shenge
Sembehun
Jaiyahun Junction and Sieromco Mokanje
Tikonko
Blama
Kenema
Tokpombu
Plantain Is.
Gbangbatok
Kpetewoma
Koribundu
Sherbro River
Sumbuya
Turtle Is.
Sherbro I.
Bonthe
Matru
Poturo
Gorahun
Pujehun
Zimmi
Kongo
Bendaja
Bopolu
Sulima
Bomi-Hills
Bong
Robertsport
Kle

Legend:

- ◉ National capital
- ◉ Provincial capital
- ○ City, town
- —·—·— International boundary
- —·—·— Provincial boundary
- ——— Main road
- ——— Secondary road
- —+—+— Railroad
- ✈ Major airport

| 0 | 20 | 40 | 60 | 80 km |
| 0 | 10 | 20 | 30 | 40 | 50 mi |

SIERRA LEONE

The boundaries and names shown and the designations used on this map do not imply official endorsement or acceptance by the United Nations.

Map No. 3902 Rev. 3   UNITED NATIONS
October 1999

Department of Public Information
Cartographic Section

tary intervention. In addition to reviewing the uneven attempts to enforce sanctions and the many violations of the arms embargo, we examine the severe humanitarian crisis in Sierra Leone resulting from war and sanctions. We conclude with an assessment of the meager results of sanctions and the implications of this case for the future.

The Roots of the Crisis

Sierra Leone has the dubious distinction of being the world's poorest and least developed nation. It ranks last on the United Nations Development Programme (UNDP) human development index and has a per capita GDP of only $167. Life expectancy is a mere forty-one years, and the infant mortality rate is 150 per 1,000 live births. The country is richly endowed with natural resources, however. Sierra Leone exports diamonds, bauxite, and titanium ore, and it supplies one-quarter of the world's supply of rutile, an ingredient in paint. The struggle for control of these resources has been at the heart of the nation's civil war. The destruction and chaos accompanying the military struggle have worsened the country's economic and social miseries and caused widespread death and human suffering.

The civil war that began in 1991 is a complex struggle involving multiple actors with often competing agendas. The RUF and its leader, former army corporal Foday Sankoh, claim to represent neglected rural areas and the country's interior. The RUF has relied on disaffected lower-class youths and forcibly conscripted child soldiers to sustain its military campaigns. In 1994 and 1995, during the first phase of the civil war, the rebels captured Sierra Leone's most important mining centers, giving them control over some $200 million in export income.[1] The rebels have become infamous for their use of terror and mutilation, often severing the limbs of their victims.

The Sierra Leone army, numbering some 10,000 soldiers, has been unable and often unwilling to combat the rebels. Army officers ruled the country prior to the 1996 election, and many profited from illegal mining and smuggling operations that the newly elected government wanted to bring under state control. The army was internally divided between opponents and supporters of the return to civilian rule. When the Kabbah regime pledged to cut the size of the army in half, army officers increasingly sided with the rebels.[2] Many officers were so-called sobels, soldiers by day and rebels by night.[3] Some government leaders drew support from the Kamajors, traditional hunters from the

SIERRA LEONE, Security Council Resolutions

Resolution Number	Action
1132	**8 October 1997** Imposed an oil embargo and an arms embargo Imposed travel sanctions on members of the AFRC junta and their families Conditioned the lifting of sanctions on the junta relinquishing power Created sanctions committee
1156	**16 March 1998** Lifted the oil embargo
1171	**5 June 1998** Confirmed the removal of sanctions on the government Reimposed the arms embargo and travel ban on the RUF and members of the former military junta

Mende tribe, with a militia of some 17,000 to 35,000 fighters.[4] The government also retained a South African mercenary firm, Executive Outcomes, which played a critical role in the conflict. Executive Outcomes won a series of military victories against the RUF in 1995 and 1996, which paved the way for the elections and the Abidjan peace agreement in November 1996.

In the Abidjan agreement, the Kabbah government agreed to recognize the RUF as a legitimate political party. The government also acceded to the RUF's demand that Executive Outcomes leave Sierra Leone. RUF leaders were granted protection from administrative or legal action against them, despite their numerous war crimes and acts of terror against civilian populations. For its part, the RUF agreed to demobilize its soldiers and accept the deployment of a UN peacekeeping force to verify the disarmament and demobilization of combatants. The rebels did not win their principal objective, however, which was representation in the government, and as a result many rebels were unwilling to accept the agreement. Sankoh refused to meet with the UN special representative or accept deployment of the UN peacekeepers, and by

February 1997 he and Kabbah had broken off communications. The RUF did not demobilize its soldiers as promised and boycotted the Demobilization and Resettlement Committee established as part of the Abidjan accords.

The Armed Forces Revolutionary Council that overthrew the Kabbah government in May 1997 was separate from the RUF, but the rebel movement quickly allied itself with the military junta. The RUF and disgruntled military officers had worked together in the past, opposing the 1996 elections. They joined forces after the coup to resist outside military intervention and preserve their control over mines and other economic resources. After the AFRC junta was forced from power in February 1998, the RUF carried on the war with substantial external assistance from Liberia, which trained and supplied the rebel group and offered its territory as a rear base, and also from Libya and Burkina Faso.

Sanctions and Military Intervention

Three months after the May 1997 military coup, the major regional organization, ECOWAS, imposed comprehensive sanctions against Sierra Leone. The stated purpose of these sanctions was to restore Sierra Leone's elected government. ECOWAS imposed comprehensive trade sanctions, including an arms embargo, an oil embargo, and a freeze on travel by and financial assets of military junta members, their families, and entities directly or indirectly controlled by them.[5] The sanctions even included a ban on the supply of humanitarian assistance, unless such deliveries were approved by a special committee with representatives from neighboring states.

Soon after imposing these regional sanctions, ECOWAS requested that the UN Security Council apply sanctions as well. The Security Council agreed to the ECOWAS request and in October adopted Resolution 1132 imposing an arms embargo, an oil embargo, and travel sanctions on members of the junta and their families. Resolution 1132 did not include comprehensive trade sanctions, in large part because the Council wanted to avoid causing further humanitarian hardships. Nor did it freeze financial assets. The declared objectives of the UN sanctions were to remove the military junta and restore the elected government, end the acts of violence, and halt interference with humanitarian relief efforts. The Security Council conditioned the lifting of sanctions on the junta's relinquishing power.

The ECOWAS and UN sanctions initially appeared to have a significant impact on the junta. Coup leaders responded to the threat of UN sanctions by agreeing to enter negotiations for a restoration of constitutional government and implementation of the Abidjan agreement. Sanctions were effective in establishing a bargaining dynamic and bringing the coup leaders to the negotiating table. The AFRC signed an agreement in Conakry, Guinea, just fifteen days after the Security Council adopted Resolution 1132. The Conakry agreement called for the restoration of the elected civilian government six months later, and the demobilization of Sierra Leone's armed forces and rebel groups. Although AFRC leaders signed the Conakry agreement, they refused to comply with its terms. The failure of the military junta to honor this agreement prompted the decision by Nigeria and its ECOWAS partners to mount a major military intervention.

In Sierra Leone as in Haiti, sanctions helped to spark initial negotiations. In both cases the military junta responded to the imposition of UN sanctions by agreeing to come to the bargaining table. But the impact of sanctions was limited and not sufficient to bring about a genuine settlement or to ensure implementation of the resulting agreement. In both countries, the bargain resulting from sanctions-induced negotiations was deeply flawed and lacked an effective means of enforcement, and sanctions gave way to military intervention.

When the ECOMOG military force succeeded in driving the junta from Freetown, the Security Council responded by adopting Resolution 1156, lifting the oil embargo against Sierra Leone. In response to the continuing rebellion by the RUF and members of the armed forces, however, the Security Council adopted Resolution 1171 in June 1998. It confirmed the removal of sanctions on the government but reimposed the travel ban and arms embargo on the RUF and members of the former military junta.

Despite ongoing UN and ECOWAS sanctions, the RUF continued its rebellion against government forces and their Nigerian supporters and steadily expanded its power base. In October 1998 the RUF launched a major military offensive that inflicted a number of defeats on government forces and terrorized civilian supporters of the government. The offensive was prompted by a court decision sentencing RUF leader Foday Sankoh to death for treason. By February 1999 the RUF had succeeded in seizing control of much of the country.

As a result of the RUF's military successes, the government was forced to negotiate a new peace settlement. The Lomé agreement of July 1999 gave the RUF significant representation in the government while affirming the same rights of political recognition and amnesty granted in the earlier Abidjan settlement. It also gave the RUF four cabinet posts and several deputy ministries and other senior-level positions. Sankoh was named chairman of the Commission for the Management of Strategic Resources, with responsibility for Sierra Leone's valuable gold, diamonds, and mineral resources. Thus Sankoh and the RUF obtained a better deal from the Lomé agreement, which followed twenty months of sanctions and the ECOMOG military intervention, than they received in the presanctions Abidjan agreement. Sanctions had no effect on the RUF's ability to wage war and strengthen its bargaining position through gains on the battlefield.

Faulty Enforcement

Sanctions against Sierra Leone failed to achieve their objectives in part because they were not properly monitored or enforced. The threat of sanctions, which led to negotiation of the Conakry agreement, proved to be more effective than the sanctions themselves. The lack of border-monitoring capabilities in neighboring states and the inability of ECOWAS or the United Nations to mount a credible implementation effort undermined the potential effectiveness of sanctions.

In theory, Sierra Leone should have been highly vulnerable to sanctions. With only three seaports and four usable airports, Sierra Leone's trade could be significantly affected by a well-enforced embargo. The country is heavily dependent on the export of diamonds and other mineral resources that can be traced and controlled. Its northern neighbor, Guinea, sharing two-thirds of the border, was strongly sympathetic to the ECOWAS and UN sanctions. Guinean authorities closed the border with Sierra Leone and attempted to enforce the sanctions, but they lacked the means to effectively prevent smuggling operations.[6] The major obstacle to carrying out an effective sanctions regime was Sierra Leone's other neighbor, Liberia, which was hostile to sanctions and the Nigerian-led military intervention and provided substantial backing for Sierra Leone's rebels.

Both the UN Security Council and ECOWAS established sanctions committees to monitor sanctions compliance. The ECOWAS Committee of Four, which later became the Group of Five, had primary responsibility for obtaining information on implementation and violations, approving requests for humanitarian deliveries, and reporting on sanctions violations. The UN sanctions committee established with Resolution 1132 had a similar mandate, with the added task of identifying junta members and their families subject to travel sanctions. The UN committee attempted to encourage greater compliance with sanctions by governments in the region. The committee's chair, Ambassador Hans Dahlgren, permanent representative of Sweden to the Security Council, met with the leaders of neighboring states and ECOWAS officials to generate greater cooperation in sanctions enforcement. The UN committee also maintained liaison with the ECOWAS monitoring group. The close relationship between the two committees served as a model for cooperation between the Security Council and regional organizations in sanctions implementation.

Despite the attempts of the UN sanctions committee to encourage compliance, the enforcement effort was impeded by a lack of institutional capacity on the part of the UN and inadequate resources in Guinea and other neighboring states. In one of the most impoverished regions of the world, with both Sierra Leone and Liberia ravaged by war, the means for enforcing sanctions simply did not exist. Nigeria and its ECOWAS partners devoted their energies to the military intervention, exhausting themselves in the process and leaving few resources available for sanctions enforcement. ECOWAS nations lacked sufficient naval vessels to blockade Sierra Leone's ports, and as a result shipping continued to reach Freetown and other ports.[7] There was also considerable smuggling across the Guinean border, despite official attempts to prevent such activities. Without a substantial infusion of outside assistance, neighboring states had no hope of enforcing the sanctions.

Violations of the arms embargo were especially egregious. The bulk of the weapons were shipped through Liberia, where Charles Taylor and the National Patriotic Front of Liberia were waging their own struggle against ECOWAS and were eager to assist the RUF. Liberia allowed the RUF to use its territory for training and resupply and provided significant military support for the rebels. Liberia's blatant violations of the arms embargo were identified by the Security Council as the major weakness in the sanctions.[8] Libya and Burkina Faso also aided the rebels, serving primarily as transit points for arms and mercenaries delivered from Ukraine and Bulgaria.[9] One of the limitations of the UN arms embargo was Resolution 1132's ambiguity about the provision of military services and training. The original resolution did not mention mercenaries or military training services, and the RUF exploited this loophole to obtain Ukrainian mercenaries and Liberian support services.

The arms embargo was a complete failure in limiting the military capabilities of the RUF and rebellious members of the armed forces.

The RUF steadily enlarged its military capabilities in spite of the sanctions, transforming itself from a guerrilla band into a well-armed force. Its improved combat prowess enabled it to regain control of much of the country in January and February 1999 and put it in position to dictate more favorable diplomatic terms in the Lomé agreement. As with nearly all UN arms embargoes during the 1990s, the embargo against Sierra Leone was a complete failure.

Humanitarian Consequences

ECOWAS sanctions included a comprehensive ban on all imports and exports. Deliveries of food and medicine were also banned unless specifically authorized by the special ECOWAS sanctions committee. The committee functioned unevenly, however, and as a result authorized shipments of food and medicine were often interrupted. In addition, the combatant groups, especially the RUF, were willing to use starvation as a weapon and on some occasions destroyed crops or blocked food shipments as a means of terrorizing the civilian population. Although the UN sanctions were more limited than the ECOWAS measures, in large part because of concern for potential adverse humanitarian consequences, they also had negative impacts. The UN sanctions included an oil embargo, which increased transportation costs and contributed to a general rise in the price of food and other necessities. Despite a 15 percent increase in crop yields in 1997, food prices tripled in 1998, mostly due to rising transportation costs and the virtual elimination of food imports into Sierra Leone.[10]

Sanctions and the intensified war brought to a standstill many commercial imports and humanitarian relief deliveries. At the time of the May 1997 coup, relief agencies in Sierra Leone had an estimated 10,000 to 14,000 metric tons of food aid stockpiled. These supplies were able to meet only 40 percent of Sierra Leone's food needs. By January 1998, these inadequate resources were exhausted, and humanitarian agencies reported only 200 metric tons of food remaining.[11] Relief agencies could have provided all of Sierra Leone's food needs, according to the UN's Office for the Coordination of Humanitarian Affairs (OCHA), but ECOWAS lacked the means to administer an exemptions approval process. Guinea and other neighboring countries were unable to establish an effective system for inspecting and approving humanitarian deliveries.[12] In February 1998 OCHA and ECOWAS took steps to correct these problems by establishing an exemptions management system. ECOWAS supplied the inspectors, and OCHA paid their salaries and provided equipment to monitor the transshipment of humanitarian goods at the major border crossing from Guinea.[13] Although the scale of the monitoring program was tiny, initially involving just two inspectors, it provided another useful precedent in cooperation between the United Nations and a regional organization in the administration of sanctions. The practical impact of the joint monitoring effort was limited, however, since ECOMOG ousted the military junta soon after the program began, and sanctions were lifted shortly thereafter.

The Sierra Leone sanctions also featured a UN assessment report on humanitarian impacts. The study was similar to the humanitarian preassessment report on Sudan released in February 1997, except that the Sierra Leone report came not before sanctions were imposed but soon afterward. The purpose of the assessment mission was similar to that in the Sudan case: to evaluate the humanitarian impacts of sanctions and recommend remedial action. The interagency report was highly critical of the ECOWAS trade embargo and confirmed that virtually no relief supplies had been able to pass along the land route from Guinea previously used by humanitarian agencies.[14] The assessment mission's report and recommendations helped to spur attempts to improve cooperative monitoring and exemptions processing. The precedent set by the Sierra Leone and Sudan humanitarian assessment missions is likely to be of value to the Security Council in future sanctions cases, since it confirmed the utility of such missions.

The human costs of war and sanctions in Sierra Leone were horrendous. From 1991 to 1999, an estimated 50,000 to 75,000 people died in Sierra Leone.[15] Two-thirds of these deaths occurred between 1997 and 1999, when sanctions were in place and the war intensified. Malnutrition rose sharply. The 1998 UN assessment mission reported a 53 percent increase in "global acute malnutrition" and a 100 percent increase in "severe acute malnutrition" among children under five.[16] Médecins Sans Frontières–Holland reported a 24 percent increase in admissions to its therapeutic feeding center in Sierra Leone in December 1997 and a 10 percent rise in the fatality rate at this center.[17]

The interagency assessment mission attributed the malnutrition crisis in Sierra Leone primarily to the ECOWAS embargo, although it also acknowledged the contributing role of military hostilities. As in other cases of sanctions-related crisis, it is hard to separate the impact of sanctions from that of war and other causes of social misery. In the Sierra Leone case, the especially savage nature of the conflict contributed directly to the starvation and death of vulnerable civilian populations. An October 1997 article in the *Christian Science Monitor* reported that the AFRC was blocking shipments of food into Mende tribal territories and systematically plowing up rice paddies to punish the local population for supporting the Kamajors and the government.[18] Even after sanctions were lifted and food and fuel prices returned to levels seen prior to the coup, the humanitarian situation in Sierra Leone remained desperate and in some cases even worsened. For example, the February 1998 UN interagency report cited an Action Contre le Faim (ACF) study in which 5.7 percent of Freetown's children were said to suffer from global acute malnutrition.[19] By July 1998, four months after sanctions were lifted, another ACF study found that global acute malnutrition had risen to 29 percent.[20] In July 1999 Reuters reported that 20,000 people were on the verge of starvation in the city of Makeni after the RUF blocked all food deliveries following its capture of the city in December 1998.[21] No doubt the sanctions, especially the total trade embargo imposed by ECOWAS, contributed to the humanitarian crisis in Sierra Leone, but the principal cause of humanitarian suffering was the war, particularly the RUF's decision to use the disruption of food supplies to civilians as a military tactic.

Conclusion

Sanctions played a minor role in the Sierra Leone tragedy. They were unable to prevent the rebels from expanding their military power and winning significant military victories that allowed them to gain favorable terms at the bargaining table. UN sanctions initially helped to spark negotiations for a political settlement, but they could not prevent the rebels from reneging on their commitments and launching a new military offensive. The ineffectiveness of the sanctions resulted from inadequate monitoring and enforcement efforts. Implementation of the arms embargo was particularly weak. The Sierra Leone case illustrated the need for more precision in Security Council resolutions to ensure that arms embargoes specifically prohibit the use of mercenaries and military support services. The case featured some innovations in cooperative monitoring between the UN sanctions committee in New York and the regional sanctions committee established by ECOWAS. It also featured a UN humanitarian assessment mission, which helped to strengthen the precedent for such reports in future sanctions episodes.

Most important, the Sierra Leone case confirmed the lesson that emerges from nearly all the sanctions cases of the 1990s: the urgent need for more effective monitoring and enforcement efforts, especially among neighboring states and in regional organizations. Without a stronger capacity for inspection and implementation, UN and regional sanctions can never achieve the purposes for which they are imposed. An arms embargo cannot restrain the military capacity of a targeted regime or military group if it is not tightly enforced. The need for greater enforcement capacity is especially acute in impoverished developing nations, which often lack basic infrastructure and have little capacity to monitor trade and border traffic even in normal times, much less during war and political turmoil. The cases of both Angola and Sierra Leone dramatically illustrate the present inadequacies of sanctions enforcement and confirm the need for strengthening the capacity of the UN system and for helping member states and regional organizations develop similar capacity.

Notes

1. William Reno, "Privatizing War in Sierra Leone," *Current History* 96 (May 1997): 227–230.

2. Richard Cornwell, "Sierra Leone: RUF Diamonds," *African Security Review* 7 (1998): 2.

3. Reno, "Privatizing War," 227.

4. Institute for International Strategic Studies, *The Military Balance 1997–1998* (London: Oxford University Press, 1997), 257.

5. United Nations Security Council, *Economic Community of West African States, Decision on Sanctions Against the Junta and Sierra Leone,* S/1997/695, annex II, 8 September 1997.

6. United Nations Security Council, *Third Report of the Secretary-General on the Situation in Sierra Leone,* S/1998/103, 5 February 1998, 4.

7. United Nations Security Council, *Economic Community of West African States, Situation Report in Sierra Leone After the Signing of the Peace Plan,* S/1997/895, 17 November 1997, 14–16.

8. United Nations Security Council, *Statement by the President of the Security Council,* S/PRST/1999/1, 7 January 1999.

9. David Pratt, *Sierra Leone: The Forgotten Crisis, Report to the Minister of Foreign Affairs, the Honorable Lloyd Axworthy,* April 1999, 8.

10. United Nations, Office for the Coordination of Humanitarian Affairs (OCHA), *Sierra Leone Situation Report, 20 December 1997–20 January 1998,* 98/0012, 20 January 1998; United Nations, OCHA, *Sierra Leone Humanitarian Situation Report, 21 January–12 February 1998,* 98/0016, 12 February 1998.

11. United States Agency for International Development, "Sierra Leone: Complex Emergency Report Number One," 28 January 1998; United Nations, OCHA, *Sierra Leone Humanitarian Situation Report,* 98/0016.

12. United Nations, OCHA, *Sierra Leone Humanitarian Situation Report,* 98/0016.

13. Ibid.

14. United Nations, OCHA, *Interagency Assessment Mission to Sierra Leone: Interim Report,* 17 February 1998, 3, 6.

15. Human Rights Watch, *Getting Away with Murder, Mutilation and Rape: New Testimony from Sierra Leone* (New York: Human Rights Watch, June 1999), 1.

16. United Nations, OCHA, *Interagency Assessment Mission.*

17. Ibid.

18. Carl Prine, "Attempt to Starve Out Opposition May Hamper Hopes for Peace," *Christian Science Monitor,* 31 October 1997, 8.

19. United Nations, OCHA, *Interagency Assessment Mission,* 4.

20. United Nations, OCHA, *Sierra Leone Humanitarian Situation Report, 9 June–6 July 1998,* 98/0068, 13 July 1998.

21. "About 20,000 Risk Starvation to Death in Leone," *Reuters,* 7 July 1999.

10

Flawed UN Arms Embargoes in Somalia, Liberia, and Rwanda*

It is difficult to find any positive results from the UN arms embargoes imposed against Somalia and Liberia in 1992 and Rwanda in 1994. Confronted with some of the decade's worst horrors—famine, war, and genocide—the Security Council responded timidly with the most minimal sanctions measures. Even when, as in Somalia, significant military force was employed, the UN did not take action through stronger sanctions. Instead, the Council opted for feeble attempts to restrict the flow of arms to countries already awash in the instruments of death. The UN made no effort to monitor and enforce these embargoes, and implementation by neighboring states, some of the poorest and least developed on earth, was minimal. Indeed, many neighboring states supported one or another faction in these conflicts and actively supplied weapons and military assistance without regard for UN sanctions. The UN arms embargoes were completely ineffective. They did not alter the policies of the targeted regimes and were unable to prevent wars from continuing and spreading.

The failings of the UN arms embargoes were part of the international community's larger inability to contain eruptions of violent conflict in Africa during the past decade. Nearly all attempts to stem the tide of war and human suffering in Africa have failed. The limitations of sanctions in Angola and Sierra Leone formed part of the same pattern. It was no accident that Secretary-General Kofi Annan's first major report in 1998 focused on the challenge of bringing peace and development to the world's most tormented continent.[1] In some cases, even UN humanitarian operations had negative consequences—for example, when Somali warlords and Hutu extremists "taxed" and manipulated UN relief programs to enhance their own power. UN military operations

---

* This chapter was coauthored by Richard W. Conroy.

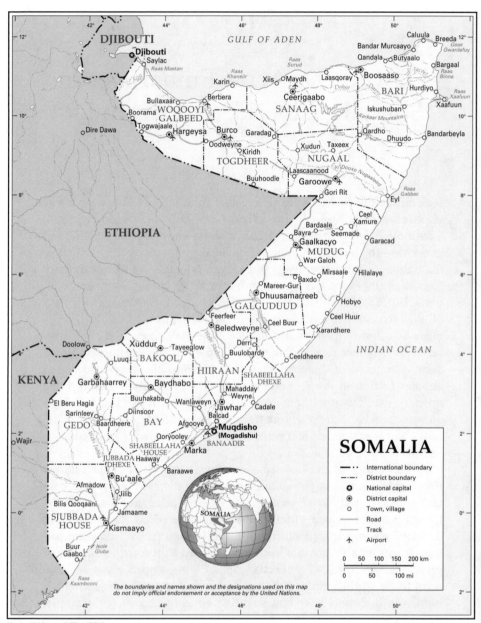

SOMALIA

- — ··· — International boundary
- — · — · — District boundary
- ⊙ National capital
- ◉ District capital
- ○ Town, village
- ——— Road
- ——— Track
- ✈ Airport

| 0 | 50 | 100 | 150 | 200 km |
| 0 | | 50 | | 100 mi |

The boundaries and names shown and the designations used on this map
do not imply official endorsement or acceptance by the United Nations.

Map No. 3690 Rev. 4   UNITED NATIONS
August 1997

Department of Public Information
Cartographic Section

in Somalia ended disastrously and soured the appetite of the United States and other nations for further military action, which in cases such as Rwanda might have helped to prevent or restrain genocide. The UN arms embargoes had fewer side effects, but that was because they were such futile efforts. In these cases UN sanctions had no impact either as instruments of bargaining pressure or military containment.

In this chapter we briefly review the UN arms embargoes in Somalia, Liberia, and Rwanda. We examine the circumstances that led to the imposition of sanctions, the relation of these measures to other UN operations, and the role of regional organizations, especially the Economic Community of West African States (ECOWAS) which imposed sanctions in Liberia. While emphasizing the general failure of the UN arms embargoes, we highlight the apparent impact of the threat of ECOWAS sanctions in Liberia and the positive precedent established in the case of Rwanda by the UN International Commission of Inquiry (UNICOI). For the most part, however, this is a story of the ineffectiveness of arms embargoes in preventing or halting mass murder and war.

Sanctions on Somalia

When fighting intensified in 1991 among Somali clan leaders and factional militia, neighboring states in the Arab League and the Organization of African Unity (OAU) urged the UN Security Council to take action. As the economy collapsed and food supplies dwindled, famine gripped the country. Factional struggles over the control of food and access to weapons were an important cause of the disastrous fighting and famine during 1991 and 1992 that took more than 300,000 lives. Armed gangs and desperate people looted whatever they could to obtain weapons and food. The country was stripped of infrastructure, right down to the underground copper wiring in Mogadishu's municipal street lights.[2] As gun battles raged around Mogadishu in late 1991, the Security Council was compelled to act.

In January 1992 the Security Council made its first attempt at peacemaking in Somalia with the imposition of an arms embargo through Resolution 733. This resolution had the declared purpose of establishing peace and security in Somalia. It did not list any specific benchmarks for the parties to achieve, however, and gave no conditions for the lifting of sanctions. Major humanitarian operations were already under way. Other efforts, including the introduction of UN peacekeepers and approval of an armed humanitarian intervention, came later. The

SOMALIA, Security Council Resolutions

Resolution Number	Action
733	**23 January 1992** Imposed arms embargo
751	**24 April 1992** Created sanctions committee
954	**4 November 1994** Requested the Somalia sanctions committee to fulfill its mandate (due to poor monitoring)

decision to take the limited step of imposing an arms embargo seemed primarily an attempt to demonstrate that some action was being taken, to deflect criticism that the Council was ignoring the tragedy in Somalia.

The Security Council made little effort to monitor and enforce the embargo. In April 1992 the Council adopted Resolution 751 establishing a sanctions committee, but the body met only fourteen times from 1992 to 1998, an average of less than three meetings per year. In 1995, 1996, and 1998, the committee met only once each year. The monitoring effort was so halfhearted that the Security Council adopted Resolution 954 in 1994 requesting the sanctions committee to fulfill its mandate.

When the Security Council imposed the embargo, Somalia was already a very heavily armed country. Substantial Cold War–era arms imports from both the East and West had turned Somalia into a militarized society. From 1979 to 1989, Somalia spent more than $1.1 billion on arms imports. In five of those years, arms constituted more than 50 percent of its total imports; in 1984 they accounted for more than 87 percent of imports.[3] These vast expenditures on weapons contributed to the economic crisis that led to Somalia's fragmentation, ironically sparking efforts to acquire even more weapons.

In addition to imposing sanctions, the Security Council approved major military operations in Somalia. The United Nations Operation in Somalia (UNOSOM) was deployed in the summer of 1992 with a mandate to conduct peacekeeping operations and protect the humanitarian relief deliveries then under way. The small UNOSOM force could not cope with the enormous scale of Somalia's famine, however, or contain the intensifying military struggle for the country's dwindling resources. The Security Council then authorized a larger and more robust military force, the Unified Task Force (UNITAF). UNITAF was empowered to use "all necessary means" to establish a secure environment for humanitarian relief. In May 1993 a larger, reinforced UNOSOM took over from UNITAF in an attempt to bring order to the spreading chaos. A force of 17,000 troops was deployed to Somalia, but these operations were costly (150 peacekeepers died) and failed to achieve their military objectives. Divisions among the participating countries undermined the effectiveness of UNITAF and UNOSOM. When a force of U.S. Army Rangers was trapped in a disastrous battle in the streets of Mogadishu in October 1993 that left eighteen Rangers dead, the United States promptly withdrew its forces and thereafter sought to limit its military exposure not only in Somalia but in other world trouble spots.

Neither UNOSOM nor UNITAF had a mandate to enforce the arms embargo and monitor arms flows into Somalia, even though their mission was to protect the humanitarian operation and reduce the level of armed conflict. The thousands of UN troops deployed to Somalia made no attempt to assist in the implementation of the embargo.[4] Although UN forces conducted arms raids to coercively disarm the combatants and reduce the supply of weapons within the country, they took no steps to halt the continuing flow of arms from outside. The attempt to control arms illustrated the critical role that disarmament efforts could have played in lowering the level of violence, but the UN never developed a sustained strategy for achieving these objectives. Disagreement among the major powers made this impossible, and the withdrawal of U.S. and other forces sealed the fate of the UN military mission.

Indications of Impact

Although the arms embargo failed in its larger goal of achieving a more peaceful and secure environment, it may have had some slight effect in constraining the combatants. The January 1992 imposition of the arms embargo was followed by a February 1992 cease-fire agreement in Mogadishu. There is no direct evidence that the cease-fire was a result of the arms embargo. Indeed, the principal clan leader, Mohammed Fareh Aidid, dismissed the UN sanctions, saying, "Generally, such action has not much effect. There are always arms sold on the black market or given as gifts. So it's very difficult to prevent the traffic of arms."[5] Nonetheless, it is at least conceivable that the UN action and the implied threat of more vigorous sanctions may have played a small role in the calculations that led clan leaders to end their hostilities. In any case, the cease-fire did not last. The arms raids conducted by UN forces in December 1992 and January 1993 also seemed to have a temporary impact. After the U.S. raid on the Bakara arms market, UN negotiators convinced the militia chiefs to sign another cease-fire agreement and agree to a mutual disarmament plan. UN forces were unable to sustain the arms raids, however, because senior officers within the UN forces questioned the wisdom of the policy.[6]

UN efforts in Somalia foundered on the ability of the warlords to manipulate the UN mission to serve their interests. Ali Mahdi, Aidid's main rival within the United Somali Congress, supported the UN role as a means of containing Aidid's faction. Others exploited the UN's relatively deep pockets and bilked "rents" and "taxes" from UN officials and humanitarian agencies to finance their activities, including the purchase of arms.[7] Agencies such as the International Committee for the Red Cross and the World Food Programme were forced to hire gunmen from the militias to protect their relief operations, diverting millions of dollars in the process and undermining the spirit, if not the letter, of the arms embargo.[8]

After UN withdrawal in 1995, the fighting in Somalia slowed. Weapons imports diminished, partly because local peacemaking efforts among Somali clans succeeded in some regions, but also because the departure of the UN meant fewer resources to exploit or loot. The arms embargo remained in place, however, and even though enforcement efforts were meager, the task of acquiring arms became more difficult. In December 1996, during a flare-up of renewed fighting in Mogadishu, the militia factions ran out of ammunition, and as a result the battle ended.[9] The Mogadishu incident indicated that the armed factions were having trouble sustaining continuous weapons imports. It is possible that the arms embargo played a role in creating this shortage or at least in making weapons more expensive, but there is no direct evidence to confirm such a connection.

In 1998 the flow of weapons into Somalia increased when the Ethiopia-Eritrea conflict intensified. Both countries supplied weapons to Somali factions sympathetic to their respective cause. Ethiopia was accused of supplying arms to Ali Mahdi's faction in Mogadishu.[10]

Eritrea was identified as a source of weapons for the Aidid faction.[11] The arms embargo remained in place but did little to prevent the Ethiopia-Eritrea war from spilling over and channeling additional arms to the Somali clans and their associated militias.

On balance, the UN arms embargo in Somalia was a failure. The sanctions had no impact on the tragic famine, did little to limit the military capabilities of the armed factions, and did not succeed in bringing greater peace and security to Somalia. The initial imposition of the embargo may have encouraged the negotiation of a temporary cease-fire and may have contributed to a shortage of ammunition in late 1996, but these possible connections cannot be proven. In any case these were meager, temporary developments that did not alter the fundamental reality of continued armed conflict. The arms embargo was never seriously enforced, and it bore no relationship to the other dimensions of the UN intervention in Somalia, including even the limited efforts to forcibly disarm the militias. The failure in Somalia was not just of the arms embargo but of the entire UN mission. Despite a massive commitment of resources, the deployment of 17,000 troops, and the expenditure of more than $2 billion, the United Nations was able neither to prevent war and famine nor to create a more peaceful and secure environment for the Somali people.

War in Liberia

In 1989 the simmering ethnic tensions in Liberia erupted in war as the insurgent National Patriotic Front of Liberia (NPFL), led by Charles Taylor, began its nearly decade-long war against the regime of President Samuel K. Doe. The NPFL was based in the Gios and Manos tribal communities, whereas the armed forces of Liberia that remained loyal to Doe were dominated by ethnic Krahn. Taylor, Doe, and other Liberian leaders manipulated ethnicity and tribal origin as part of a conscious political strategy. They sought to inflame intergroup hatreds to gain political power and cement intragroup solidarity around their leadership.[12] As NPFL forces launched military attacks, government forces responded brutally and carried out terrible atrocities. The NPFL responded in kind, and the conflict became a savage war replete with massacres, the use of coerced labor, and the conscription of child soldiers. By the time the war ended in 1997, ironically with Taylor's election as president, an estimated 150,000 Liberians had been killed.

LIBERIA

Department of Public Information
Cartographic Section

GUINEA

CÔTE D'IVOIRE

SIERRA LEONE

Atlantic Ocean

Legend

- International boundary
- County boundary
- ⊛ National capital
- ◉ County capital
- ○ Town, village
- Road
- +—+ Railroad
- ✈ Airport

Scale:
0 10 20 30 40 50 mi
0 20 40 60 80 km

The boundaries and names shown on this map do not imply official endorsement or acceptance by the United Nations.

Map No. 3775 Rev. 2   UNITED NATIONS
August 1996

Counties / regions: LOFA, BONG, NIMBA, GRAND GEDEH, SINOE, RIVER CESS, GRAND BASSA, MARGIBI, MONTSERRADO, GRAND CAPE MOUNT, BOMI, GRAND KRU, MARYLAND

Places (selection): Monrovia, Guéckédou, Voinjama, Kolahun, Mendekoma, Vahun, Zigida, Belle Yella, Zorzor, Yella, Gbarnga, Suakoko, Zienzu, Bong Town, Gbange, Wiesua, Bopolu, Tubmanburg, Klay, Brewerville, Careysburg, Kakata, Marshall, Harbel, Hartford, Edina, Buchanan, Robertsport, Kongo, Bendaja, Bo, Sulima, Pujehun, Kenema, Kailahun, Pendembu, Iníé, Nzérékoré, Danané, Saniquellie, Yekepa, Kahnple, Gahnpa (Ganta), Kpein, Sagleipie, Butlo, Toulépleu, Toui, Kola (Kola Town), Guiglo, Taï, Drubo (Zwedru), Tchien, Towabli (Towai Town), Babio, Galio, Pelokehn, Yakahn, Duabo, Duabo, Tiehnpo, Tawake, Yibuke (Kaobli), Ködeke, Nyaake, Nemeke, Tabou, Harper, Pliba, Barclayville, Grand Cess, Sasstown, Nana Kru, Kopo, Juazohn, Sehnkwehn, Greenville, Timbo, River Cess, Trade Town, Gonglee, Bokoa, Ghapo, Shabli, Debli, Gboyi, Tobli, Poabli, Guata, Tapeta, Zekera, Kpeaple, Gbange, Palala, Belefuanai, Yela, Gbarnga, Sinoe Bay

Physical features: Atlantic Ocean, Sassandra, Cavalla, Cavally, Cess, Cestos, Saint Paul, Saint John, Lofa, Nuon, Mano, Morro, Wologisi Range, Nimba Range, Putu Range, Mt. Wutivi, Gbi, Dube, Dwoke, C. Palmas, Gbeyn Creek, Lake Piso

Although the Liberian war was primarily a civil struggle, it had important external linkages. Ivory Coast and Burkina Faso opposed the Doe regime and supplied arms to the NPFL throughout the conflict.[13] Libya also provided training and arms to the NPFL through Burkina Faso. The Doe regime received $500 million in U.S. economic and military aid during the 1980s, making it the largest recipient of U.S. assistance in sub-Saharan Africa. These external connections, especially within the region, made the conflict harder to resolve and became a source of weapons supply in violation of regional and UN sanctions.

The Role of Sanctions

The most important external actor in the Liberian conflict was ECOWAS and its military arm (ECOMOG). The Doe regime was closely allied with the government of Nigeria, the main force in ECOMOG. Nigeria strongly opposed the NPFL insurgency and took both military and economic action to defeat the rebellion. In August 1990, as Taylor's forces closed in on Monrovia, Nigerian-led ECOMOG forces entered the capital to prevent NPFL from capturing it. As a military stalemate developed, the Liberian factions signed the Yamoussoukro IV peace agreement in October 1991. The NPFL refused to honor the settlement, however. In response to NPFL violations of the agreement, ECOWAS threatened to impose comprehensive trade sanctions on NPFL territory. Declaring the ECOWAS threat an act of aggression, Taylor launched a new military offensive that almost captured Monrovia. ECOWAS followed through on its threat and in October 1992 imposed an arms embargo, financial sanctions, and a general trade embargo on NPFL-controlled territory.

The regional sanctions imposed against Liberia were extremely severe. They aimed to stop all traffic into and out of NPFL territory, which covered more than half the country. ECOWAS declared that the sanctions would remain in place until the NPFL complied fully with the Yamoussoukro IV peace agreement.[14] ECOWAS set up a sanctions committee, the so-called Committee of Five, to monitor compliance with the sanctions and obtain information from member states on implementation measures. ECOMOG was empowered to take "all necessary measures" to ensure compliance with the sanctions.

ECOWAS appealed to the Security Council to impose the same form of comprehensive sanctions it had enacted against the NPFL. In November 1992 the Council approved Resolution 788, imposing a lim-

---

LIBERIA, Security Council Resolutions

Resolution Number	Action
788	**19 November 1992** Imposed limited arms embargo (exempted ECOMOG forces)
985	**13 April 1995** Created sanctions committee
1071	**30 August 1996** Welcomed proposed ECOWAS punitive measures (including travel and voting restrictions) but did not threaten additional UN sanctions

---

ited arms embargo. The resolution halted all deliveries of weapons and military equipment to Liberia but exempted ECOMOG forces. The Council's reluctance to enact stronger sanctions reflected skepticism over ECOMOG's role in the conflict, Western antipathy toward Nigeria's military government, and French commercial connections to the NPFL.[15] Members of the Council hoped that an arms embargo would be sufficient to limit the flow of weapons to the NPFL and thereby reduce the scale of violence. They also hoped that the embargo would serve as a form of pressure to encourage NPFL compliance with the Yamoussoukro IV peace agreement. The arms embargo remained in place even after the Liberian war ended and Taylor was elected because of Liberia's support for the Revolutionary United Front in neighboring Sierra Leone.

As in other cases of UN arms embargoes, the Security Council did little to monitor and enforce the sanctions against Liberia. The Council did not even establish a sanctions committee until more than two years after the imposition. In April 1995 the Council approved Resolution 985, establishing a committee to monitor compliance and make recommendations to the Council on ways to improve the embargo. UN decisionmakers assumed that ECOMOG would enforce the arms embargo, so they took little action to contribute UN resources to the effort. ECOMOG did indeed attempt to restrict the flow of weapons and other goods into NPFL zones, but the organization violated the arms embargo by supplying weapons to various Liberian proxies and splinter groups. In the early years of the ECOMOG intervention, when its forces numbered some 16,000 troops, the alliance was able to seal Liberia's border with Ivory Coast.[16] In subsequent years, ECOMOG's military strength fell to approximately 7,000 troops, and it was stretched too thin to be able to exert effective border control or limit commerce into NPFL territory. The UN sanctions committee was mostly a bystander in this process and did little to assist in the implementation effort.

During the initial phase of the ECOWAS sanctions, the economic and humanitarian impact of these measures was considerable. Although the NPFL managed to raise sufficient money and smuggle enough arms to maintain its military operations despite the sanctions, commerce within "Taylorland" was severely disrupted. The combination of war and ECOWAS sanctions cut Monrovia's port traffic to less than 5 percent of its prewar level.[17] Food, fuel, and medicine became scarce in NPFL territory. By March 1993 there was little electricity or running water in these areas, shops were closed or empty, and few vehicles plied the streets.[18] As a result of the sanctions and intensifying military pressure, including Nigerian air raids, humanitarian conditions in NPFL territory deteriorated. ECOMOG attempted to create a humanitarian corridor from Ivory Coast into NPFL zones. It also created a relief distribution system in Monrovia. But ECOMOG kept up the military pressure and even attacked some shipments that were marked as aid deliveries. Amos Sawyer, Liberia's interim president, accused the NPFL of importing weapons using trucks that bore the markings of humanitarian agencies. As a result, Nigerian jets strafed aid convoys it suspected of arms smuggling.[19] There are no statistics on humanitarian conditions within NPFL territory during the ECOWAS sanctions, but it is likely that the trade blockade, in combination with continuing military pressures, contributed significantly to Liberia's appalling toll of human misery.

The United Nations and ECOWAS mounted a number of peacemaking efforts in Liberia, but their joint efforts failed to end the war or prevent Taylor from achieving political power. Between 1990 and 1997 ECOWAS brokered more than a dozen peace agreements, most of which had little impact on the continued fighting. ECOWAS sanctions and the ECOMOG military intervention for a time constrained Taylor's advances, but Nigeria and its partners were unable to sustain these efforts. The United Nations sent the UN Observer Mission in Liberia (UNOMIL) to monitor implementation of the demobilization agreements, but it had no means of responding to the numerous violations.

ECOWAS sanctions and the UN arms embargo had little impact on these developments. Taylor's NPFL continued to control wide swaths of Liberian territory, including gemstone mines, timber forests, rubber plantations, and the seaport at Robertsport. Taylor's government at Gbarnga carried on a lively trade in diamonds and other commodities with European countries, earning more than enough revenue to purchase the weapons necessary to continue its military campaigns.[20] France carried on a particularly active trade with Liberia and was its largest customer for timber.[21]

As Taylor consolidated his de facto regime, at times controlling up to 90 percent of Liberian territory, ECOWAS negotiators were forced to grant bargaining concessions that reflected political and military realities on the ground. Each successive major peace agreement brought Taylor closer to his ultimate objective. The October 1991 Yamoussoukro IV peace agreement barred military faction leaders from holding office. In the July 1993 Cotonou agreement, however, this restriction was relaxed. In the September 1994 Akosombo agreement, faction leaders were allowed to hold seats in an interim government and transition council. These concessions reflected not only Taylor's military and economic position but the growing war weariness of Nigeria and its ECOWAS partners.

Even concessions to Taylor did not bring an end to the violence. In April and May 1996, NPFL forces went on a rampage of fighting and looting in Monrovia. The renewed outbreak of fighting was partly an effort by Taylor to eliminate his critics within Liberia's small but influential professional and commercial class in the capital. In response to the flare-up of hostilities, ECOWAS and the OAU threatened to impose additional sanctions against the NPFL and to ask the United Nations to convene a Liberian war crimes tribunal.[22] ECOWAS threatened to restrict the travel of faction leaders, exclude them from the electoral process, expel family members from ECOWAS states, and ask the UN to impose visa restrictions.[23] The Security Council responded by adopting Resolution 1071 in August 1996, which "welcomed" the proposed ECOWAS punitive measures but did not specifically threaten additional UN sanctions.

The threat of renewed, more targeted sanctions and the prospect of a war crimes tribunal seemed to have an impact in putting the peace process back on track. The NPFL and other factions agreed to participate in the Liberian Transition National Council. The contending groups worked together to begin actual disarmament and demobilization efforts and prepare for national elections. Whether the sanctions threat played a role in the NPFL's more cooperative approach is unknown, although the sequence of threat followed by compliance suggested a connection. One factor that may have given greater credibility to these pressures was the support they enjoyed not only among major external actors, including ECOWAS and the OAU, but also within Liberian society. Liberian religious organizations and civil society groups, fed up with the continuing war and eager for a political solution, expressed strong support for the proposed ECOWAS and OAU sanctions.[24] The combination of internal pressure and external threat seemed to provide the catalyst for cooperation among the warring parties. The result was a commitment to give all factions, including the NPFL, an opportunity to contend in the proposed national elections.

In the end Taylor succeeded in achieving his goals through electoral means, winning more than 70 percent of the vote in the July 1997 election. This outcome probably reflected a realization by Liberian voters that an electoral victory for Taylor was the only way to end the war. Taylor himself suggested that a loss at the polls would lead to renewed fighting. ECOWAS officials were forced to acknowledge the legitimacy of the election and proceeded to lift sanctions. ECOWAS military intervention and sanctions played some role in delaying Taylor's advances and applying pressure for negotiations, but they were unable to prevent the NPFL from achieving victory. Indeed, the ECOWAS/Nigerian intervention may have prolonged the war and worsened the humanitarian crisis. Had Taylor faced less opposition in 1990, it is likely that he would have captured Monrovia and installed himself as president well before his election to that office in 1997. Instead, a military stalemate ensued, with civilians as primary victims as each side battled the other and sought out proxies that could be armed to fight in their interest.

The UN arms embargo played no role whatsoever in these events. The Security Council imposed the arms embargo as a gesture of support for the ECOWAS mission, but the Council was unwilling to approve stronger sanctions and took no action to ensure compliance with the measures it did adopt. As in Somalia, the UN arms embargo in Liberia was an exercise in futility, a failed attempt to do something about a crisis in which it had neither the will nor the means to act.

The Rwandan Genocide and the UN Response

The horrors of genocidal murder that gripped Rwanda in the spring of 1994 did not come without warning. The struggle between Tutsis who

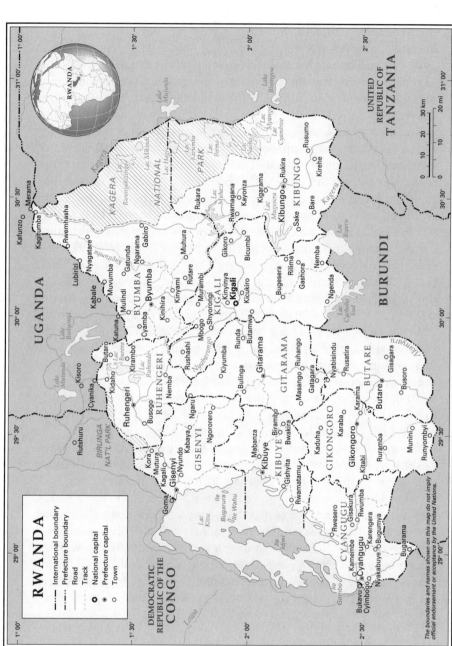

RWANDA

- --·--· International boundary
- --·--· Prefecture boundary
- ———— Road
- - - - - Track
- ⊛ National capital
- ◉ Prefecture capital
- ○ Town

UGANDA

DEMOCRATIC
REPUBLIC OF THE
CONGO

UNITED
REPUBLIC OF
TANZANIA

BURUNDI

KAGERA   NATIONAL   PARK

BIRUNGA
NAT'L PARK

BYUMBA

RUHENGERI

GISENYI

KIGALI

KIBUYE

GITARAMA

GIKONGORO

KIBUNGO

BUTARE

CYANGUGU

Kigali

Merama
Kafunzo
Kagitumba
Rwemhasha
Lubirizi
Nyagatare
Kabale
Muvumba
Ngarama
Gabiro
Mulindi
Gatunda
Byumba
Mutura
Katuna
Cyamba
Kinihira
Kinyami
Rutare
Rukara
Rwamagana
Kayonza
Kigarama
Rukira
Kibungo
Bare
Kirehe
Rusumo
Sake
Nemba
Gashora
Rilima
Ngenda
Bugesera
Bicumbi
Gikoro
Kinyinya
Murambi
Kicukiro
Shyorongi
Mbogo
Rushashi
Kirambo
Butaro
Kidaho
Cyanika
Kisoro
Rutshuru
Kora
Mutura
Kagali
Gisenyi
Goma
Nyundo
Kabaya
Ngororero
Busogo
Nemba
Ngaru
Kiyumba
Bulinga
Runda
Butamwa
Gitarama
Masango
Ruhango
Gatagara
Nyabisindu
Rusatira
Karama
Karaba
Gikongoro
Gisagara
Busoro
Butare
Munini
Runyombyi
Rurama
Kitabi
Gishyita
Rwamatamu
Kaduha
Gisakura
Rwumba
Bugumya
Karengera
Nyakabuye
Cyimbogo
Bukavu
Cyangugu
Kamembe
Rwesero
Bugarama
Mabanza
Kibuye
Brambo
Bwakira
Kibungo
Lubirizi
Muhura
Mutura
Nyabisindu

The boundaries and names shown on this map do not imply
official endorsement or acceptance by the United Nations.

Map No. 3717 Rev. 7   UNITED NATIONS
December 1997 (Colour)

Department of Public Information
Cartographic Section

formed the Rwandan Patriotic Front (RPF) and the Hutu-dominated government of Juvenal Habyarimana became increasingly bitter in the early 1990s. The signing of the 1993 Arusha agreement and the negotiation of a power-sharing arrangement within the government and army did little to dampen rising animosities. The UN Observer Mission for Uganda and Rwanda (UNOMUR) and its successor, the UN Assistance Mission in Rwanda (UNAMIR), reported on the increasing tensions and the flow of arms into Rwanda from Uganda, the RPF's principal patron. Hutu extremists within the government were opposed to any power-sharing plan. They spoke of eliminating their Tutsi opponents. Toward that end, they developed militia forces, acquired arms, and broadcast anti-Tutsi hate propaganda. In January 1994 the UNAMIR commander, Romeo Dallaire, faxed UN headquarters in New York with detailed information on the military training and weapons-stockpiling activities of the Hutu extremists.[25] When the gruesome killing spree began in April, close observers were not surprised, although all were shocked by the appalling scale and ferocity of the slaughter.

When the genocide began, ten Belgian soldiers were murdered, prompting the Security Council to withdraw most of UNAMIR, whose troops were protecting thousands of Rwandans. The Security Council later changed its mind and decided to expand and redeploy the force, but delays prevented this from occurring until well after the genocide was over. By then, understandably, UNAMIR enjoyed no credibility, and it was unable to provide protection or security for returning Rwandan refugees, who in any case were prevented from leaving camps in eastern Zaire by the armed Hutu militants who had perpetrated the genocide. UNAMIR withdrew at the request of the Rwandan government in April 1996.

Unwilling to prevent the genocide or to provide protection for its victims, the Security Council decided in May 1994 to impose an arms embargo.[26] Resolution 918 prohibited the sale or supply to Rwanda of weapons and military-related material. It also established a sanctions committee with the standard mandate to seek information on implementation and make recommendations for improving the effectiveness of the embargo. Resolution 918 was an extremely limited measure, given the enormity of the catastrophe unfolding in Rwanda. Hutu extremists killed more than 500,000 Tutsis and Hutu moderates in the space of just three months.[27] The imposition of an arms embargo in the face of such mass murder seemed an utterly inadequate, almost pathetic response. This was the only action the Security Council could agree upon, howev-

---

RWANDA, Security Council Resolutions

Resolution Number	Action
918	**17 May 1994** Imposed arms embargo Created sanctions committee
997	**9 June 1995** Specified that the arms embargo applied to groups in other countries operating against Rwanda
1011	**16 August 1995** Suspended the arms embargo on the Rwandan government Maintained the sanctions on the rebel Hutu groups in eastern Zaire
1013	**6 September 1995** Established the UN International Commission of Inquiry (UNICOI) to investigate and report arms embargo violations

---

er. By the time the Council decided to impose sanctions, the crisis was already out of control.

The arms embargo against Rwanda was too little, too late. So much propaganda and hate had already developed, and so much of the killing was "up-close" involving machetes and small arms, that even the most effective arms embargo would have been powerless to change the course of events. No form of sanctions pressure could have been effective in bringing an immediate halt to the killing. Only a major armed intervention would have had a chance of ending the carnage, and that was a policy the members of the Security Council were not prepared to support.

Despite the fundamental limitations of its chosen policy, the Security Council gamely carried on with attempts to adapt the arms embargo to changing circumstances. When the Tutsi-dominated RPF overthrew the Hutu government in Rwanda in July 1994, hundreds of thousands of Hutus, including the leaders of the genocide, fled to refugee camps in eastern Zaire. The Hutu extremists took control of the camps, manipulating UN relief operations to their benefit. The rebels also carried on armed attacks against the new RPF government in Kigali. In response, the Security Council adopted Resolution 997 in June 1995, specifying that the arms embargo be applied to groups in other countries operating against Rwanda. In August 1995 the Council adopted Resolution 1011, suspending the arms embargo on the Rwandan government but maintaining sanctions on the rebel Hutu groups in eastern Zaire. These were meaningless actions, however, for the UN made no effort to enforce these measures. The prospects for effective implementation of an arms embargo were even lower in the chaotic conditions of eastern Zaire than they were in Rwanda.

Investigations of Violations

Enforcement of the UN arms embargo was practically nonexistent. Not only did the Security Council fail to provide resources for implementation, but many of the neighboring states openly refused to cooperate with the UN action. Indeed, most countries in the region actively supported either the Hutu extremists or the RPF government. Many sent arms and even troops as the conflict later widened. The Mobutu government in Zaire and the UNITA rebels in Angola supported the Hutu extremists, whereas Uganda aided the RPF regime in Kigali. When UN officials approached neighboring countries about the stationing of UN monitors on their territory, they were rebuffed. With no support from neighboring countries and lacking any independent means to monitor the embargo, the UN sanctions committee for Rwanda had little to do. From 1994 through 1998, the committee met only five times, the least active of any of the UN sanctions committees.

Recognizing the futility of the committee's monitoring mandate, yet concerned about the continuing warfare and large supplies of arms flowing into the region, the Security Council took the unusual step of creating an independent commission of inquiry. In September 1995, the Council adopted Resolution 1013, establishing the UN International Commission of Inquiry to investigate and report violations of the arms embargo. Unlike the sanctions committees, which usually lack investigative authority and are political bodies representing Security Council member states, the commission, composed of experts chosen for their legal, military, and policy expertise, was an independent body with a broad mandate to investigate and report on violations. Instead of merely receiving reports from member states, the commission was empowered to travel, collect documents, interview officials, and uncover whatever information it could find. UNICOI performed its mission well and assembled detailed documentation on the extensive arms-trafficking networks and financing schemes that sustained and strengthened the Hutu extremists and fueled the war as it spread to eastern Zaire.

UNICOI issued five reports between January 1996 and November 1998.[28] These documents offer the most thorough examination of arms embargo violations of any UN sanctions case during the 1990s. In its December 1997 report, UNICOI described "huge, loose, overlapping webs of more or less illicit arms deals, arms flights and arms deliveries spanning the continent from South Africa as far as Europe."[29] The Hutu extremists used arms-trafficking networks from the apartheid and Cold War eras that the government of South Africa had used to circumvent the UN arms embargo imposed there in 1977. In addition, the Hutu rebels also received support through arms-smuggling networks established to support UNITA's war against the government of Angola and in 1996 formed partnerships with Hutu parties and rebels from neighboring Burundi. As a result of these supply networks and because of the spread of the war to eastern Zaire, the Hutu extremists remained a formidable force and became a growing menace throughout central Africa.

When the Tutsi RPF government in Rwanda launched a military offensive in 1996 and 1997 to expel the Hutu rebels from the refugee camps in eastern Zaire, they set in motion a series of cascading rebellions that led to the overthrow of the Mobutu government in Zaire and a widening regional war. The Rwanda conflict thus became part of a larger, interconnected series of conflicts that converged in Zaire (now the Democratic Republic of Congo) and involved Uganda, Burundi, Zimbabwe, Sudan, and Angola, among others. The Hutu extremists remained at the heart of this network of conflict. In the process this twice-defeated international pariah was transformed into a quasi-legitimate force operating with international allies in a regional war. In its final report in November 1998, UNICOI described this as a "profoundly shocking state of affairs" and warned of a possible repetition of the Rwanda genocide on a subregional scale.[30]

Conclusion

Like the other UN arms embargoes in Africa, the sanctions against Rwanda failed completely. In this case the tragedy was much greater. The UN proved helpless to prevent the Rwandan genocide that killed

500,000 or more people. The international community was also unable to halt the spread of the war into Zaire/Congo and hundreds of thousands of additional deaths. These horrors resulted from deliberate policies by governments and rebel regimes in the region to arm the agents of genocide and their opponents and to seek ever more costly military solutions. The major powers shared some of the responsibility by their inability to take more forceful action and their unwillingness to commit greater resources to the prevention and resolution of conflict in Africa.

The only positive note in the Rwanda sanctions experience was the creation of UNICOI and the precedent it established for more aggressive, independent reporting of embargo violations and illicit arms trafficking. UNICOI provided a model for the kind of effective, professional investigative efforts that are needed to uncover the shadowy networks of those who supply weapons to the perpetrators of genocide. The model was so successful that Belgium advocated making UNICOI a permanent mechanism. A number of UN officials and academic experts have made similar proposals. In our own program of policy recommendations in the final chapter, we support the call for the creation of independent investigative commissions.

The UN arms embargoes imposed in Somalia, Liberia, and Rwanda were utterly ineffective responses to the catastrophes of famine, war, and genocide that afflicted Africa during the last decade. In each case the sanctions came too late, after huge stockpiles of weapons were already in place and many of the atrocities had already occurred. They were also far too little, a woefully timid and unworkable response to the challenge of ending mass murder and genocide. Even the most pervasive and comprehensive sanctions would have been inadequate to the task. The more limited instrument of an arms embargo had no chance of success. The arms embargoes in Somalia, Liberia, and Rwanda constituted a desperate attempt to do something in the face of disaster, but they were a fundamentally flawed policy that did nothing to stem the tide of war and human suffering.

Notes

1. Kofi Annan, *The Causes of Conflict and the Promotion of Durable Peace and Sustainable Development in Africa: The Secretary-General's Report to the United Nations Security Council* (New York: United Nations, 16 April 1998).

2. Paul Watson, "Engineer Lights Up Corner of Somalia," *Toronto Star,* 6 March 1993, 1.

3. United States Arms Control and Disarmament Agency, *World Military*

Expenditures and Arms Transfers: 1990 (Washington, D.C.: United States Arms Control and Disarmament Agency, November 1991), 122. See also Jeffrey A. Lefebvre, *Arms for the Horn: U.S. Security Policy in Ethiopia and Somalia, 1953–1991* (Pittsburgh: University of Pittsburgh Press, 1991).

4. Associated Press, "Weapons Flowing into Somalia Despite U.S. Presence, Experts Say," *Toronto Star,* 15 January 1993, 16.

5. Quoted in Paul Watson, "Somali Guerrilla Scoffs at UN Arms Embargo," *Toronto Star,* 26 January 1992, 12.

6. Diana Jean Schemo, "The World Moves on Somalia: The Warlords Move Faster," *New York Times,* 21 February 1993, 6.

7. Andrew Natsios, "Humanitarian Relief Interventions in Somalia: The Economics of Chaos," *International Peacekeeping* 3 (Spring 1996): 74–80; Enrico Augelli and Craig Murphy, "Lessons of Somalia for Future Multilateral Humanitarian Assistance Operations," *Global Governance* 1 (September–December 1995): 348.

8. Robert Press, "Somali Civil War Is Fueled by Huge Stockpiles of Weapons," *Christian Science Monitor,* 14 October 1992, 1, 4.

9. Saferworld, *Undermining Development: The European Arms Trade with the Horn of Africa and Central Africa* (London: Saferworld, January 1998), 27.

10. Haroun Hassan, "Arrival of Arms Shipment Heightens Tensions in Mogadishu," *Associated Press,* 3 January 1997.

11. "Weapons Flowing into Somalia," *Xinhua News Agency,* 21 February 1999.

12. Stephen Ellis, "Liberia 1989–1994: A Study of Ethnic and Spiritual Violence," *African Affairs* (April 1995): 183.

13. Ademola Adeleke, "The Politics and Diplomacy of Peacekeeping in West Africa: The ECOWAS Operation in Liberia," *Journal of Modern African Studies* 33 (1995): 378–379.

14. United Nations Security Council, *Letter Dated 30 October 1992 from the Permanent Representative of Benin to the United Nations,* S/24811, 16 November 1992.

15. Binaifer Nowrojee, "Joining Forces: UN and Regional Peacekeeping— Lessons from Liberia," *Harvard Human Rights Journal* 8 (Spring 1995): 142; and David Wippman, "Enforcing the Peace: ECOWAS and the Liberian Civil War," in Lori Fisler Damrosch, ed., *Enforcing Restraint: Collective Intervention in Internal Conflicts* (New York: Council on Foreign Relations, 1993), 174.

16. "Peacekeepers Tighten Blockade of Rebels," *Agence France Presse,* 10 May 1993.

17. United Nations, Department of Humanitarian Affairs Integrated Regional Information Network for West Africa, "IRIN-WA Weekly Roundup 11–97 of Main Events in West Africa," 1 September 1997, 2.

18. Nickolas Kotch, "Defiant Taylor 'Will Not Surrender': Sanctions and Air Raids Are Crushing Liberia's Rebel," *Guardian,* 27 March 1993, 15.

19. "Peacekeepers Tighten Blockade of Rebels."

20. William Twaddell, "Bloody Hands: Foreign Support for Liberian Warlords," testimony in Hearings Before the Subcommittee on Africa of the Committee on International Relations, United States House of Representatives, 104th Cong., 2d sess., 26 June 1996, 6, 14–15, 37–38.

21. William Reno, "The Business of War in Liberia," *Current History* 95 (May 1996): 212–213.

22. Tarcey Munaku, "OAU Considers Possible Sanctions Against Liberia," *PanAfrican News Agency,* 5 July 1996.

23. "Liberia Sanctions Package Unveiled by ECOWAS," *Deutsch Presse-Agentur,* 19 August 1996.

24. Harry Mouzala, "Call for Sanctions Against Warlords," *PanAfrican News Agency,* 18 July 1996.

25. Philip Gourevitch, "The Genocide Fax," *New Yorker* 74 (11 May 1998): 42–46.

26. The Security Council, might have been able to prevent the catastrophe that took place. A report from the Carnegie Commission on Preventing Deadly Conflict concluded that the rapid response operation proposed by France was feasible and could have saved hundreds of thousands of lives. See Scott R. Feil, "Preventing Genocide: How the Early Use of Force Might Have Succeeded in Rwanda," *A Report to the Carnegie Commission on Preventing Deadly Conflict,* Carnegie Corporation of New York, April 1998; and Philip Gourevitch, *We Wish to Inform You That Tomorrow We Will Be Killed with Our Families: Stories from Rwanda* (New York: Farrar, Straus, and Giroux, 1998). For an opposing, more skeptical view, see Alan J. Kuperman, "Rwanda in Retrospect," *Foreign Affairs* 79, no. 1 (January–February 2000): 94–118.

27. Reuters, "New Report Spotlights UN Failures in Rwanda," *New York Times,* 16 December 1999; Kuperman, "Rwanda in Retrospect," 101.

28. The most important of these were United Nations Security Council, *Report of the International Commission of Inquiry,* S/1996/195, 14 March 1996; United Nations Security Council, *Report of the International Commission of Inquiry,* S/1997/1010, 24 December 1997; and United Nations Security Council, *Final Report of the International Commission of Inquiry,* S/1998/1096, 18 November 1998.

29. United Nations Security Council, *Report of the International Commission of Inquiry,* S/1997/1010.

30. United Nations Security Council, *Final Report of the International Commission of Inquiry,* S/1998/1096, 12.

11

Case Findings

At first glance it appears that the cases of United Nations sanctions over the past decade were so diverse and idiosyncratic that a cross-case comparison would be futile. There is reason to examine each episode sui generis. The type of sanctions imposed, the relationship of sanctions to regional or national forces involved, and the extent to which sanctions were comprehensive or partial all varied according to the situation at hand. The resolutions that the Council passed or the adaptations that the sanctions committee made (or did not make) were primarily related to the particular circumstances of each case. The prospects of enforcement, or the lack thereof, derived primarily from local realities.

Upon closer scrutiny, however, the differing cases yield some reasonable commonalties that provide useful insights in making recommendations for future UN sanctions policy. In this chapter, we summarize these trends and findings. Using the generalizations reviewed in Chapter 1 and testing the theories of effectiveness examined in Chapter 2, we attempt to ascertain whether the cases of the 1990s support the assumptions we and others have made about how sanctions work, or do not work.

We isolate both patterns and particulars, seeking clues from the latter for understanding the former. Our assessment has four broad categories: the type of sanctions, the degree of compliance by the target, the general impact of the sanctions in the humanitarian and political sectors, and the factors that contributed to success or failure. We also review the implications of these findings for sanctions formulation and implementation.

In Chapter 1 we articulated a number of generalizations that have gained credence among policymakers and the informed public regarding UN-mandated sanctions. Of those presented in that chapter, four are particularly useful to this examination of findings across the cases:

- The economic impact of sanctions does not guarantee political success.
- Sanctions have serious unintended consequences.
- The UN system lacks the resources and the capacity to properly administer sanctions.
- There is implicit tension between UN goals and those of member states.

We find supporting evidence for each of these generalizations, but we also discover grounds for qualifying or modifying some of them.

Success Rates

Table 11.1 provides a comprehensive, summary assessment of eleven UN sanctions cases examined in this volume.[1]

The most important finding from the case data is that sanctions appear to be more effective in gaining target compliance than is widely acknowledged. Although in no instance did sanctions achieve full and immediate compliance, in three cases—Iraq, Yugoslavia, and Libya—sanctions achieved moderate to high success. And in Cambodia, sanctions contributed in a limited fashion to the successful isolation of the Khmer Rouge. Three or four of the eleven cases thus could be judged as at least partially successful. In four other episodes—Haiti, Angola, Sierra Leone, and Somalia—sanctions had a very limited, temporary effect in sparking negotiations, but they had no longer-term impact in containing armed violence or changing the policies of the targeted regime. In three cases—Sudan, Liberia, and Rwanda—UN sanctions were a complete failure and had no policy impact whatsoever. Our assessment of success in three out of eleven cases translates into a 27 percent effectiveness rate. If we add the Cambodia case, the effectiveness rate is 36 percent.

This scoring of the UN sanctions cases in the 1990s conforms generally with the 34 percent overall rate of effectiveness found by the Institute for International Economics in its analysis of a much broader set of more diverse cases over a longer period of time.[2] By our scoring system, UN sanctions during the 1990s were reasonably successful, more so than is generally acknowledged.

Our assessments are consistent with the case evidence, even if they appear contrary to conventional wisdom. We judge sanctions a success if they had a positive, enduring impact on bargaining dynamics or if they helped isolate or weaken the power of an abusive regime. Our

Table 11.1 Summary of Impacts of UN Sanctions in the 1990s

Target and Type of Sanctions[a]	Political Effectiveness of UN Sanctions (success in pressuring the target rated as high, moderate, low, or none)	Humanitarian Impacts	Special Factors/ Other Considerations
Iraq 1990 Comprehensive	**moderate to high** Of eight provisions in SCR 687, six partially or fully met; weapons dismantlement partially achieved; Iraqi military threat reduced	Severe social impacts, especially on children; significant rise in rates of malnutrition and child mortality	Longest, most comprehensive UN sanctions; accompanied by major use of military force; oil for food program largest relief operation in UN history
Yugoslavia 1991, 1992, and 1998 Comprehensive, 1992 to 1995; limited arms embargo, 1998	**moderate to high** Sanctions were major bargaining chip in negotiations leading to Dayton accord	Major economic damage and weakening of civil society, but no evidence of significant humanitarian consequences	Croatian military offensive/NATO bombing contributed to Dayton negotiations; SAMs regional monitoring and enforcement system was the most effective ever mounted
Haiti 1993 Comprehensive	**low** UN sanctions led to Governors Island agreement, but inconsistency and hesitancy reduced impact	Significant humanitarian consequences; evidence of rise in child mortality	Preceded by OAS sanctions; gave way to U.S.-led military force; major international relief efforts

(Table 11.1 *continues*)

(Table 11.1 *continued*)

Target and Type of Sanctions[a]	Political Effectiveness of UN Sanctions	Humanitarian Impacts	Special Factors/ Other Considerations
Libya 1992 Aviation sanctions; partial assets freeze, and ban on oil equipment imports	**moderate to high** Sanctions a factor in negotiations that brought suspected terrorists to the Netherlands for trial in 1999; Libyan support for international terrorism reportedly reduced	Libyan claims of negative consequences, but no independent confirmation of major social or humanitarian effects	Threat of withdrawal from sanctions by OAU and Arab League sparked negotiating flexibility by Western powers
Sudan 1996 Diplomatic sanctions; aviation sanctions threatened but not imposed	**none** No response to demand for extradition of terrorist suspects; no reported change in support for international terrorism	No social impacts since travel sanctions never imposed	Humanitarian preassessment mission cautioned against sanctions imposition
Cambodia (Khmer Rouge) 1992 Oil embargo and ban on exports of timber, minerals, and gems	**moderate** Paris accord and sanctions contributed to isolation and weakening of Khmer Rouge	No evidence of humanitarian impacts from UN sanctions	Accompanied by large UNTAC mission and nation-building effort; UN stood firm against Khmer Rouge resistance
Angola (UNITA) 1993, 1997, and 1998 Oil and arms embargo, 1993; travel and diplomatic sanctions, 1997; financial sanctions and diamonds embargo, 1998	**none** Sanctions provided little or no bargaining leverage and did not prevent UNITA from waging war and becoming a large well-armed military force	Hundreds of thousands died from war and political violence; no discernible evidence of additional impacts from sanctions	Crisis linked to widening war in Congo and central Africa; almost complete lack of enforcement; 1999 mission by chair of UN sanctions committee attempted to gain greater compliance

Sierra Leone 1997 Oil and arms embargo and travel ban	**none** Sanctions sparked negotiations but did not prevent rebel movement from accumulating arms and launching military offensives	Tens of thousands died from war and political terror; ECOWAS sanctions contributed to shortages; Sierra Leone factions denied food to civilian populations; no evidence of additional impacts from UN sanctions	ECOWAS trade sanctions; major ECOMOG military intervention; cooperation between UN sanctions committee and ECOWAS in sanctions monitoring; humanitarian assessment report
Somalia 1992 Arms embargo	**low** UN embargo sparked limited cease-fire; fighting in 1996 ended due to lack of ammunition	300,000 died in famine and military conflicts; no evidence of additional impacts from UN arms embargo	Accompanied by major UNOSOM and UNITAF missions; overall UN mission weakened by divisions among participating states; linked to Ethiopia/Eritrea conflict
Liberia 1992 Arms embargo	**none** UN arms embargo ineffective in constraining NPFL; threat of ECOWAS sanctions following NPFL military rampage in 1996 put peace process back on track and led to elections	Tens of thousands died from military conflict; ECOWAS sanctions imposed economic and social hardships on NPFL-controlled territory; no discernible impacts from UN arms embargo	Accompanied by ECOWAS sanctions and major ECOMOG military intervention; linked to conflict in Sierra Leone
Rwanda 1992 Arms embargo	**none** UN arms embargo too late and too little to prevent genocide; unable to halt widening of conflict to eastern Congo	More than 500,000 died in genocide, and hundreds of thousands more died in widening war in Congo; no evidence of additional impacts from UN arms embargo	Linked to conflicts in Democratic Republic of Congo and Angola; UNICOI established precedent of independent investigation of violations

Note: a. Cases ordered as they appear in the volume.

standard for success is not complete capitulation by the target but some indication that sanctions produced at least partial compliance. These are modest, but we believe, realistic benchmarks for evaluating the overall effectiveness of UN sanctions. By these standards, UN sanctions during the decade achieved a reasonable degree of success.

Types of Sanctions: Comprehensive or Selective

One of the most striking findings of the cases is that two of the four examples of partial success—Iraq and Yugoslavia—involved comprehensive trade sanctions. The cases in which economic damage was most severe were also the ones in which political impacts were greatest. On the other side of the ledger, several of the worst failures—Sudan, Liberia, and Rwanda—involved cases where the Security Council imposed the most minimal measures and took no enforcement action. The obvious lesson is that comprehensive, rigorously enforced sanctions are more likely to be successful than limited, unenforced measures. Again, this confirms the findings of the Institute for International Economics study.

Comprehensiveness is no guarantee of success, however. UN sanctions became increasingly comprehensive against Angola during the 1990s without apparent impact. In Haiti, sanctions became comprehensive during the latter stages of the episode but gave way to the use of military force without affecting the final outcome. In some cases selective sanctions were effective. In Libya, an aviation ban and other partial measures helped in applying bargaining pressure that eventually produced a settlement. In Cambodia, limited sanctions contributed to the successful political isolation of the Khmer Rouge. It is difficult to draw conclusions from these differing results. Comprehensive sanctions worked in some cases, whereas selective measures had an impact in others. The one constant theme was that limited, poorly enforced sanctions had no chance of success.

Many sanctions policymakers and analysts, ourselves included, have expressed enthusiasm for the potential of targeted sanctions to achieve political impacts without causing unintended humanitarian hardships. As noted in the opening chapters and the final chapter, there is growing interest in smart sanctions strategies as an alternative to comprehensive trade restrictions. The evidence from the UN cases of the 1990s offers only limited support for the viability of this strategy, however, while raising a number of questions and concerns. Selective or targeted measures were partially effective in Libya and Cambodia but not in Angola and Sierra Leone. Arms embargoes were generally unsuccessful. By contrast, as noted earlier, comprehensive sanctions were partially effective in Iraq and Yugoslavia. Our judgment is not that targeted or selective sanctions are ineffective, but that the policy steps necessary to enhance the impact of these more limited measures have not been taken.

Compliance

The most important constant in the success of sanctions is not the type of measure applied but the degree to which sanctions are enforced. Compliance ultimately determines effectiveness. When member states and regional organizations cooperated in the enforcement of Security Council resolutions, the political impact was greatest. The most extensive enforcement efforts were mounted in Iraq and Yugoslavia. In both cases sanctions had substantial impacts. In the Libya case, international compliance with the aviation ban was nearly universal. Even member states and regional organizations that were skeptical of the continuing UN sanctions adhered to the flight ban and maintained the political and diplomatic isolation of the Qaddafi regime. In the case of Cambodia, enforcement was less effective, especially along the border with Thailand, but the diplomatic and political isolation of the Khmer Rouge was virtually total.

By contrast, the comprehensive trade sanctions imposed against Haiti were porous until the very end of the episode and were inconsistently applied, lifted, and then reapplied. In the case of Angola, increasingly forceful measures were applied in 1997 and 1998, but the inability to enforce the diamond and financial sanctions and the overall lack of compliance with these measures undermined their potential effectiveness. In the cases in which no UN enforcement efforts were mounted—Somalia, Liberia, and Rwanda—sanctions had no impact. The experience of the 1990s confirms that sanctions have no chance of succeeding without a credible enforcement effort and concerted international cooperation. Whether the sanctions are comprehensive or selective, general or targeted, their political impact depends on effective implementation.

Were Targeted Sanctions Smart?

The track record for targeted, or "smart," UN sanctions during the 1990s was uneven. Financial sanctions, arms embargoes, and travel bans were applied with frequency during the decade, but they produced mixed results. The role and place of financial sanctions was particularly uncertain. Financial sanctions were a critical part of the package imposed on Iraq in 1990. They were so extensive that they even included, at the request of the Kuwaiti government, a freeze on Kuwaiti financial assets so that these would not fall into the hands of Saddam Hussein. The United States and Great Britain acted swiftly to freeze Kuwaiti assets even before the Security Council voted to impose sanctions. These efforts succeeded in protecting a substantial portion of Kuwaiti financial assets from Iraqi control. But neither national action nor efforts by the United Nations succeeded in locating or freezing many of the assets held by Hussein and his immediate family. The financial sanctions on Iraq involved governmental assets alone. These measures were effective in denying income and assets to the Baghdad government, but they did not impose the kind of targeted pressure on decisionmaking elites that financial sanctions are capable of applying.

UN financial sanctions were also applied in varying degrees against Yugoslavia, Haiti, and the UNITA faction in Angola. As was the case with Iraq, these financial sanctions were targeted against the assets of governments and government-controlled entities. Only in the case of Yugoslavia, in which nearly $3 billion of Yugoslav government assets were frozen, did these measures have much of an impact.[3] No attempt was made by the Security Council to impose mandatory asset freezes on the financial accounts of designated individuals and decisionmaking elites. The UN system lacks the legal authority and institutional capacity to target individual leaders and their personal assets. By contrast, the United States and the European Union have developed considerable experience and institutional capacity for freezing assets of both governments and designated individuals. During the Kosovo crisis, for example, U.S. and EU sanctions froze not only Yugoslav government assets but those of Milosevic and several hundred of his closest military and political supporters and business associates. The denial of access to financial accounts and a ban on visas proved to be very effective forms of pressure on these decisionmaking elites.[4] Until the UN system develops a similar capacity for freezing the assets of individuals as well as governments, the impact of UN financial sanctions will be limited.

Arms embargoes were the most frequently imposed but also the most visibly impotent of UN sanctions during the 1990s. Five of the seven cases in which Security Council sanctions had little or no effectiveness—Angola, Sierra Leone, Somalia, Liberia, and Rwanda—involved arms embargoes as the sole or primary action. A number of factors seem to account for this failure. The most important is that member states were in most cases unwilling or unable to enforce these measures. The problem was partly political, with neighboring states and regional organizations often taking sides and providing military support for particular factions in conflicts the Security Council was attempting to resolve. The challenge of enforcing arms embargoes was also economic, with the lure of profit from the sale of weapons often proving irresistible. Arms trafficking provides such diverse, lucrative reward structures that it is extremely difficult to halt the flow of weapons. Indeed, the prevailing concern that prompts frontline states to interdict arms bound for a sanctioned neighbor is that such a shipment might displace the frontline state's own gun runners.[5] Without a substantial system of monitoring and enforcement and without compensating inducements to encourage compliance, arms embargoes do not work.

The states in which arms embargoes have been ineffective share some common characteristics other than the general political and economic considerations noted above. These states have very poor transportation structures, especially regarding air transport, which is dominated by private entrepreneurs. Under these conditions, not only is there a lack of regulation and registration of aircraft and routes that might be used to transport illicit arms, but the very same planes might carry humanitarian supplies and medicine alongside a few crates of banned AK-47s. This means that arms embargoes fail partly due to the absence of a modern cargo management and air traffic control system. More generally, many of these countries lack even rudimentary control over their borders and have few resources to maintain and ensure the reliability of customs agencies. In many cases, control over weapons flows was itself a major source of contention and precluded the development of an effective arms interdiction system separate from the tide of battle.

In theory, arms embargoes are one of the best tools available to the Security Council for limiting violent conflict and applying pressure on warring parties without causing hardships to vulnerable populations. Arms embargoes have the potential to raise the price of weapons, reduce their availability, limit humanitarian suffering, and coax warring actors into negotiations. The problems that have occurred with the actual practice of arms embargoes result not from the instrument itself but from the flawed implementation of these measures. These problems include

- lack of attention to the purposes of an arms embargo, beyond the symbolic act of "doing something" and

- insufficient resources devoted to monitoring and enforcement, both among member states and within the UN system.

These problems are not immutable. They can be solved if member states are willing to take the practical steps necessary (as outlined in Chapter 12) to ensure effective implementation.

Travel restrictions have been perceived as the weak link in the cluster of sanctions options available to the Security Council, but they have featured more prominently in the 1990s than many acknowledge. They played a particularly important role in the Libya case. Travel sanctions were also part of the comprehensive sanctions packages imposed against Iraq, Yugoslavia, and Haiti and were imposed as part of the selective measures against Angola and Sierra Leone. They were threatened but not imposed against Sudan. In light of the relative success of sanctions in Libya, Iraq, and Yugoslavia, there may be reason to believe that these travel bans are relatively effective means of isolating and pressuring targeted regimes.

The Humanitarian Impacts of Sanctions

The generalization that the impacts of sanctions are difficult to predict and lead to unintended consequences is partly confirmed by the cases of the 1990s. But the experience of the decade also offers grounds for qualifying this assumption. The cases provide an answer to those who charge that sanctions lack moral legitimacy because they target vulnerable populations and indiscriminately punish those least able to change policy.[6] This is a valid critique for the case of Iraq, but it does not apply in most of the other episodes. In only two cases, Iraq and Haiti, did sanctions generate serious humanitarian consequences. In Iraq a severe crisis developed, and in Haiti human suffering was also widespread, although in this case humanitarian hardships were caused as well by the effects of violence and political repression. In both cases major humanitarian relief efforts were mounted. In Iraq the oil for food program began to ameliorate some aspects of the crisis, although only after a long delay caused in large part by Baghdad's initial rejection of the program. In Haiti, large-scale relief efforts were immediate and had a significant impact in preventing a more severe humanitarian crisis.

In most of the cases of the 1990s, comprehensive trade sanctions were not the norm. In only one other case, Yugoslavia, were general

trade sanctions imposed, and in this instance the impact of these broader measures on public health and nutrition was limited. The more common pattern during the decade was the imposition of selective or targeted measures, including embargoes on oil, arms, and other commodities.
These more limited measures had few humanitarian consequences. Thus
the devastating humanitarian crisis that developed in Iraq was the
exception to the rule. The more general pattern across the twelve cases
is clear: far-reaching, negative humanitarian consequences of sanctions
occurred only in cases where comprehensive trade sanctions were
imposed. More selective, targeted sanctions resulted in fewer humanitarian difficulties. In most of the cases, sanctions-related humanitarian
consequences were limited. Even where the impacts were severe,
efforts to provide humanitarian relief received priority attention.
Procedures for providing humanitarian exemptions improved during the
decade, from the better formulation of sanctions resolutions to the more
effective functioning of the sanctions committees, although further
streamlining remained necessary. Consciousness about the need to
avoid serious humanitarian impacts became a priority in sanctions policymaking.

In our examination of the cases, we recognized that any attempt to
assess the effectiveness and humanitarian consequences of sanctions
runs into an insoluble methodological dilemma: how to separate the
effects of sanctions from other causes of political and social disruption.
By their very nature sanctions are imposed in situations of conflict and
political turmoil, where political systems function poorly and civilian
populations face multiple stresses and hardships. In most of the cases
examined, Libya being perhaps the only exception, the targeted country
experienced multiple disasters, including war, armed rebellion, ethnic
atrocities, the overthrow of governments, and massive involuntary population displacement. Any of these conditions would be sufficient to
induce political and social changes within the target society. In combination with one another and with the added pressure of externally imposed
sanctions, these conditions created highly chaotic and unpredictable settings in which specific causal factors were difficult to isolate. This does
not mean that tracing the influence of sanctions is impossible, but it does
suggest the need for humility and caution in drawing conclusions about
sanctions effects. Attempts to attribute exclusive or primary responsibility for a given policy change or social outcome to the imposition of economic sanctions are inherently uncertain and subject to debate.

Nonetheless, social impacts are easier to predict and assess than political effects. Countries already on the verge of humanitarian crisis clearly are more likely to be pushed over the edge by effectively imposed economic sanctions. A country such as Iraq that is heavily dependent on the export of a single commodity will be devastated economically and socially by an effective embargo against that commodity. The political impacts of these measures will be more uncertain and diffuse. Policymakers must decide how to apply economic pressure on a vulnerable regime to bring about compliance with international norms without simultaneously causing harmful social effects that may undermine or impede the achievement of those norms.

Unintended Political Impacts

A different, more nuanced perspective on unintended consequences focuses on the diverse and far-reaching impacts sanctions can have on political groups and constituencies within the targeted regime. One of the most consistent patterns across the twelve sanctions cases was that disaffected political groups, usually opponents of the regime being targeted, found themselves caught in a double bind. On the one hand, such sanctions as travel and participation bans severely limited their ability to maintain contact with NGOs and other transnational actors who provided support for their domestic political efforts. When trade sanctions reduced the availability of newsprint, as was the case in Yugoslavia, democratic opposition groups interested in maintaining a free flow of information and countering xenophobia were unable to publish. On the other hand, sanctions provided authoritarian governments with leverage to create a rally 'round the flag effect as a means of suppressing domestic opposition.

The cases of the 1990s reveal that sanctions can be self-defeating in the domestic political arena, which is especially troublesome when sanctions are imposed to restore democracy and improve human rights. When sanctions are applied, the Security Council should recognize that restrictions on commerce and travel may have the effect of marginalizing opposition groups and strengthening a regime's control over its society and economy. To some extent these unintended consequences may be unavoidable. But the Security Council should make every possible effort to ensure that sanctions do not unduly victimize or harm the interests of reform groups or opposition constituencies within a targeted regime that support the very norms the United Nations is seeking to uphold.

Structure, Innovation, and Adaptation in UN Sanctions

We made the claim in Chapter 1 that the United Nations lacks the capacity to effectively administer sanctions as a means of international enforcement. We also noted the tension that emerges when member states hijack the sanctions process to serve purposes separate from those approved by the Security Council. Nonetheless, the United Nations was given the task of administering the twelve sanctions cases during the 1990s, and in the process the UN system gained valuable experience about the institutional structures and policies that contribute to effectiveness. Although the sanctions cases of the past decade unfolded under very different circumstances, with differing structural arrangements, some generalizations flow from these experiences:

- Swift, forceful sanctions tend to be more effective than slow, incremental measures.
- With greater cooperation from frontline states and the major trading partners of the target, sanctions will be more successful.
- When a sanctions committee is more engaged, as evidenced by frequency of meetings and the active role of its chair, implementation will be enhanced.
- A greater effort devoted to sanctions monitoring, both regarding violations and political and humanitarian impacts, will produce more effective sanctions.
- The involvement of regional organizations can greatly enhance sanctions implementation.

Each of these findings warrants amplification, as detailed briefly below.

The Scope and Intensity of Sanctions

The cases of the 1990s illustrate that the effectiveness of sanctions depends greatly on swift and forceful implementation. This finding confirms the conclusion reached in the original IIE study of 1990, which argued that swift and comprehensive measures are most effective, but does not deny the value of ratcheting up pressure in cases in which previous sanctions pressures have not been sufficient to induce policy change.[7] In the Yugoslavia case, the progressive strengthening of these measures in Resolutions 787 (1992) and 820 (1993) contributed to the effectiveness of sanctions as bargaining leverage on the Milosevic regime. Nor does this emphasis on swift and forceful imposition deny the importance of inducement strategies as part of the sanctions-generated bargaining dynamic. Offering rewards for compliance can generate positive reciprocity and enhance the effectiveness of the bargaining process. The combination of forceful sanctions and concrete incentives for compliance can be highly effective.

The Yugoslavia case illustrates the effectiveness of a ratcheting down of pressure as an inducement for greater compliance. The lack of such inducements in the Iraq case, by contrast, impeded the prospects for greater compliance. Although the United Nations is limited in the incentives it can offer (lacking financial resources and the ability to provide security assurances), the Security Council can offer a very significant inducement—the lifting or suspending of sanctions. The cases of the 1990s show that the desire for a lifting of sanctions is a priority for most targeted regimes. The effective use of this potential reward is crucial to successful bargaining dynamics.

One of the creative inducement concepts that developed in UN circles with regard to the Iraq and Libya episodes was the notion of sanctions suspension. Rather than raising the issue of an end to sanctions, which would have forced an acrimonious debate within the Security Council, some member states proposed instead a suspension of sanctions. Although some questioned the difference between termination and suspension, arguing that it was only a matter of semantics, for UN diplomats the distinction was important. The latter term implied the maintenance of some sanctions controls and an ability to bargain with a targeted state regarding its continued compliance. This suspension concept was critical in resolving the Libya sanctions situation and in ensuring compliance. The term has also been the subject of debate regarding an easing of trade sanctions against Iraq, although to date without success.

Member State Cooperation

The cooperation of a targeted regime's neighboring states and principal trading partners is essential. In many of the cases in Africa, where neighboring states were either unwilling or unable to cooperate with UN sanctions, sanctions were completely ineffective. In Haiti the lack of compliance by the Dominican Republic weakened the impact of sanctions. The problem of noncooperation is largely a political question, arising from the disagreement of neighboring states with the UN agenda, but it is also a structural issue. The lack of legal, administrative, and institutional capacity for sanctions implementation among many member states is a major impediment to political effectiveness.

The two cases with the greatest degree of cooperation from neighboring states, Iraq and Yugoslavia, were also the most successful cases. Compliance in the Iraq case was greatly aided by the cooperation of Turkey, a part of the U.S.-led coalition, and Iran, Iraq's military adversary. The special arrangement allowing Iraq to export oil to Jordan also played an important role. In the case of Yugoslavia, the extensive monitoring and enforcement effort mounted by European regional institutions was decisive in applying economic pressure on Belgrade. The Yugoslavia case confirms that the active participation of regional security and economic institutions can be crucial to sanctions effectiveness.

However, where regional organizations lack sufficient resources, their ability to enhance sanctions implementation is limited. In Liberia and Sierra Leone, the Economic Community of West African States (ECOWAS) established regional monitoring and enforcement efforts aided by its military arm, ECOMOG. But these efforts were hampered by an emphasis on military operations and a lack of infrastructure and institutional capacity for customs control and border monitoring. In the Sierra Leone case, the UN sanctions committee in New York maintained liaison with ECOWAS, and the Office for the Coordination of Humanitarian Affairs (OCHA) provided support for the monitoring of humanitarian relief. Although this assistance was minimal and came too late in the short-lived sanctions effort to have much impact, it could serve as a model for recognizing and supporting the implementation efforts of regional organizations in less developed areas of the world. In many parts of Africa, Latin America, and Asia, the infusion of resources and technical capacity can make a significant difference in the ability of regional organizations to ensure effective implementation of Security Council sanctions.

Administration of Sanctions

The role of sanctions committees and the associated administrative structure in the UN Secretariat can affect the implementation of sanctions and the administration of humanitarian relief. The most effective sanctions, those imposed on Iraq and Yugoslavia, had the most active and engaged sanctions committees. The Iraq committee, in particular, was constantly involved in a wide range of activities, especially the processing of humanitarian exemption applications. The oil for food program implemented in 1996 became a huge operation with a substantial bureaucratic apparatus. By the end of the decade the budget for the UN Iraq program grew to more than $10 billion per year, exceeding that of the United Nations itself.

The oil for food program itself was unique due to the combination of the humanitarian crisis related to the sanctions and the ability of Iraq to generate huge oil revenues to pay for the needed supplies. The presence of cash-generating oil exports gave the Security Council inventive possibilities for dealing with the humanitarian crisis. Very few instances are likely to arise in which the sanctioned nation will be able or willing to pay for offsetting its own economic strangulation.

One of the more remarkable features of the Iraq sanctions was the manner in which so many member states, including those who became vocal in their opposition to the continuation of sanctions in the latter half of the decade, nonetheless maintained the embargo. This was due in part to the relative ease of enforcing the oil embargo, especially when key neighboring countries remained committed to keeping the pipelines shut. The celebrated exemption for the Jordanian importation of oil, based on its dependence on Iraqi oil, was a particularly useful innovation. It recognized a trading partner's legitimate Article 50 injury claims while making an exemption that would keep the coalition of sanctions-supporting states intact.

In many of the cases in which sanctions were ineffective, the sanctions committees played little or no role. In the Somalia case, the oversight effort was so minimal that the Security Council had to adopt a special resolution (Resolution 954 in 1994) requesting that the sanctions committee fulfill its duties. In the Liberia and Rwanda cases as well, the sanctions committees played little or no role in attempting to implement the arms embargoes. The limitations of these sanctions regimes were reflected in the inactivity of the associated sanctions committees.

The Rwanda committee was supplanted by the International Commission of Inquiry (UNICOI), which served as an innovative approach to monitoring sanctions violations. Although UNICOI had no enforcement capabilities, its independence and vigorous investigative powers allowed it to assemble a detailed record of the extensive arms trafficking and financing networks that sustained the perpetrators of the Rwandan genocide. UNICOI was an expert group rather than a committee of political representatives, and it thus had greater latitude to pursue evidence of violations without political constraint. The precedent of convening a special investigative commission may prove useful in future sanctions episodes.

In the Angola case, as the Security Council strengthened sanctions measures in 1997 and 1998, the sanctions committee became more active and attempted to play a more assertive role in encouraging compliance with the sanctions, especially among neighboring states in Africa. Committee chair Robert Fowler, permanent representative of Canada to the Security Council, made an innovative effort in 1999 to mobilize support for the sanctions. The convening of expert panels by the Angola committee, following the example of the Iraq committee, marked another creative attempt by the sanctions committee to enhance monitoring and effectiveness. Whether these efforts by the Angola committee will result in greater cooperation with sanctions among member states and ultimately bring about some compliance by the targeted UNITA regime, however, remains to be seen.

Play it Again, SAM: Monitoring as Essential

One of the most significant developments in sanctions enforcement over the past decade was the introduction of sanctions assistance missions (SAMs) to monitor and enforce the sanctions against Yugoslavia. SAMs were the most elaborate and highly developed monitoring program ever established. Western European governments sent customs officers to the countries surrounding Yugoslavia, and the Western European Union and NATO established patrol missions on the Danube and in the Adriatic. As noted in the Yugoslavia case study, the SAMs contributed significantly to the success of the sanctions against Belgrade, making them the most rigorously enforced in history.

In other cases, the lack of anything resembling SAMs among regional organizations meant that implementation efforts were either limited or nonexistent. When the Organization of American States imposed sanctions against Haiti in 1991, it had no means of assuring the implementation of these measures. When ECOWAS imposed sanctions against Liberia and Sierra Leone, it created sanctions committees to monitor and enforce these measures, but the committees lacked the necessary financial resources and technical capacity for ensuring effective implementation. Only in the Sierra Leone case, as noted, did UN agencies provide limited assistance. Regional organizations can and must play a central role in the monitoring and enforcement of sanctions, but the realization of this potential will depend on the greater availability of financial and technical resources and a stronger political commitment to the objectives of UN sanctions.

Conclusion

In part because no comparative and summary assessment of UN-imposed multilateral sanctions has been undertaken until now, the conclusions and findings offered here are tentative in nature. But as we have tried to demonstrate in this chapter, certain patterns of experience and policy trends have become clear during the past decade. One of the challenges has been to see beyond the Iraq case. The debate over Iraq has so dominated the discourse on sanctions that it has skewed public understanding of the real data of sanctions and the successful adaptations that have occurred in recent years. The UN community has learned a great deal more about the conditions under which sanctions are successful than the general debate on these questions (as discussed in Chapter 1) might suggest. The understanding of humanitarian and social consequences resulting from sanctions has also expanded.

This volume has identified some of the factors that account for effectiveness, in some instances specific to particular cases and in other instances more generic. We have also learned much from the failures, especially from the ineffectiveness of arms embargoes. By drawing on the experience of the past decade and gleaning appropriate lessons from both the successes and failures, we can identify a set of policy recommendations for the future. That is the task to which we now turn.

Notes

1. Afghanistan is not included because sanctions went into effect in November 1999 and as of this writing have not had a chance to have an impact.

2. Gary Clyde Hufbauer, Jeffrey J. Schott, and Kimberly Ann Elliott, *Economic Sanctions Reconsidered: History and Current Policy,* 2d ed. (Washington, D.C.: Institute for International Economics, 1990).

3. Stephen Engelberg, "Conflict in the Balkans: UN Steps Said to Dry Up Serbs' Cash," *New York Times,* 13 May 1993, A8.

4. Robert Black and Neil King, Jr., "Milosevic's Cronies Struggle for Removal from West's Blacklist," *Wall Street Journal,* 1 October 1999, A1, A6.

5. See Jeffrey Boutwell and Michael T. Klare, *Lethal Commerce: The Global Trade in Small Arms and Light Weapons* (Cambridge, Mass.: American Academy of Arts and Sciences, 1995), and R. T. Naylor, *Patriots and Profiteers: On Economic Warfare, Embargo Busting and State-Sponsored Crime* (Toronto: McClelland and Stewart, 1999).

6. The most serious of these critiques is that of Joy Gordon, "A Peaceful, Silent, Deadly Remedy: The Ethics of Economic Sanctions," *Ethics and International Affairs* 13 (1999): 123–142.

7. Hufbauer, Schott, and Elliott, *Economic Sanctions Reconsidered,* 100–102.

12

Recommendations for a New Sanctions Policy

If economic sanctions are to serve as an alternative to military force, or even as a viable complement to more forceful forms of coercion, many improvements will be necessary. As the case studies in this volume illustrate, sanctions too often suffer from poor design, loose commitment from member states, inadequate monitoring, and lax enforcement. The present limitations of sanctions stem in part from the shortcomings of the UN system. They also result from the lack of sanctions enforcement capability in many member states. The widespread use of multilateral sanctions is a very recent development and has no parallel in the political economy of nations. The systematic study of UN sanctions is also in its infancy. Only in the last few years have policymakers and scholars concentrated on the requirements for more effective use of the instrument. Although many uncertainties and questions remain, it is now possible to outline a widely shared set of principles and operational guidelines to make economic sanctions more humane and effective.

In this chapter we build from the summary findings of the last chapter to bring various reform proposals together into a comprehensive strategy for achieving more successful sanctions policies. Many recommendations have been made, both from official quarters and private sources, for improving the use of economic sanctions. Despite the many reform suggestions, however, to date no attempt has been made to synthesize the various proposals into an integrated program for enhancing sanctions' effectiveness. We offer such a synthesis in these pages. Our task is made easier by the commonality that exists among the various reform proposals. The reports that have emanated from UN agencies and private research groups show a high degree of congruity and reflect an emerging consensus on many of the most important requirements and conditions for effective sanctions. Some points of disagreement and uncertainty remain, but sufficient clarity exists on the main points to present a relatively coherent platform of principles and policy proposals for making sanctions a viable instrument of international peace-making.

The recommendations presented here are drawn from reports of the UN Secretary-General;[1] an issue paper of the chairs of the Security Council sanctions committees;[2] reports of the UN General Assembly Special Committee on the Charter of the United Nations and the Sanctions Subgroup of the Informal Open-Ended Working Group on "An Agenda for Peace";[3] a letter from the five permanent members of the Security Council to the president of the Council;[4] the Copenhagen Roundtable on the Sanctions against Yugoslavia;[5] private reports of the Carnegie Commission on Preventing Deadly Conflict, the Institute for International Economics, and the United Nations Association–USA;[6] and a special symposium on targeted sanctions cosponsored by the Fourth Freedom Forum and the Joan B. Kroc Foundation in New York in December 1998.[7] We also draw extensively on our own previous work and from the suggestions and writings of a variety of academic colleagues and policymakers.[8] We believe that these proposals, taken together, offer a credible blueprint for increasing the viability and effectiveness of sanctions as instruments of United Nations policy.

Our goal in these recommendations is to assist the UN community at a critical, introspective moment regarding sanctions. As we have shown, over the course of the 1990s momentum has developed to transform sanctions policy from the ad hoc, often poorly implemented instrument it presently is into a more refined tool for preventing and resolving conflict. The imposition of economic sanctions can and should begin to resemble the workings of an international regime, with standardized policy guidelines and operational principles equivalent to those that exist in other international arenas, such as humanitarian action or the use of military force.

The recommendations outlined here will require a substantial commitment of political and financial capital. Implementing effective sanctions is a highly complex and expensive proposition. Decisionmakers who think of sanctions as "policy on the cheap" are sadly mistaken and are ensuring that the halfhearted efforts that often pass as sanctions policy fail. Attempting to harness market forces for political ends can only be successful with a substantial commitment of resources. Anything less than a large-scale effort, guided by sound strategy and concerted international participation, is not worth attempting.

Setting the Policy Framework

Sanctions are best considered as instruments of coercive diplomacy to persuade decisionmakers in the targeted state to reassess the costs and benefits associated with policies that have attracted the ire of the international community. As such, the decision to employ sanctions requires three elements for ensuring compliance. First, much like the place of aerial bombing in a wider military campaign, the larger strategy of coercion-persuasion in which sanctions play a component part must be clear and specified. Within that larger strategy, the exact role and place of sanctions must be realizable. Second, since sanctions will always have broad impacts, it is essential to assess those impacts on the diverse actors and conditions within the targeted state and to adjust sanctions accordingly. Third, to form the first and to guarantee the second, sanctions must have multiple layers of institutional support during the various phases of implementation.

Sanctions are only as effective as the overall policy they are designed to support and the structures within which they are implemented. If the assumptions underlying that policy are flawed, major states are unwilling to carry out that policy, or the organizations that impose sanctions are unable to administer them, sanctions will inevitably fail. Sanctions are simply one of a varied set of policy instruments designed to serve an overall diplomatic strategy and by themselves cannot achieve major policy objectives. When they are combined with other policy tools, however, and especially when they are tied to a carrot-and-stick bargaining process, they can be effective instruments of persuasion. Realistic expectations about what sanctions can accomplish and how they fit with other tools of policy are essential to their effective use.

The strategic targeting of sanctions is now considered a crucial element of policy. Such was not the case in the early 1990s. As Secretary-General Kofi Annan stated in his 1998 Africa report, "Better targeting of sanctions is necessary to help ensure that they will achieve their intended purpose."[9] The issue paper by the chairs of the UN Security Council sanctions committees likewise observed: "Targeted sanctions such as arms embargoes, flight bans, travel bans, freezing of financial assets . . . represent a valuable alternative to other, more comprehensive types of sanctions."[10] Although the actual practice of targeted sanctions has yet to be tested fully, the logic of this approach is convincing. Sanctions are likely to be most effective when they target the decisionmakers responsible for wrongdoing and deny the assets and resources that are most valuable to these decisionmaking elites. At the same time, care must be taken to avoid measures that cause unintended humanitarian hardships or inadvertently enrich or empower decisionmakers or criminal elements. The essence of a smart sanctions strategy is tailoring sanctions to meet specific objectives and focusing coercive pressure on particular groups and resources. We will address these points in more detail below.

Flexibility is key to effective strategy. In military conflict, the capacity to maneuver is a valuable strategic asset. The same holds true with the implementation of sanctions. Too often, however, sanctioning authorities are inflexible in their approach and unwilling to make adjustments as conditions change. The issue paper by the chairs of the sanctions committees argued that the "Security Council should be able to adjust the sanctions regimes" in response to humanitarian needs, the concerns of neighboring states, and other considerations.[11] Flexibility also helps in responding to partial concessions from targeted regimes. The Security Council should reward partial compliance by easing pressures, as it did in the sanctions against Yugoslavia during the Bosnian war. Conversely, an unyielding sanctions policy, as in the failure of the Security Council to reciprocate partial Iraqi concessions, often leads to political stalemate. Flexibly targeted sanctions within the framework of carrot-and-stick diplomacy remain essential to effective policy.

Minimizing Unintended Consequences

Is it possible to make sanctions both more effective and more humane, to maximize their impact on policy while minimizing unintended effects on third parties and vulnerable populations? Many public commentaries on sanctions assume there is an irreconcilable contradiction between these two purposes. Civilian pain is an inevitable and even intended result of sanctions, many assume, and is essential to achieving political success. Although there indeed can be tensions between humanitarian impacts and political objectives, addressing these concerns together is both possible and necessary.[12] Much political learning and institutional adaptation has occurred in this regard over the past decade. The greater the attention to minimizing adverse humanitarian impacts, the deeper and broader the support for such sanctions within the coalition of sender states. Also, the more sensitive sanctions designers are to limiting the harm on innocent bystanders, the less likely sanctioned leaders will be able to mobilize support within the targeted state. Efforts to reduce unintended humanitarian impacts also make it more likely that sanctions will be targeted against decisionmaking elites.

Preparing Preassessment Reports

Numerous proposals have been offered to address and minimize the humanitarian consequences of sanctions. The UN Department of Humanitarian Affairs commissioned two major studies, one in 1995 and the other in 1997, which proposed a wide array of reforms.[13] A central recommendation of these studies is that humanitarian assessments should be conducted before, during, and after the imposition of UN sanctions. A detailed multistep methodology has been developed that allows the United Nations to assess the likely impact of sanctions before they are imposed and then after sanctions are in place to determine if changes in sanctions policy are warranted. A preassessment prior to the imposition of sanctions would establish baseline data. This would be followed by an actual assessment of impacts after sanctions are applied, with recommendations for any necessary alterations or policy changes.

UN reports have also defined a series of indicators for assessing humanitarian impact. The indicators are divided into five categories: public health, economics, migration, governance and civil society, and humanitarian activities.[14] Specific indicators within these categories include infant mortality rates, the nutritional status of children, market prices of foodstuffs, changes in migratory population flows, the status of civil society, and the ability of humanitarian agencies to meet the needs of vulnerable populations. These indicators were selected not only on the basis of their importance for analyzing impacts within a particular category but according to their ease of access. To be functional, an assessment methodology must be based on readily available information that can be collected quickly without extensive field research. The proposed assessment methodology meets these standards and would enable sanctioning authorities to anticipate potential adverse consequences and adjust sanctions policies accordingly.

Although some observers question the viability of preassessment when the Security Council must act swiftly, many UN officials favor the idea of assessing potential humanitarian impacts before sanctions are imposed. An indication of the growing support for this concept can be found in the decisions of the Security Council to send preassessment missions to Sudan (1997) and Sierra Leone (1998) to study the potential impact of sanctions on those two countries.[15] The reports from these missions provided useful information on the humanitarian situation in both countries. The Sudan report influenced the Council's decision to withhold the imposition of aviation sanctions in order to avoid unintended adverse consequences (although the decision not to proceed was also based on Egypt's reluctance to support these stronger measures).

Preassessment of humanitarian and other impacts should be adopted as a general principle of sanctions policy. Whenever the Security Council considers the imposition of sanctions, it should commission a quick report of likely humanitarian impacts, both within the targeted country and in neighboring states. This process would provide the information necessary to design sanctions so that they avoid unintended adverse consequences. A special representative or experts group should also be appointed to oversee the continuing assessment of humanitarian needs and recommend any needed changes in sanctions policy.[16]

A special comment is in order regarding the political impact of preassessment studies. Some member states caution that such reports could be used to undermine consensus and weaken political resolve in the Security Council. This is a valid concern that impinges on the prospects for political effectiveness. The findings from the analyses of UN sanctions during the 1990s suggest that swift, forceful implementation increases the chances of success. A prolonged process of preassessment could undermine the decisiveness that brings effectiveness. This need not be the case if the assessment report is conducted quickly, and if the Council is united in its dual commitment to minimize unintended humanitarian hardships and apply concerted pressure on those responsible for objectionable behavior. In fact, the commissioning of a preassessment report could be a form of political signaling, a message to the targeted state that the Security Council is serious about applying coercive pressure and is taking the necessary preparatory steps to mobilize international cooperation.

Some worry that such advance warning of impending sanctions would permit a targeted regime to stockpile materials and prepare various sanctions countermaneuvers. Although self-protective adjustments no doubt will occur, this type of action is, ironically, a sign that sanctions are already having an impact. The threat of sanctions forces decisionmakers to reexamine the costs and benefits of their objectionable policies and to reallocate domestic resources as a result of international pressure. These adjustments may help the target withstand sanctions initially, but over the long term, the impacts of stronger and more effectively implemented sanctions are likely to be considerable. If taking the time to examine the potential impact of sanctions helps to build international consensus, the likelihood of implementation will increase. Broader support within the international arena increases the bite of sanctions by making them enforceable over the medium to long term.

Streamlining Exemptions Procedures

The other key mechanism for ameliorating humanitarian hardships is the system of sanctions exemptions. The humanitarian agencies that operate within countries targeted by sanctions have frequently noted the difficulties of obtaining exemptions and have urged improvements in the system.[17] The administration of exemptions by the sanctions committees has been widely criticized as overly bureaucratic, opaque, and insensitive to the needs of both humanitarian agencies and suffering populations.[18] In response to these concerns, the Security Council has adopted measures to make the procedures of the sanctions committees more transparent, but the committees still meet behind closed doors, and many of the concerns previously expressed about the inadequacy of humanitarian exemptions procedures remain unresolved.[19] Although the committees have expedited the process for approving exemption applications, humanitarian agencies continue to face difficulties in gaining approval for the prompt delivery of relief supplies.

Three basic options exist for improving the management of humanitarian exemptions. Each would ease the administrative burdens of reviewing exemption applications and ensure more rapid delivery of nonstrategic humanitarian goods to vulnerable populations. The three options are listed below.

Institution-specific exemptions.   Established international humanitarian organizations, such as the United Nations High Commissioner for Refugees (UNHCR), would receive blanket authority to import items in support of their activities. A 1995 Department of Humanitarian Affairs study recommended this approach. A Russian Federation proposal has also called for "the complete exemption of international humanitarian organizations from sanctions restrictions."[20]

Item-specific exemptions.   Essential items, such as certain drugs, water purification materials, and standard agricultural equipment, would be automatically granted exemption without review. The World Health

Organization and other groups have attempted to develop generic lists of such items, but attempts to win political approval for this approach have failed.

Country-specific exemptions.   This approach, similar to the one above, would develop lists of items to be automatically exempted for each particular sanctions episode, taking into account the idiosyncratic nature of each situation. This approach evolved in 1994 and 1995 during the latter stages of the sanctions against Yugoslavia, when institution-specific exemptions were granted to UNHCR and other UN agencies and NGOs.[21]

We recommend a combination of the country-specific and institution-specific approach. The innovative approach adopted in Yugoslavia eliminated a huge backlog in exemption applications and facilitated the work of UN humanitarian agencies. Some UN member states oppose granting blanket exemptions to humanitarian agencies for fear that this will weaken sanctions and open the door to black marketing. But offering such exemptions to trusted humanitarian organizations within the UN system would not prevent the sanctions committees from continuing to monitor and block prohibited commercial imports. The vast majority of exemption applications to the sanctions committees (95 percent in the cases of Iraq and Yugoslavia) originate from commercial companies. Items requested by humanitarian organizations constitute less than 5 percent of the total requests.[22] Granting exemptions to UN humanitarian agencies in specific sanctions episodes would not prevent the Security Council from maintaining tight enforcement of economic sanctions. It would facilitate the provision of necessary humanitarian relief and thereby enhance the moral legitimacy and potential political effectiveness of sanctions.

Addressing Third Party Impacts

Closely related to the problem of preventing unintended humanitarian consequences is the challenge of minimizing impacts on nontarget countries. States that border or have major trading relations with a sanctioned country inevitably suffer when commercial restrictions are imposed against that country. Article 50 of the UN Charter recognizes this problem but offers no remedies for addressing it. Nontarget countries affected by sanctions are given the right to "consult" with the Security Council, but no fixed mechanisms or procedures exist to resolve such problems. Former Secretary-General Boutros Boutros-Ghali addressed these concerns in his *Supplement to An Agenda for Peace,* when he argued that the costs of sanctions "should be born equitably by all member states and not exclusively by the few who have the misfortune to be neighbors or major economic partners of the target country."[23] He proposed creating a permanent UN mechanism that, among other tasks, would "explore ways of assisting member states that are suffering collateral damage and evaluate claims submitted . . . under Article 50."[24]

The challenge of mitigating third party impacts is crucial to enhancing the effectiveness of economic sanctions. Without the support and cooperation of neighboring states and major trading partners, sanctions cannot work. Nontarget states need special assistance to compensate for economic losses and adverse social impacts if they are to be expected to cooperate with UN sanctions. A failure by sanctioning authorities to address the need for burden sharing will undermine support for sanctions and thus limit their effectiveness. Addressing the special needs of nontarget countries is more than an issue of justice and humanitarianism. It is a vital contribution to making sanctions more effective.

The United Nations has convened a number of experts groups to address the problem of third party impacts, and they have produced a range of proposals. We will highlight only a few of what seem to us the most important and credible reform recommendations. Some of the suggestions that UN member states have offered, such as the creation of a permanent compensation fund to meet Article 50 requests, make sense logically, but they are completely unrealistic politically and economically and have no chance of being adopted. We focus here on just a few recommendations that seem to have the best chance for gaining the political support necessary for implementation.[25]

Strategies for minimizing third party impacts should be integrated into the initial design of sanctions. Steps to address the problem of third party impacts should be taken before and while sanctions are being imposed, not as an afterthought. A preassessment study is an essential first step that should be combined with the humanitarian preassessment process recommended earlier. When the Security Council is considering the imposition of sanctions, it should conduct an assessment not only of potential humanitarian impacts within the targeted state but of likely consequences for nontarget countries. The latter analysis should apply to states immediately surrounding the target and major trading partners. The assessment of third party impacts need not be elaborately detailed, but it should address the general character of trade dependency on the targeted state and should include suggestions for the kinds of assistance and compensatory measures that might be needed to ameliorate these impacts.

Security Council resolutions imposing sanctions should include specific provisions addressing the problem of third party impacts. The recommendations of the preassessment report might be incorporated into the initiating resolutions. In many of the resolutions imposing sanctions, including the cases of Iraq, Yugoslavia, and Haiti, the Council made no mention of the need to help nontarget states. A far better procedure would be to issue instructions for addressing this problem and to indicate to member states the availability of Article 50 procedures.

If member states are to be encouraged to seek assistance for unintended impacts, the UN system will need greater expertise and administrative capability not only for assessing these impacts but for evaluating requests for assistance from member states. To aid this process, the UN Secretariat should develop standardized categories of impact that could be tailored to each case and that could be used by technical experts to evaluate the merit and priority of member state requests for assistance. For each sanctions episode, the Secretary-General might appoint an experts group or special representative to work with affected member states and the relevant sanctions committee to monitor unintended impacts and make recommendations to the Security Council for appropriate remedial action. This suggested experts group or special representative might be combined with the similar group or special representative addressing humanitarian impacts within the targeted country.

Specific compensatory actions must be taken in response to demonstrated needs in nontarget states. In some cases support can be provided through special arrangements, such as the agreement allowing Jordan to import oil from Iraq. In most cases, however, it will be necessary to convene special donor conferences. Such gatherings have been employed in the past, for example, among the frontline states in the Rhodesia case, and they have been used recently as a tool of postconflict reconstruction in the Balkans. Donor conferences would bring together major economic powers, relevant regional organizations, international financial institutions such as the World Bank and the International Monetary Fund, and the affected nontarget states. The conference would identify possible forms of direct financial assistance, such as grants or concessionary loans, debt relief, and the extension of credit. Other possible indirect measures of assistance might include tariff adjustments, the provision of compensatory supplies of essential commodities, and technical and financial support for sanctions monitoring and enforcement efforts, perhaps modeled on the sanctions assistance missions employed in the Yugoslavia case.

Compensatory measures such as these will be expensive, but they cannot be avoided if sanctions are to be taken seriously. The expenses involved in addressing humanitarian needs and third party impacts should be weighed against the costs of either using military force or doing nothing in the face of a major crisis. Economic sanctions and incentives can be an effective, less costly means of resolving international conflict, but as noted at the outset, they are not cheap. They can only work if those imposing such measures are prepared to meet the costs for themselves and for nontarget states that bear the greatest burden of such measures.

Another suggestion for addressing the needs of neighboring states is to provide infrastructure support for bolstering the civil society protections of legitimate business interests. When sanctions are imposed, sanctions-busting entrepreneurs in neighboring states grab control of markets in the sanctioned country. Frontline state leaders who are willing to arrest "sanctions smugglers" from other countries may turn their back on such criminal and black market activity within their own borders. Political leaders may derive short-term benefit from this, but important economic sectors often suffer. The new challenge for a sanctions regime within the UN system, then, becomes how to convince leaders that long-term economic transparency and legal commerce serve them better than personal gain from corruption and a new, booming criminal sector that will skew the economy increasingly in its favor.

Strengthening Institutions and Policies

Below we specify a series of needed reforms and actions within a range of institutions and groups that are involved in sanctions policymaking and implementation. We begin by considering policy actions within the Security Council, both in the narrow sense of formulating resolutions and guidelines and in the broader context of developing policy. Then we address the programmatic and institutional changes that must occur among member states, the sanctions committees, and the UN Secretariat.

Security Council Policymaking

The sanctions episodes of the last decade have revealed the need for substantial improvements in the workings of the Security Council. One of the highest priorities is developing greater clarity and uniformity in Security Council resolutions. The language of Council resolutions is the result of political jockeying and compromise and may leave ambiguities and loopholes that greatly complicate the task of implementation. Whether imposing comprehensive trade sanctions or more selective measures such as arms embargoes or travel bans, the Security Council too often employs vague terms and sets general conditions for compliance that make it difficult to determine whether a targeted country has met the Council's requirements. This concern was addressed as part of the Interlaken process sponsored by the Swiss government. At the second Interlaken seminar in March 1999, draft language was presented for Security Council resolutions.[26] The proposed technical language included standard definitions for financial sanctions so that they conform to the terms employed in the global financial sector.[27] Similar efforts are under way as part of a German government initiative to improve the effectiveness of arms embargoes and travel bans. The clarification of terms and objectives are essential steps toward improving the implementation of sanctions.

It is especially important that Security Council resolutions specify criteria for lifting or suspending sanctions. Former Secretary-General Boutros-Ghali addressed this issue in his *Supplement to An Agenda for Peace:*

> While recognizing that the Council is a political body rather than a judicial organ, it is of great importance that when it decides to impose sanctions, it should at the same time define objective criteria for determining that their purpose has been achieved.[28]

The language of Council resolutions should be as clear as possible on these criteria. If the lifting of sanctions is to serve as an effective inducement, the targeted regime must know what it will take. When there are multiple conditions in Security Council resolutions, as there often are, compliance with each of those specific conditions could be reciprocated with a partial easing of sanctions. By clearly spelling out the specific steps required for compliance, the Council could signal a willingness to reciprocate these steps and in the process could establish a momentum for cooperation that could accelerate the resolution of the crisis. The more precise the Security Council can be in clarifying terms, the better the prospects for negotiating an acceptance of Security Council concerns.

Enhancing Member State Cooperation

Along with greater clarity of resolutions and more precise definitions of terms must come better guidelines for member states regarding the implementation of Security Council resolutions. At present the sanctions committees ask member states to report on their efforts to comply with Security Council sanctions, but no guidelines or instructions are offered for how states should report on compliance efforts. Since there is no enforcement machinery to ensure that member states respond, these notices from the sanctions committees are often ignored or answered in a perfunctory manner. A more concerted effort to obtain compliance information from member states and to collect it in a standardized manner would help to improve the monitoring and enforcement of sanctions resolutions.

Much of the momentum for improving sanctions compliance must come from individual member states and regional organizations, given that member states bear the bulk of the responsibility for implementing Security Council decisions. The challenge is to help member states feel more of an obligation to support Security Council resolutions. Sanctions violations are often motivated by the promise of financial reward from smuggling or result from a lack of political support for the policy objectives of sanctions. The former concern can be addressed through greater attention to Article 50 requests and adequate compensatory measures for neighboring states and companies, as noted earlier. The latter concern can be addressed by making sure that sanctions are imposed only for the most serious offenses. When a strong international consensus for action exists, states are more likely to support sanctions and to make a significant commitment to implementation.

The Security Council can also encourage member state participation and support through the use of incentives strategies. The Security Council lacks the financial resources to offer much in the way of rewards or incentives on its own, but member states and international organizations can assist UN peacemaking efforts by providing "carrots" to encourage cooperation and compliance with Security Council resolutions. This model was followed with success in the international partnerships that helped bring an end to the civil wars in Central America. Similar partnerships in other settings could increase the benefits of member state compliance with Security Council resolutions and enhance the overall effectiveness of conflict resolution efforts.

The United States has by far the most highly evolved legal and administrative infrastructure for implementing sanctions. This is the result of the extensive U.S. experience with sanctions and the tendency in Washington to impose sanctions frequently against a wide range of targets—a policy that has been described by Richard Haass as "sanctions madness."[29] Although the United States resorts to sanctions perhaps too frequently, its legal and institutional capabilities can serve as a model for nations in developing a greater capacity to monitor and enforce such measures. No other country can match U.S. capabilities, but the major industrial countries within the Organization for Economic Cooperation and Development (OECD) have at least some legal and institutional capability for implementing sanctions. Beyond the major industrial countries, however, sanctions enforcement capability is almost totally lacking. It was estimated at the December 1998 symposium on targeted sanctions in New York that only twelve nations have laws enabling them to enforce Security Council financial sanctions. Given the meager state of sanctions capabilities around the world, it is no wonder that compliance with Security Council sanctions is often so inadequate.

To remedy this situation, assistance should be provided for member states to develop the capacity for sanctions implementation. This support could take the form of model legislation, adaptable to varying political and social systems, that would enable member states to make necessary adjustments in their domestic laws and regulations to permit cooperation with UN sanctions. Considerable progress has been made in developing such model legislation, especially for the purpose of enforcing targeted financial sanctions. Secretary-General Kofi Annan has highlighted the need for a similar strengthening of legal authority for the enforcement of arms embargoes. In most countries of the world today, it is not a violation of the law to circumvent or ignore Security Council arms embargoes. In his 1998 report on Africa, Annan urged member states to "adopt legislation making the violation of a Security Council arms embargo a criminal offence under their national laws."[30] If Security Council sanctions are to become an effective instrument of international policy, it is essential that member states develop the necessary legal authority and institutional capability to enforce these measures.

The Sanctions Committees

The sanctions committees established by the Security Council for each major sanctions case have become increasingly important over the past decade. Initially the committees functioned as a kind of import-export licensing bureau, processing thousands of requests for humanitarian exemptions but paying little attention to other dimensions of sanctions policy. The committees were criticized in the past for their arbitrariness in reviewing exemptions requests, their lack of transparency and accountability, and the absence of any procedures for evaluating compliance and acting upon the noncompliance of member states.[31] Reforms were introduced in 1995 and 1996 to improve the functioning of the committees, but many problems remain. In more recent years, the chairs of the committees have become active in exerting leadership within the Security Council to improve both the work of the committees and the overall design of sanctions policy. The result has been a series of proposals and initiatives for further reform in the functioning of the committees and better overall coordination of sanctions policies. The reform recommendations are contained in *The Work of the Sanctions Committee: Notes by the President of the Security Council*, issued in January 1999.[32] This report provides a vitally important road map for enhancing Security Council policymaking.

The committee chairs recommend greater transparency and improved communications. According to their report, "the transparency of work of the Security Council and its sanctions committees should be improved." Communications must be improved with agencies within the UN system, as well as with intergovernmental and regional organizations, neighboring states, and the international community in general.[33] Summary records of the proceedings of the sanctions committees should be made available to the public and posted on the United Nations website. The sanctions committees should also consider holding periodic open meetings to gain wider public involvement in the monitoring and review of sanctions cases.[34] These recommendations for greater openness would enhance the legitimacy of sanctions committee operations and would enable the Security Council to mobilize public opinion for sanctions implementation.

The reform recommendations also include a number of suggestions for improving sanctions implementation by the Security Council. Some of these have been addressed already, including periodic assessments of humanitarian and economic impacts of sanctions, streamlined exemptions procedures for humanitarian agencies, and clear guidelines to member states for the reporting of alleged violations of sanctions. The committee chairs also recommend that the internal sanctions reviews now conducted by the Security Council become more detailed and substantive. These reviews should include an opportunity for the targeted regime to present its point of view to the sanctions committee. Each review should encompass the full range of humanitarian and policy impacts and the extent of implementation by member states. A formalized process of periodic review would enable the Security Council to make adjustments, either strengthening or easing sanctions pressures as appropriate, and would help to ensure that sanctions are implemented in a more predictable, transparent, and politically acceptable manner.

The most important recommendation concerns the role of committee chairs themselves and the suggestion that the chairs of the relevant sanctions committees make visits to the regions concerned. The purpose of the visits would be to obtain firsthand accounts of the humanitarian and economic impacts of the sanctions, assess both results and difficulties in sanctions implementation, and sensitize neighboring states to the need for more effective enforcement.[35] The proposal for visits by sanctions committee chairs has generated considerable support and interest. In May 1999, Ambassador Robert Fowler, the Canadian permanent representative to the UN and chair of the Angola sanctions committee, acted upon the recommendation and conducted an extensive assessment of and diplomatic mission to the affected region.[36]

The Fowler mission was a major undertaking that included visits to seven countries in central and southern Africa as well as subsequent meetings with international diamond traders in Europe. The specific objectives of the Fowler mission were to engage governments, private companies, and opinion leaders of the region in discussions of ways to improve the effectiveness of sanctions against the UNITA faction in Angola and to remind neighboring states of their obligation to implement these sanctions. The mission also sought to obtain information from member states, companies, and individuals on violations of the sanctions.[37] Fowler's report confirmed that African countries were implicated in "systematic violation" of the sanctions, but his report also identified a number of specific steps that could be taken by the Security Council to improve the implementation of the UNITA sanctions.[38]

The Fowler mission helped to overcome the relative lack of attention paid to the UNITA sanctions and effectively reminded key players in the region that more concerted action was needed to carry out the Security Council's mandates. The very presence of the committee chair in the region helped to raise awareness and increased the visibility of the sanctions. On a practical basis, the Fowler mission identified several concrete steps that could greatly improve the implementation of the sanctions, although these will require a commitment from the Security Council and leading member states. Resources and technical assistance will be needed to help the countries of central and southern Africa in sanctions monitoring and enforcing. The Fowler mission established a valuable precedent for the Security Council and its sanctions committees. Visits by committee chairs to affected regions can become an effective tool for enhancing the legitimacy and effectiveness of sanctions.

The Secretariat

The numerous United Nations programs that have operated effectively in recent years in such areas as humanitarian assistance and peacekeeping share a common characteristic: serious and sustained involvement from the UN Secretariat. Unfortunately, the scope of Secretariat involvement with Security Council sanctions has been minimal. As noted in most of the case studies, UN monitoring and enforcement efforts have been extremely limited. The Secretariat has virtually no capacity to ensure the implementation of sanctions and must rely entirely on the participation of member states. In most cases, member state involvement is nonexistent. Only in the cases of Iraq and Yugoslavia were credible enforcement operations mounted by the United States and European countries, although even here major gaps existed. In every other case, little or no effort was made to monitor compliance and prevent violations. The problem of poor implementation exists both at the level of the Security Council and UN Secretariat and in the lack of legal authority and administrative systems among member states.

The Secretariat has very little staff capacity to monitor and enforce sanctions. Fewer than a dozen professionals currently work on sanctions policy in the Department of Political Affairs, not counting the staff of the Iraq oil for food program. By contrast, the U.S. Treasury's Office of Foreign Assets Control, the principal U.S. agency responsible for sanctions implementation, has a staff of some fifty investigators and enforcement specialists. The minuscule UN sanctions staff cannot possibly cope with the tasks at hand. There is no capability for planning and analysis to match sanctions options with policy objectives, a lack of basic information on compliance in the field, and little understanding of the actual humanitarian and policy impacts of sanctions.[39] These staff inadequacies have become "glaringly apparent" within the United Nations and among member governments and have prompted growing calls for an upgrading of the UN's technical and administrative capabilities for sanctions implementation.[40]

Security Council support is growing for an institutional strengthening of sanctions-monitoring capacity. The envisioned changes may not be the full-blown "mechanism" that Boutros-Ghali recommended in 1995, but they would definitely increase the UN's staff and resource commitment to sanctions implementation.[41] The report of the December 1998 sanctions symposium attended by UN officials recommended "a credible monitoring capacity . . . within the UN Secretariat both to assess sanctions impacts and report on implementation efforts by member states and regional organizations." The report urged "greater technical expertise within the UN Secretariat, especially on administrative and legal matters" and called for establishing this institutional capacity in cooperation with regional organizations, UN agencies, and other organizations.[42] Strengthening institutional arrangements through the UN and regional organizations would significantly enhance the implementation of sanctions. As Lisa Martin and other researchers have demonstrated, international institutions foster cooperation among member states and help to maintain cohesion and commitment among political coalitions, which are otherwise subjected to centrifugal tendencies.[43]

To meet these needs and manage the tasks necessary for more effective sanctions management, the United Nations should establish a new Office of Sanctions Affairs within the Secretariat. This would elevate the political importance of sanctions management within the UN system. It would create a focal point for coordinating the work of the sanctions committees, managing preassessment and Article 50 concerns, and ensuring more concerted monitoring and enforcement efforts. Creating this office would not mean establishing a large new bureaucracy within the UN. Function would be more important than form in the proposed office. Some enlargement and upgrading of staff capacity would be necessary, but much of the needed enhancement of capacity could be achieved through partnerships with other agencies and the use of outside experts. The necessary changes could be realized through a modest strengthening of the technical capacity of the existing Secretariat, combined with the strategic use of expert panels, special representatives, and investigative commissions. Already the Security Council is using such methods, establishing expert panels for the Iraq and Angola sanctions committees and creating the UN Commission of Inquiry to investigate violations of the arms embargo against Rwanda. As noted, special visits to affected areas by sanctions committee chairs can also jump-start diplomatic and information-gathering efforts. The use of such "virtual capability" would allow for the creation of a new administrative unit without the burden of a large staff bureaucracy.

Whenever the Security Council imposes sanctions and creates a new sanctions committee, it should be required to adopt a budget for the administration of these measures. Budgets are developed for humanitarian operations and peacekeeping missions, and the same should be required for sanctions cases. A budgeting exercise would focus greater attention on the steps necessary for effective implementation of sanctions and lend a greater sense of realism to the imposition of sanctions, thereby helping to impress targeted authorities with the seriousness of the UN effort. A budget approval process and the accompanying appeal for contributions would also vest member states more thoroughly in the sanctions undertaking.

As the Secretariat enhances its sanctions administration capacity, special attention must be given to better and more reliable data collection. Specific forms of expertise are necessary for different types of sanctions. In the cases of Angola and Sierra Leone, for example, information on the diamond trade was necessary, whereas in Iraq the focus was on the international petroleum industry. The investigation of sanctions violations would be aided by the creation of a permanent registry of sanctions violations, which was recommended in the area of arms embargoes and could be applied to all sanctions. Such a database would allow investigators from the United Nations and member states to check reports of violations and develop enforcement strategies.

Developing and Implementing "Smarter" Sanctions

The reforms and institutional arrangements proposed here address some of the glaring inadequacies that became manifest in the 1990s. But, as we have noted throughout this book, the UN sanctions environment was hardly static during the 1990s. The evolution of sanctions shifted away from the imposition of general trade sanctions toward the use of sanctions instruments that target elites and operate in particular sectors of the political economy. This trend away from comprehensive sanctions toward smarter targeted measures gives greater urgency to specialized reforms that can enhance the effectiveness of financial sanctions, arms embargoes, and aviation and travel bans. Although many of the general improvements recommended earlier—better design, clearer Security Council resolutions, a stronger UN Secretariat, and enhanced legal and administrative capacity among member states—apply as much to targeted measures as to general trade sanctions, specific policy changes are needed in each of the categories of targeted sanctions.

Strategic Design

At the heart of the smart sanctions strategy lies the assumption that sanctions should be used not as blunt instruments for punishing an entire society, but as more refined instruments for exerting pressure on specific decisionmaking groups. Targeted sanctions have also been referred to as "designer sanctions." They seek to direct coercive pressure against designated individuals and groups, and they apply restrictions on very specific goods and commodities. The use of targeted or smart sanctions depends on a careful strategic analysis of the targeted society. This analysis seeks to identify the assets and resources that are most valuable to the specific groups and individuals responsible for objectionable policies. Sanctions are then designed in such a way as to deny these individuals and groups access to their most treasured assets and resources. Strategic analysis also identifies any reform groups or opposition constituencies that may exist within the targeted society and crafts sanctions so that they do not adversely affect these constituencies and, if possible, provide support for them.[44] Thus smart sanctions are designed to maximize internal opposition effects while minimizing the prospect of a rally 'round the flag effect.

Improving Targeted Financial Sanctions

Financial sanctions are the centerpiece of a targeted sanctions strategy. A great deal of attention has focused recently on ways to enhance international cooperation in the enforcement of Security Council financial sanctions.[45] One of the conclusions of the Interlaken process is that significant lessons can be learned from international efforts to control drug-money laundering. Much progress has been achieved in recent years in the struggle against the financing of illegal drug transactions. The menace of corruption and criminality from money laundering has been acknowledged internationally as a major threat to financial integrity and social stability, as codified in the 1988 UN Convention Against Illicit Traffic in Narcotic Drugs and Psychotropic Substances, Vienna Convention. The leaders of the industrial nations created a Financial Action Task Force at their Group of 7 summit in 1989 to coordinate international efforts against money laundering. The task force meets regularly under the auspices of the OECD and recently issued forty recommendations for enhancing international cooperation to prevent illegal financial transactions. These efforts received priority attention at the 1998 Group of 8 summit in Birmingham, England. The participants at the Interlaken seminars agreed that many of the laws and technologies used in the battle against money laundering can be applied to the implementation of financial sanctions.

The United States has provided leadership for these international efforts through its Financial Crimes Enforcement Center (FINCEN), which has helped to create financial intelligence units in dozens of countries and provided technical assistance to help nations strengthen anti–money laundering laws and institutions.[46] More than forty financial intelligence units now exist, and these have formed their own association, the Egmont Group, to share intelligence data and facilitate rapid international response to financial crimes. This increasing international cooperation against financial crimes should be harnessed to ensure similar cooperation in the enforcement of targeted financial sanctions.

The success of financial sanctions hinges on the ability to identify and target specific individuals and entities whose assets are to be frozen. Partly this is a technical and administrative challenge. The speed with which financial assets can be transferred, the growth of cybercurrency, and the presence of offshore financial centers pose major, although not insurmountable problems. Improved international enforcement efforts and private sector cooperation, especially by U.S. financial institutions, have helped to address the challenge of tracking financial transfers. Continuing efforts to improve legal and administrative systems, both internationally and among member states, can limit the ability of targeted individuals and entities to avoid financial sanctions.

The greater problem for the Security Council is the reluctance of member states to approve a mandatory system for targeting the assets of designated individuals and companies. Only in the case of Haiti did the Security Council issue a list of individuals whose assets were to be frozen, but even that was on a recommended rather than required basis. Major political and jurisdictional questions have been raised about the UN's ability to target specific individuals and entities. The Security Council's legal authority to seize property and block financial transactions is uncertain, although the Haiti precedent suggests that this authority may fall within the Council's obligations under Chapter VII of the UN Charter. The Council has not been reluctant to target specific individuals and entities for travel bans and aviation sanctions. This same authority must be applied to the implementation of targeted financial sanctions if the promise of these measures is to be realized.

Toward More Effective Arms Embargoes

Arms embargoes hold promise as potentially effective forms of targeted sanctions. They are intended to deny wrongdoers the resources needed for repression and military aggression. They apply pressure only on ruling elites and arms traffickers and avoid harm to vulnerable populations. Although arms embargoes are frequently imposed, they are seldom enforced. Arms embargoes were included in nearly all of the Security Council sanctions imposed during the 1990s, but in most cases they failed completely. Only in the case of Iraq were sanctions against weapons enforced vigorously. Otherwise, as the case studies amply illustrate, the implementation of arms embargoes was woefully inadequate. In some cases, such as Somalia and Yugoslavia, the targeted country was already overflowing with arms, which meant that the practical effect of an arms embargo was nil. In nearly every case the effectiveness of arms embargoes was impeded by the economic self-interest of arms traffickers, the complicity in the arms trade of ruling elites and neighboring governments, and the major legal and institutional weaknesses that exist at the United Nations and among many member states.

Nowhere is the need for reform and a strengthening of enforcement greater than in the area of arms embargoes. The Security Council has imposed arms embargoes more frequently than any other measure over the past decade, but in most cases the results of these actions have been meager to nonexistent. As our case studies demonstrate, member states have blatantly disregarded Security Council arms embargoes, and the UN has been powerless to stem the tide of weapons inundating zones of conflict, especially in Africa. The problem is so serious that the Security Council adopted a special resolution in 1998 recommending a series of steps for improving the effectiveness of arms embargoes. Many of the recommendations of Resolution 1196 fall within the framework of the general reforms identified earlier, including a strengthening of technical capacity within the Security Council and the UN Secretariat and an improvement in the ability of member states to monitor and enforce sanctions. As noted above, one of the most important recommendations in the Secretary-General's 1998 Africa report was that member states should make violations of UN arms embargoes a criminal offense in their domestic laws. This is an absolutely essential precondition for making arms embargoes effective and enabling nations to prosecute embargo violations.

Another valuable recommendation in Security Council Resolution 1196 is for greater use of special investigative commissions to uncover and report on violations of arms embargoes. The Security Council specifically acknowledged the innovative role of the UN International Commission of Inquiry (UNICOI) in Rwanda, which was created in September 1995 to investigate violations of the arms embargo on the Hutu rebels responsible for the Rwandan genocide. As noted in the Rwanda case study, UNICOI produced several useful reports documenting embargo violations and recommending improved enforcement.[47] After completing its initial mandate in October 1996, UNICOI remained dormant until April 1998, when it was revived by the Security Council to investigate and make recommendations on ways to halt the renewed flow of money and arms to former Rwandan armed forces and militia in central Africa.[48] Although UNICOI lacked resources, staffing, and adequate judicial authority, its work was a "useful means for strengthening the effectiveness" of arms embargoes[49] and marked an important advance in focusing attention on the enforcement of arms embargoes.[50] The United Nations should consider creating similar investigative commissions and providing them with greater institutional capacity and legal authority to investigate violations of other arms embargoes.

The recommendation offered earlier for greater clarity and specificity in Security Council resolutions becomes particularly important with regard to arms embargoes. Too often Council resolutions call for an embargo on arms but never identify exactly what weapons and military services are prohibited. This leaves giant loopholes for arms traffickers to exploit. To prevent such violations, Security Council resolutions should specifically prohibit military assistance and military contract services and identify dual-use items to be banned. A specific registry of dual-use goods should be published for each case of arms embargoes, which could be derived from existing databases that have been developed as part of the Wassenaar Arrangement controlling conventional arms proliferation.[51]

Efforts to strengthen the UN's capacity to monitor and enforce arms embargoes must be integrated with parallel efforts to control and limit trafficking in conventional weapons and small arms. Greater international participation in the UN Register of Conventional Arms would facilitate the process of monitoring arms embargoes. In addition, a number of UN and nongovernmental experts have called for an international agreement to ban the deadly commerce in weapons. The UN Panel of Governmental Experts on Small Arms and the UN Economic and Social Council Commission on Crime Prevention and Criminal Justice have urged member states to negotiate a convention on the prevention of arms trafficking. The development of such a convention would go hand in hand with the strengthening of UN arms embargoes and would establish a solid foundation in international law for reducing the flow of prohibited arms into conflict zones.

Improving Travel and Aviation Sanctions

The Security Council has imposed two types of travel bans: restrictions on the travel of targeted individuals and restrictions on air travel to and from a targeted state. Travel sanctions are attractive because they focus pressure on specific decisionmaking elites or particular aviation companies while minimizing adverse humanitarian impacts on vulnerable populations. Although travel sanctions have limited economic impact on the target regime, they can be a potent psychological tool for isolating and denying legitimacy to targeted individuals or groups. Even as it seeks to impose the strictest possible ban on the mobility of targeted leaders, the Security Council must allow exemptions for particular purposes, especially for humanitarian deliveries and emergency medical evacuations. In addition, specific exemptions should be provided for targeted leaders to participate in negotiations for the settlement of conflicts.

The enforcement of travel bans is easier than the enforcement of financial sanctions and arms embargoes, but substantial challenges exist. The names of sanctioned individuals and companies must be transmitted to customs officials in many countries, especially states neighboring the targeted regime. Some less developed countries may not have adequate border-monitoring and enforcement capabilities. In these cases sanctions assistance missions may be necessary. Technical assistance and financial backing should be provided, ideally through regional organizations, to strengthen border controls and aviation-monitoring capabilities.

Many countries face legal uncertainties about their ability to enforce UN travel bans. If the targeted individual has a passport, permanent residency, or citizenship in the country being visited, customs officials may lack legal authority to expel or detain that individual. The United States and some European countries have laws that give officials the authority to override these protections in the case of UN mandatory measures—another example of a category of domestic law within member states in which reform is needed. As proposals are developed for model legislation to assist in the enforcement of financial sanctions, arms embargoes, and other aspects of UN sanctions, attention should also be paid to improving member states' legal and administrative capacity for implementing travel bans.

The effectiveness of travel bans would be greatly enhanced if they included a requirement that member states detain targeted individuals who attempt to travel.[52] Just as individuals indicted in the Rwanda and Yugoslavia tribunals must limit their mobility for fear that they will be detained if they travel abroad, so well-enforced travel bans could be a deterrent against the mobility of targeted individuals. The effectiveness of travel bans would also be increased through the use of secondary sanctions against individuals and companies who travel to meet sanctioned individuals in their countries. In the cases of Angola and Sierra Leone, international diamond traders and oil company executives have traveled to these countries to do business with the targeted leaders, thereby weakening the impact of the Security Council's travel bans. Under current conditions, such travel to meet with sanctioned individuals is not prohibited. Extending travel bans to include penalties against corporations and individuals that do business with targeted wrongdoers would help the Security Council achieve its objectives. Banning contact and trade with sanctioned leaders would also prevent the further looting of the target country's resources for private gain. This extension of the travel ban concept would in effect impose full trade sanctions, but these would be narrowly directed against specific individuals and companies rather than an entire nation.

Whether financial sanctions, arms embargoes, and aviation and travel bans will replace comprehensive sanctions remains to be seen. Many questions and uncertainties persist about the effectiveness of these measures. Skeptics doubt whether such mild forms of pressure as sanctioning a national airline are sufficiently forceful to change the decisionmaking calculus of political leaders. Freezing financial assets or denying weapons and related technology are potentially stronger measures, but their enforcement poses major challenges. Many doubt whether the reforms necessary to make financial sanctions and arms embargoes effective will be applied broadly enough to constrain the lucrative worlds of money laundering and arms trafficking. Targeted sanctions are no panacea, but they are far less costly in human terms and have much greater political viability and moral legitimacy than general sanctions. The trend toward smart sanctions in UN policymaking is unmistakable. Whether these measures succeed depends on the soundness of the overall policy of which they are part and on how well they are integrated into a carrot-and-stick diplomacy designed to achieve a negotiated resolution of conflict.

Conclusion: Toward a New Era of Economic Statecraft

The myriad changes and proposals recommended here would significantly advance the art of economic statecraft and create new opportunities for the effective use of economic sanctions and incentives. To reach their full potential, sanctions must be developed, implemented, and monitored with two key policy considerations in mind. First, accompanying the use of smart sanctions should be a parallel set of strategically targeted incentives. A wide range of incentive tools is available from member states and international organizations, including foreign assistance; concessionary loans and credits; debt relief; technology transfers; trade benefits; security assurances; and the provision of specific goods, such as broadcast equipment and newsprint, that directly benefit opposition groups. Rewards and benefits should be directed to the groups most likely to support reform policies. This means avoiding incentives that benefit oppressive elites, such as providing military assistance to an authoritarian regime that is responsible for gross violations of human rights. Misdirected incentives may be counterproductive politically, strengthening the very forces of repression that are often responsible for conflict while weakening the status of reform constituencies. Incentives should be designed instead to empower reform constituencies while undermining the power and stature of decisionmaking groups.

Second, sanctions policies must be guided by a widely accepted code of conduct and basic international legal principles. At present, sanctions have little or only controversial standing in international law. They fall into a gray area between humanitarian law and the rules of warfare. Because of the minimal use of multilateral sanctions prior to the last decade, legal standards and guarantees for the practice of economic statecraft have not been elaborated. Many of the dilemmas associated with the use of sanctions could be addressed through the codification of legal standards. As Roger Normand argued:

> The imposition of sanctions by the Security Council, as well as by individual states, needs to be governed by an explicit legal regime, drafted by a panel of international experts and informed by both human rights and humanitarian law principles. Under this regime, future cases of sanctions could be assessed according to universal criteria, in contrast to the current situation in which sanctions increasingly are imposed without reference to any legal or ethical standard.[53]

Normand's proposals for more formalized legal standards in the conduct of sanctions merit support. The policy guidelines that could serve as the foundation for these legal standards have been discussed here and are articulated in the major UN sanctions reform documents of recent years, including the 1998 issue paper of the chairs of sanctions committees and the 1997 General Assembly resolution on *An Agenda for Peace* and the question of UN sanctions. The principles for developing more authoritative and humane sanctions are increasingly well understood. The challenge now is to translate these principles into legal standards and operational capability.

The road to creating more effective and humane sanctions is a long one, but the journey has begun, and the lessons from the UN experiences over the past decade can shed important light on the way forward. If the necessary changes are made, sanctions can serve as an effective policy tool for UN peacekeeping and peace enforcement in the next decade and beyond. The following pages present a summary of the policy recommendations identified in this chapter.

Summary of Policy Recommendations

Policy Framework

- Apply sanctions flexibly within the framework of a carrot-and-stick diplomacy designed to resolve conflict.
- Target pressures against decisionmaking elites responsible for wrongdoing; avoid measures that cause unintended humanitarian hardships.
- Design sanctions that deny assets and resources of value to decisionmaking elites; avoid measures that adversely affect reform groups or opposition constituencies within the targeted society.

Humanitarian Consequences

- Conduct humanitarian assessment reports in the early stages of sanctions, using the multistep methodology and humanitarian indicators developed for the UN Office for the Coordination of Humanitarian Affairs.
- Streamline humanitarian exemption applications. Adopt country-specific and institution-specific procedures that grant blanket exemptions to trusted UN humanitarian agencies in specific cases.

Third Party Impacts

- Conduct third party assessment studies in the early stages of sanctions.
- Specify the availability of Article 50 procedures in the Security Council resolutions imposing sanctions.
- Develop standardized reporting procedures for member states seeking assistance under Article 50.
- Arrange special compensatory measures and convene donor conferences to address the needs of particular member states adversely affected by Security Council sanctions.

Security Council Policymaking

- Employ more precise technical terms and definitions in Security Council resolutions imposing sanctions.
- Identify the specific policy changes a targeted regime must undertake in order for sanctions to be lifted. Indicate benchmarks for compliance and link these to reciprocal steps to ease sanctions.

Member State Cooperation

- Assist member states in developing legal authority and administrative capacity for the administration and enforcement of Security Council resolutions.

The Sanctions Committees

- Enhance the transparency of the work of the Security Council and its sanctions committees. Improve communications with member states, other agencies, and the international community in general.
- Encourage the chairs of sanctions committees to visit regions affected by sanctions, for the purpose of gathering information on implementation and encouraging member state compliance with Security Council resolutions.

The UN Secretariat

- Establish a new Office of Sanctions Affairs within the Secretariat. Enhance the technical expertise and staff capacity of the Secretariat to administer UN sanctions. Develop a "virtual capability" for more effective sanctions implementation through the use of expert panels, special representatives, and investigative commissions.

- Develop and approve a budget and financing plan for the administration of each new sanctions episode.

Financial Sanctions

- Implement the recommendations of the Financial Action Task Force of the OECD for enhancing international cooperation to prevent illegal financial transactions.
- Freeze the financial assets not only of government entities but of targeted decisionmaking elites and their supporters.
- Employ standardized terms in Security Council resolutions that conform with definitions used in the financial sector.

Arms Embargoes

- Encourage and help member states to pass laws criminalizing violations of UN arms embargoes.
- Prohibit military contract services, military training, and a specific list of dual-use items in resolutions imposing arms embargoes.
- Create additional investigative commissions such as UNICOI to investigate and publicize violations of UN arms embargoes.
- Support recommendations for a UN convention on the prevention of illicit arms trafficking.

Travel Bans

- Provide assistance to member states and regional organizations in customs assistance and border monitoring.

Notes

1. Kofi Annan, *The Causes of Conflict and the Promotion of Durable Peace and Sustainable Development in Africa, Secretary-General's Report to the United Nations Security Council* (New York: United Nations, 16 April 1998); United Nations General Assembly, *Annual Report of the Secretary-General on the Work of the Organization*, A/53/1, 16 April 1998; Boutros Boutros-Ghali, *An Agenda for*

Peace 1995 (New York: United Nations, 1995); Boutros Boutros-Ghali, *Supplement to An Agenda for Peace: Position Paper of the Secretary-General on the Occasion of the 50th Anniversary of the United Nations,* A/50/60 (New York: United Nations, 3 January 1995).

2. United Nations Security Council, Chairs of the Sanctions Committees, *Issue Paper Concerning the Sanctions Imposed by the Security Council,* 30 October 1998; see also United Nations Security Council, *Note by the President of the Security Council,* S/1999/92, 29 January 1999.

3. United Nations General Assembly, *Implementation of the Provisions of the Charter of the United Nations Related to Assistance to Third States Affected by the Application of Sanctions Under Chapter VII of the Charter, Report of the Secretary-General,* A/50/361, 1995; United Nations General Assembly, *Report of the Special Committee on the Charter of the United Nations and on the Strengthening of the Role of the Organization,* Supplement no. 33, A/53/33, 1998.

4. United Nations Security Council, *Letter Dated 13 April 1995, Addressed to the President of the Security Council,* S/1995/200, annex, 13 April 1995.

5. United Nations Security Council, *Letter Dated 24 September 1996 from the Chairman of the Security Council Committee Established Pursuant to Resolution 724 (1991) Concerning Yugoslavia Addressed to the President of the Security Council, Report of the Copenhagen Roundtable on United Nations Sanctions in the Case of the Former Yugoslavia, Held at Copenhagen on 24 and 25 June 1996,* S/1996/776, 24 September 1996.

6. John Stremlau, "Sharpening International Sanctions: Toward a Stronger Role for the United Nations," a report to the Carnegie Commission on Preventing Deadly Conflict (New York: Carnegie Corporation of New York, November 1996); Gary C. Hufbauer, Jeffrey J. Schott, and Kimberly Ann Elliott, *Economic Sanctions Reconsidered: History and Current Policy,* 2d ed. (Washington, D.C.: Institute for International Economics, 1990); and Lisa L. Martin and Jeffrey Laurenti, "The United Nations and Economic Sanctions: Improving Regime Effectiveness," a paper of the United Nations Association–USA International Dialogue on the Enforcement of Security Council Resolutions, New York, August 1997.

7. *Towards Smarter, More Effective United Nations Sanctions,* report of a Symposium on Security Council Sanctions, New York, 7 December 1998, Fourth Freedom Forum, Goshen, Indiana.

8. See Larry Minear, David Cortright, Julia Wagler, George A. Lopez, and Thomas G. Weiss, *Toward More Humane and Effective Sanctions Management: Enhancing the Capacity of the United Nations System,* Occasional Paper no. 31 (Providence, R.I.: Thomas J. Watson Jr. Institute for International Studies, 1998); and Thomas G. Weiss, David Cortright, George A. Lopez, and Larry Minear, eds., *Political Gain and Civilian Pain: Humanitarian Impacts of Economic Sanctions* (Lanham, Md.: Rowman and Littlefield, 1997).

9. Annan, *The Causes of Conflict,* par. 25.

10. United Nations Security Council, Chairs of the Sanctions Committees, *Issue Paper,* par. 12.

11. Ibid., par. 11.

12. Larry Minear et al., *Toward More Humane and Effective Sanctions Management.*

13. Claudia von Braunmühl and Manfred Kulessa, *The Impact of UN Sanctions on Humanitarian Assistance Activities: Report on a Study Commissioned by the United Nations Department of Humanitarian Affairs* (Berlin: Gesellschaft für

Communication Management Interkultur Training, December 1995); and Larry Minear et al., *Toward More Humane and Effective Sanctions Management.*

14. A detailed description of this methodology is available in Minear et al., *Toward More Humane and Effective Sanctions Management,* 23–54.

15. The reports in question are United Nations, Department of Humanitarian Affairs, *Note from the Department of Humanitarian Affairs Concerning the Possible Humanitarian Impact of the International Flight Ban Decided in Security Council Resolution 1070 (1996),* 18 February 1997; and United Nations, Office for the Coordination of Humanitarian Affairs, *Interagency Assessment Mission to Sierra Leone: Interim Report,* 17 February 1998.

16. Stephen Marks has emphasized the role of independent teams of health and human rights specialists in investigating humanitarian impacts. See Stephen P. Marks, "Economic Sanctions as Human Rights Violations: Reconciling Political and Public Health Imperatives," *American Journal of Public Health* 89, no. 10 (October 1999): 1512.

17. Weiss et al., *Political Gain and Civilian Pain,* especially chaps. 1 and 7; and Minear et al., *Toward More Humane and Effective Sanctions Management,* chap. 3.

18. See, for example, Paul Conlon, "The UN's Questionable Sanctions Practice," *Aussenpolitik* 46, no. 4 (1995): 327–338; an assessment of the limitations of exemptions procedures is also contained in von Braunmühl and Kulessa, *The Impact of UN Sanctions.*

19. United Nations Security Council, *Note by the President of the Security Council,* S/1995/234, 29 March 1995.

20. Working paper submitted by the Russian Federation, document A/AC.182/L.94, 27 January 1997, par. 9.

21. United Nations Security Council, *Letter Dated 15 November 1996 from the Chairman of the Security Council Committee Established Pursuant to Resolution 724 (1991) Concerning Yugoslavia Addressed to the President of the Security Council,* S/1996/946, 15 November 1996, pars. 11, 12.

22. The review was conducted in August 1992 by former Secretariat official Paul Conlon and is referenced in his article, "Mitigation of UN Sanctions," *German Yearbook of International Law* 39 (1996): 262 ff.

23. Boutros-Ghali, *Supplement to An Agenda for Peace,* par. 73.

24. Ibid., par. 75e.

25. We are indebted for many of these suggestions to Margaret Doxey, "United Nations Economic Sanctions: Minimizing Adverse Effects on Non-Target States," paper prepared for the Symposium on Targeted Sanctions, New York, 7 December 1998.

26. Natalie Reid, Sue E. Eckert, Jarat Chopra, and Thomas J. Biersteker, "Targeted Financial Sanctions: Harmonizing National Legislation and Regulatory Practices," a research project on Targeted Financial Sanctions, Thomas J. Watson Institute for International Studies, Brown University, Providence, Rhode Island, December 1998.

27. Rolf Jeker, *Chairman's Report: 2nd Interlaken Seminar on Targeting United Nations Financial Sanctions, 29–31 March, 1999,* Swiss Federal Office for Foreign Economic Affairs in Cooperation with the United Nations Secretariat, 7.

28. Boutros-Ghali, *Supplement to An Agenda for Peace,* par. 68.

29. Richard N. Haass, "Sanctioning Madness," *Foreign Affairs* 76, no. 6 (November–December 1997): 74–85.

30. Annan, *The Causes of Conflict,* par. 26.

31. Conlon, "UN's Questionable Sanctions Practice," and Conlon, "Mitigation of UN Sanctions."

32. United Nations Security Council. *Note by the President of the Security Council,* S/1999/92, 29 January 1999.

33. United Nations Security Council, Chairs of the Sanctions Committees, *Issue Paper,* par. 2.

34. Ibid., par. 9.

35. Ibid., par. 7; United Nations Security Council, *Note by the President of the Security Council,* S/1999/92, par. 2.

36. The report of Fowler's mission is available from the United Nations Security Council as *Letter from the Chairman of the Security Council Concerning the Situation in Angola,* S/1999/644, 4 June 1999.

37. Ibid., par. 2.

38. Ibid., par. 7.

39. Martin and Laurenti, "United Nations and Economic Sanctions," 10–11.

40. Stremlau, "Sharpening International Sanctions," 48.

41. Boutros-Ghali, *Supplement to an Agenda for Peace,* pars. 66–76. Scholars have also proposed the creation of a new UN sanctions agency; see Donald G. Boudreau, "On Creating a United Nations Sanctions Agency," *International Peacekeeping* 4, no. 2 (Summer 1997): 115–137; and Lloyd (Jeff) Dumas, "A Proposal for a New Economic United Nations Council on Economic Sanctions," in David Cortright and George A. Lopez, eds., *Economic Sanctions; Panacea or Peacebuilding in a Post–Cold War World* (Boulder, Colo.: Westview Press, 1995), 187–200.

42. *Towards Smarter, More Effective United Nations Sanctions.*

43. See Lisa L. Martin, *Coercive Cooperation: Explaining Multilateral Economic Sanctions* (Princeton, N.J.: Princeton University Press, 1992).

44. This discussion of strategic design draws heavily from Elizabeth Gibbons, *Sanctions in Haiti: Human Rights and Democracy Under Assault,* Center for Strategic and International Studies, Washington Papers 177 (Westport, Conn.: Praeger, 1999), 100–110.

45. The IIE study defines financial sanctions to include the suspension of foreign assistance and concessionary loans and grants, but these measures can have economic and social impacts equivalent to those caused by general trade sanctions. Measures that halt the funding of investment and trade are practically indistinguishable in their social impact from broader trade sanctions. Because such measures can have serious humanitarian consequences across an entire society, they do not properly fall within the rubric of targeted or smart sanctions.

46. United States, General Accounting Office, *Money Laundering: FINCEN's Law Enforcement Support, Regulatory, and International Roles,* T-GGD-98-83 (Washington, D.C.: GAO, 1 April 1998).

47. The third report is available as United Nations Security Council, *Letter Dated 1 November 1996 from the Secretary-General Addressed to the President of the Security Council,* S/1997/1010, 24 December 1997.

48. The report of the 1998 investigation is available in *Letter Dated 18 November 1998 from the Secretary-General Addressed to the President of the Security Council,* S/1998/1096, 18 November 1998.

49. *United Nations Security Council Resolution 1196,* S/RES/1196, 16 September 1998.

50. We are indebted for this analysis to Loretta Bondi, "Arms Embargoes," paper delivered at the Symposium on Targeted Sanctions, New York, 7 December 1998.

51. Ibid., 7.

52. We are indebted for these suggestions on travel ban enforcement to Richard W. Conroy, "UN Travel Sanctions: An Evaluation with Policy Recommendations," paper presented at the Symposium on Targeted UN Sanctions, New York, 7 December 1998.

53. Roger Normand, "Iraqi Sanctions, Human Rights, and Humanitarian Law," *Middle East Report* (July–September 1996): 43.

Bibliography

Adeleke, Ademola. "The Politics and Diplomacy of Peacekeeping in West Africa: The ECOWAS Operation in Liberia." *Journal of Modern African Studies* 33 (1995).

American Friends Service Committee, Working Group on International Economic Sanctions. *Dollars or Bombs: The Search for Justice Through International Economic Sanctions.* Philadelphia: American Friends Service Committee, 1993.

Amini, Gitty M. "A Larger Role for Positive Sanctions in Cases of Compellence?" Working Paper no. 12, Center for International Relations, University of California at Los Angeles, May 1997.

Annan, Kofi. *The Causes of Conflict and the Promotion of Durable Peace and Sustainable Development in Africa, Secretary-General's Report to the United Nations Security Council.* New York: United Nations, 16 April 1998.

Augelli, Enrico, and Craig Murphy. "Lessons of Somalia for Future Multilateral Humanitarian Assistance Operations." *Global Governance* 1 (September–December 1995).

Axelrod, Robert. *The Evolution of Cooperation.* New York: Basic Books, 1984.

Baldwin, David A. *Economic Statecraft.* Princeton, N.J.: Princeton University Press, 1985.

———. "The Power of Positive Sanctions." *World Politics* 24, no. 1 (October 1971).

Boudreau, Donald G. "On Creating a United Nations Sanctions Agency." *International Peacekeeping* 4, no. 2 (Summer 1997): 115–137.

Boutros-Ghali, Boutros. *An Agenda for Peace 1995.* New York: United Nations, 1995.

———. *Supplement to an Agenda for Peace: Position Paper of the Secretary-General on the Occasion of the 50th Anniversary of the United Nations.* A/50/60. New York: United Nations, 3 January 1995.

Boutwell, Jeffrey, and Michael T. Klare. *Lethal Commerce: The Global Trade in Small Arms and Light Weapons.* Cambridge, Mass.: American Academy of Arts and Sciences, 1995.

British Foreign Office. "Foreign Office Paper on Iraqi Threat and Work of UNSCOM." London, 4 February 1998.

Clawson, Patrick. "Sanctions as Punishment, Enforcement, and Prelude to Further Action." *Ethics and International Affairs* 7 (1993).

Conlon, Paul. "Mitigation of UN Sanctions." *German Yearbook of International Law* 39 (1996).

————. "The UN's Questionable Sanctions Practice." *Aussenpolitik* 46, no. 4 (1995).

Cordesman, Anthony H. "The Iraq Crisis: Background Data." Washington, D.C.: Center for Strategic and International Studies, 1998.

Cortright, David, and George A. Lopez. "Are Sanctions Just? The Problematic Case of Iraq." *Journal of International Affairs* 52, no. 2 (Spring 1999).

————. "Trouble in the Gulf, Pain and Promise." *The Bulletin of the Atomic Scientists* 54, no. 3 (May–June 1998).

Cortright, David, and George A. Lopez, eds. *Economic Sanctions: Panacea or Peacebuilding in a Post–Cold War World.* Boulder, Colo.: Westview Press, 1995.

Crawford, Neta C., and Audie Klotz, eds. *How Sanctions Work: Lessons from South Africa.* New York: St. Martin's Press, 1999.

Damrosch, Lori Fisler, ed. *Enforcing Restraint: Collective Intervention in Internal Conflicts.* New York: Council on Foreign Relations, 1993.

Delevic, Milica. "Economic Sanctions as a Foreign Policy Tool: The Case of Yugoslavia." *International Journal of Peace Studies* 3, no. 1 (January 1998).

Dolley, Steven. "Iraq and the Bomb: The Nuclear Threat Continues." Washington, D.C.: Nuclear Control Institute, 19 February 1998.

Dowty, Alan. "Sanctioning Iraq: The Limits of the New World Order." *Washington Quarterly* 17, no. 3 (Summer 1994).

Doxey, Margaret P. *International Sanctions in Contemporary Perspective.* 2d ed. New York: St. Martin's Press, 1996.

Durch, William J., ed. *The Evolution of UN Peacekeeping: Case Studies and Comparisons.* New York: St. Martin's Press, 1993.

Elliott, Kimberly Ann, and Gary Clyde Hufbauer. "Ineffectiveness of Economic Sanctions: Same Song, Same Refrain? Economic Sanctions in the 1990s." Papers and proceedings of the 111th Annual Meeting of the American Economic Association, 3–5 January 1999. *American Economic Review* (May 1999).

Ellis, Stephen. "Liberia 1989–1994: A Study of Ethnic and Spiritual Violence." *African Affairs* (April 1995).

Evans, Gareth. *Cooperating for Peace.* Sydney: Allen and Unwin, 1993.

Feil, Scott R. "Preventing Genocide: How the Early Use of Force Might Have Succeeded in Rwanda." A report to the Carnegie Commission on Preventing Deadly Conflict. Carnegie Corporation of New York, April 1998.

Food and Agricultural Organization. *Evaluation of Food and Nutrition Situation in Iraq.* Rome: FAO, 1995.

Garfield, Richard. *Morbidity and Mortality Among Iraqi Children from 1990 to 1998: Assessing the Impact of Economic Sanctions.* Occasional Paper Series 16:OP:3. Paper commissioned by the Joan B. Kroc Institute for International Peace Studies at the University of Notre Dame and the Fourth Freedom Forum, March 1999.

Gibbons, Elizabeth. *Sanctions in Haiti: Human Rights and Democracy Under Assault.* Center for Strategic and International Studies, Washington Papers 177. Westport, Conn.: Praeger, 1999.

Global Witness. *A Rough Trade: The Role of Companies and Government in the Angolan Conflict.* London: Global Witness, December 1998.

Gordon, Joy. "A Peaceful, Silent, Deadly Remedy: The Ethics of Economic Sanctions." *Ethics and International Affairs* 13 (1999).

Gourevitch, Philip. "The Genocide Fax." *New Yorker* 74 (11 May 1998).

————. *We Wish to Inform You That Tomorrow We Will Be Killed with Our Families: Stories from Rwanda.* New York: Farrar, Straus, and Giroux, 1998.

Gurney, Judith. *Libya: The Political Economy of Oil.* Oxford: Oxford University Press for the Oxford Institute for Energy Studies, 1996.

Haass, Richard N. "Sanctioning Madness." *Foreign Affairs* 76, no. 6 (November–December 1997).

Harvard University School of Public Health. *Sanctions in Haiti: Crisis in Humanitarian Action.* Program on Human Security, Working Papers Series. Cambridge, Mass.: Harvard University Center for Population and Development Studies, November 1993.

Holbrooke, Richard. *To End a War.* New York: Random House, 1998.

Hufbauer, Gary C., Jeffrey J. Schott, and Kimberly Ann Elliott. *Economic Sanctions Reconsidered: History and Current Policy.* 2d ed. Washington, D.C.: Institute for International Economics, 1990.

Human Rights Watch. *Angola Unravels: The Rise and Fall of the Lusaka Peace Process.* New York: Human Rights Watch, September 1999.

————. *Arms Trade and Violations of Laws of War Since the 1992 Elections.* Washington, D.C.: Human Rights Watch, November 1994.

————. *Between War and Peace: Arms Trade and Human Rights Abuses Since the Lusaka Protocol.* Washington, D.C.: Human Rights Watch, February 1996.

————. *Getting Away with Murder, Mutilation and Rape: New Testimony from Sierra Leone.* New York: Human Rights Watch, June 1999.

Institute for International Strategic Studies. *The Military Balance 1997–1998.* London: Oxford Press, 1997.

International Atomic Energy Agency. *Fifth Consolidated Report of the Director General of the International Atomic Energy Agency Under Paragraph Sixteen of Security Council Resolution 1051 (1996).* S/19989/312. United Nations, New York.

Jeker, Rolf. *Chairman's Report: 2nd Interlaken Seminar on Targeting United Nations Financial Sanctions, 29–31 March 1999.* Swiss Federal Office for Foreign Economic Affairs in Cooperation with the United Nations Secretariat.

Kaempfer, William, and Anton Lowenberg. "Unilateral Versus Multilateral International Sanctions: A Public Choice Perspective." *International Studies Quarterly* 43, no. 1 (March 1999).

Kuperman, Alan J. "Rwanda in Retrospect." *Foreign Affairs* 79, no. 1 (January–February 2000).

League of Arab States. *Arab Libyan Maternal and Child Health Survey.* 1996.

Lefebvre, Jeffrey A. *Arms for the Horn: U.S. Security Policy in Ethiopia and Somalia, 1953–1991.* Pittsburgh: University of Pittsburgh Press, 1991.

Leurdijk, Dick A. *The United Nations and NATO in Former Yugoslavia, 1991–1996: Limits to Diplomacy and Force.* The Hague: Netherlands Atlantic Commission, 1996.

Lukic, Reneo, and Allen Lynch. *Europe from the Balkans to the Urals: The Disintegration of Yugoslavia and the Soviet Union.* New York: SIPRI, Oxford University Press, 1996.

Luttwak, Edward M. "Toward Post-Heroic Warfare." *Foreign Affairs* 74, no. 3 (May–June 1995).

Maguire, Robert, et al. *Haiti Held Hostage: International Responses to the Quest for Nationhood, 1986 to 1996.* Occasional Paper No. 23. Providence, R.I.: Thomas J. Watson Jr. Institute for International Studies, 1996.

Malone, David. *Decision-Making in the UN Security Council: The Case of Haiti.* Oxford: Oxford University Press, 1998.

Marks, Stephen P. "Economic Sanctions as Human Rights Violations: Reconciling Political and Public Health Imperatives." *American Journal of Public Health* 89, no. 10 (October 1999).

Martin, Ian. "Haiti: Mangled Multilateralism." *Foreign Policy* 95 (Summer 1994).

Martin, Lisa L. *Coercive Cooperation: Explaining Multilateral Economic Sanctions.* Princeton, N.J.: Princeton University Press, 1992.

Martin, Lisa L., and Jeffrey Laurenti. "The United Nations and Economic Sanctions: Improving Regime Effectiveness." A paper of the United Nations Association–USA International Dialogue on the Enforcement of Security Council Resolutions, New York, August 1997.

Minear, Larry, David Cortright, Julia Wagler, George A. Lopez, and Thomas G. Weiss. *Toward More Humane and Effective Sanctions Management: Enhancing the Capacity of the United Nations System.* Occasional Paper No. 31. Providence, R.I.: Thomas J. Watson Jr. Institute for International Studies, 1998.

Natsios, Andrew. "Humanitarian Relief Interventions in Somalia: The Economics of Chaos." *International Peacekeeping* 3 (Spring 1996).

Naylor, R. T. *Patriots and Profiteers: On Economic Warfare, Embargo Busting and State-Sponsored Crime.* Toronto: McClelland and Stewart, 1999.

Nincic, Miroslov, and Peter Wallensteen, eds. *Dilemmas of Economic Coercion: Sanctions and World Politics.* New York: Praeger, 1983.

Normand, Roger. "Iraqi Sanctions, Human Rights, and Humanitarian Law." *Middle East Report* (July–September 1996).

Nossal, Kim Richard. "Liberal Democratic Regimes, International Sanctions and Global Governance." In *Globalization and Global Governance,* ed. Raimo Väyrynen. Lanham, Md.: Rowman and Littlefield, 1999.

Nowrojee, Binaifer. "Joining Forces: UN and Regional Peacekeeping—Lessons from Liberia." *Harvard Human Rights Journal* 8 (Spring 1995).

Organization of African Unity, Assembly of Heads of State and Government. "The Crisis Between the Great Socialist People's Libyan Arab Jamahiriya and the United States of America and the United Kingdom." AHG/DEC.127 XXXIV, 8–10 June 1998.

Owen, David. *Balkan Odyssey.* New York: Harcourt, Brace and Company, 1995.

Pape, Robert A. "Why Economic Sanctions Do Not Work." *International Security* 22, no. 1 (Fall 1997).

Political Risk Services. "Libya." *International Country Risk Guide: Middle East and Africa* (May 1995).

Reno, William. "The Business of War in Liberia." *Current History* 95 (May 1996).

———. "Privatizing War in Sierra Leone." *Current History* 96 (May 1997).

Rose, Gideon. "Libya." In *Economic Sanctions and American Diplomacy,* ed. Richard Haass. New York: Council on Foreign Relations, 1998.

Rowe, David M. "Surviving Economic Coercion: Rhodesia's Responses to International Economic Sanctions." Ph.D. diss., Duke University, 1993.

Saferworld. *Undermining Development: The European Arms Trade with the Horn of Africa and Central Africa.* London: Saferworld, January 1998.

Shawcross, William. *Cambodia's New Deal: A Report.* Washington, D.C.: Carnegie Endowment for International Peace, 1994.

———. *Sideshow: Kissinger, Nixon, and the Destruction of Cambodia.* New York: Simon and Schuster, 1987.

Stremlau, John. "Sharpening International Sanctions: Toward a Stronger Role for the United Nations." A report to the Carnegie Commission on Preventing Deadly Conflict. Carnegie Corporation of New York, November 1996.

Tetlock, Philip E., and Aaron Belkin. *Counterfactual Thought Experiments in World Politics.* Princeton, N.J.: Princeton University Press, 1996.

Twaddell, William. "Bloody Hands: Foreign Support for Liberian Warlords." Testimony in Hearings Before the Subcommittee on Africa of the Committee on International Relations, 104th Cong., 2d sess., 26 June 1996.

Ullman, Richard H. "The Wars in Yugoslavia and the International System After the Cold War." In *The World and Yugoslavia's Wars,* ed. Richard H. Ullman. New York: Council on Foreign Relations, 1996.

United Nations. *The United Nations and the Iraq-Kuwait Conflict 1990–1996.* The United Nations Blue Book Series, vol. 9. New York: United Nations Department of Public Information, 1996.

———. *The United Nations and Cambodia 1991–1995.* The United Nations Blue Book Series, vol. 2. New York: United Nations Department of Public Information, 1995.

United Nations, Department of Humanitarian Affairs. *Note from the Department of Humanitarian Affairs Concerning the Possible Humanitarian Impact of the International Flight Ban Decided in Security Council Resolution 1070 (1996).* 20 February 1997.

———. *Report of the DHA Mission to Afghanistan.* 15 May 1997.

United Nations, General Assembly. *Annual Report of the Secretary-General on the Work of the Organization* (1998). A/53/1. 16 April 1998.

———. *Implementation of the Provisions of the Charter of the United Nations Related to Assistance to Third States Affected by the Application of Sanctions Under Chapter VII of the Charter, Report of the Secretary-General.* A/50/361. 1995.

———. *Report of the Special Committee on the Charter of the United Nations and on the Strengthening of the Role of the Organization.* Supplement no. 33, A/53/33. 1998.

———, Subgroup on the Question of United Nations Imposed Sanctions of the Informal Open-Ended Working Group of the General Assembly on "An Agenda for Peace." *Provisionally Agreed Texts.* 10 July 1996.

———. *Supplement to "An Agenda for Peace."* A/RES 51/242. 26 September 1997.

United Nations, Inter-Agency Standing Committee. *Report for Humanitarian Mandates in Conflict Situations.* 1996.

United Nations, Office for the Coordination of Humanitarian Affairs. *Interagency Assessment Mission to Sierra Leone: Interim Report.* 17 February 1998.

United Nations, Security Council. *Economic Community of West African States, Decision on Sanctions Against the Junta and Sierra Leone.* S/1997/695, annex II. 8 September 1997.

———. *Economic Community of West African States, Situation Report in Sierra Leone After the Signing of the Peace Plan.* S/1997/895. 17 November 1997.

———. *Final Report of the International Commission of Inquiry.* S/1998/1096. 18 November 1998.

———. *Fourth Progress Report of the Secretary-General on UNTAC.* S/25719. 3 May 1993.

———. *Letter Dated 28 July 1999 from the Chairman of the Security Council Committee Established Pursuant to Resolution 864 (1993) Concerning the*

Situation in Angola Addressed to the President of the Security Council. S/1999/829. 28 July 1999.

———. *Letter Dated 26 February 1999 from the Chairman of the Security Council Committee Established Pursuant to Security Council Resolution 1160 (1998) Addressed to the President of the Security Council.* S/1999/216. 4 March 1999.

———. *Letter Dated 15 January 1998 from the Secretary-General Addressed to the President of the Security Council.* S/1998/201. 6 March 1998.

———. *Letter Dated 22 November 1997 from the Executive Chairman of the Special Commission Established by the Secretary-General Pursuant to Paragraph Nine (b)(i) of Security Council Resolution 687 (1991) Addressed to the President of the Security Council.* S/1997/922. 24 November 1997.

———. *Letter Dated 27 May 1997 from the Permanent Representative of the Libyan Arab Jamahiriya to the United Nations Addressed to the Secretary-General.* S/1997/404. 27 May 1997.

———. *Letter Dated 15 November 1996 from the Chairman of the Security Council Committee Established Pursuant to Resolution 724 (1991) Concerning Yugoslavia Addressed to the President of the Security Council.* S/1996/946. 15 November 1996.

———. *Letter Dated 24 September 1996 from the Chairman of the Security Council Committee Established Pursuant to Resolution 724 (1991) Concerning Yugoslavia Addressed to the President of the Security Council, Report of the Copenhagen Roundtable on United Nations Sanctions in the Case of the Former Yugoslavia, held at Copenhagen on 24 and 25 June 1996.* S/1996/776. 24 September 1996.

———. *Letter Dated 13 April 1995, Addressed to the President of the Security Council.* S/1995/200, annex 1. 13 April 1995.

———. *Letter Dated 30 November 1992 from Thailand Outlining the Position of the Royal Thai Government with Regard to Security Council Resolution 792 (1992).* S/24873. 30 November 1992.

———. *Letter Dated 30 October 1992 from the Permanent Representative of Benin to the United Nations.* S/24811. 16 November 1992.

———. *Letters Dated 27 and 30 March 1999, Respectively, from the Chairman of the Panels Established Pursuant to the Note by the President of the Security Council of 30 January 1999, S/1999/100, Addressed to the President of the Security Council.* S/1999/356. 30 March 1999.

———. *Letter from the Chairman of the Security Council Committee Concerning the Situation in Angola.* S/1999/644. 4 June 1999.

———. *Letter from the Chairman of the Security Council Committee Concerning the Situation in Angola.* S/1999/509. 4 May 1999.

———. *Letter from the Chairman of the Security Council Committee Concerning the Situation in Angola.* S/1999/147. 12 February 1999.

———. *Letter from the Permanent Observer of the League of Arab States.* S/1998/895. 29 September 1998.

———. *Letter from the Permanent Representative of Qatar.* S/1998/926. 7 October 1998.

———. *Note by the President of the Security Council: Work of the Sanctions Committees.* S/1999/92. 29 January 1999.

———. *Note by the President of the Security Council.* S/1995/234. 29 March 1995.

———. *Report of the Executive Chairman on the Activities of the Special Commission Established by the Secretary-General Pursuant to Paragraph 9 (b)(i) of Resolution 687 (1991).* S/1998/332. 16 April 1998.

————. *Report of the International Commission of Inquiry.* S/1997/1010. 24 December 1997.

————. *Report of the International Commission of Inquiry.* S/1996/195. 14 March 1996.

————. *Report of the Secretary-General Pursuant to Paragraph 6 of Security Council Resolution 1210 (1998).* S/1999/187. 22 February 1999.

————. *Report of the Secretary-General on the United Nations Observer Mission in Angola.* S/1999/49. 17 January 1999.

————. *Report of the Secretary-General Pursuant to Paragraph 10 of Security Council Resolution 1153 (1998).* S/1998/1100. 19 November 1998.

————. *Report of the Secretary-General Pursuant to Paragraph 7 of Security Council Resolution 1143 (1997).* S/1998/90. 1 February 1998.

————. *Report of the Secretary-General Pursuant to Paragraph 3 of Resolution 1111 (1997).* S/1997/935. 28 November 1997.

————. *Report of the Secretary-General Pursuant to Security Council Resolution 1070.* S/1996/940. 14 November 1996.

————. *Report of the Secretary-General on the Question of Haiti.* S/1994/1012. 26 August 1994.

————. *Report of the Secretary-General on the Question of Haiti.* S/1994/871. 26 July 1994.

————. *Report of the Secretary-General on the Situation in Angola.* S/26872. 13 December 1993.

————. *Report of the Secretary-General in Pursuance of Paragraph 6 of Security Council Resolution 810 (1993) on Preparations for the Election for the Constituent Assembly in Cambodia.* S/25784. 15 May 1993.

————. *Report of the Secretary-General on the Implementation of Security Council Resolution 792 (1992).* S/25289. 13 February 1993.

————. *Report of the Secretary-General on the Implementation of Security Council Resolution 783 (1992) on the Cambodia Peace Process.* S/24800. 15 November 1992.

————. *Report to the Secretary-General Dated 15 July 1991 on Humanitarian Needs in Iraq, Prepared by a Mission Led by the Executive Delegate of the Secretary-General for Humanitarian Assistance in Iraq.* S/22799. 17 July 1991.

————. *Report to the Secretary-General on Humanitarian Needs in Kuwait and Iraq in the Immediate Post-Crisis Environment by a Mission to the Area Led by Mr. Martti Ahtisaari, Under-Secretary-General for Administration and Management, 10–17 March 1991.* S/22366. 20 March 1991.

————. *Review and Assessment of the Implementation of the Humanitarian Programme Established Pursuant to Security Council Resolution 986 (1995) December 1996–November 1998.* S/1999/481. 28 April 1999.

————. *Third Progress Report of the Secretary-General on UNTAC.* S/25154. 25 January 1993.

————. *Third Report of the Secretary-General on the Situation in Sierra Leone.* S/1998/103. 5 February 1998.

United Nations, Security Council, Chairs of the Sanctions Committees. *Issue Paper Concerning the Sanctions Imposed by the Security Council.* 30 October 1998.

United States Agency for International Development. "Sierra Leone: Complex Emergency Report Number One." Washington, D.C.: USAID, 28 January 1998.

United States, Central Intelligence Agency. *Report of Proliferation-Related Acquisition in 1997*. Langley, Va.: Central Intelligence Agency, 1998.

United States, Department of State. *Patterns of Global Terrorism 1996*. Publication 10535. Washington, D.C.: Government Printing Office, 1996.

———. *UN Sanctions Against Belgrade: Lessons Learned for Future Regimes*. Paper prepared by the Interagency Task Force on Serbian Sanctions, Washington, D.C., June 1996.

United States, Department of the Treasury, Office of Foreign Assets Control. *Terrorist Assets Report*. Washington, D.C.: U.S. Department of the Treasury, January 1998.

United States, General Accounting Office. *Economic Sanctions: Effectiveness as Tools of Foreign Policy*. Washington, D.C.: GAO, 1993.

———. *GAO Evidence Regarding Non-Compliance with the OAS Embargo*. GAO/NSIAD B-248828. Washington, D.C.: GAO, 27 May 1992.

———. *International Trade: Issues Regarding Imposition of an Oil Embargo Against Nigeria: Report Prepared for the Chairman, Subcommittee on Africa, Committee on Foreign Relations, U.S. House of Representatives*. 103rd Cong., 2d sess. GAO/GGD-95-24. Washington, D.C.: GAO, November 1994.

———. *Money Laundering: FINCEN's Law Enforcement Support, Regulatory, and International Roles*. T-GGD-98-83. Washington, D.C.: GAO, 1 April 1998.

von Braunmühl, Claudia, and Manfred Kulessa. *The Impact of UN Sanctions on Humanitarian Assistance Activities: Report on a Study Commissioned by the United Nations Department of Humanitarian Affairs*. Berlin: Gesellschaft für Communication Management Interkulter Training, December 1995.

Walker, Peter. "Sanctions: A Blunt Instrument." *Red Cross, Red Crescent*, no. 3 (1995).

Webster, William H. "Iraq: The Domestic Impact of Sanctions." Testimony of the director of the Central Intelligence Agency before the House Armed Services Committee, 5 December 1990. Reprint in *Congressional Record*, 10 January 1991.

Weiss, Thomas G., David Cortright, George A. Lopez, and Larry Minear, eds. *Political Gain and Civilian Pain: Humanitarian Impacts of Economic Sanctions*. Lanham, Md.: Rowman and Littlefield, 1997.

Woodward, Susan L. *Balkan Tragedy: Chaos and Dissolution After the Cold War*. Washington, D.C.: Brookings Institution Press, 1995.

World Health Organization and United Nations Children's Fund. *Joint WHO/UNICEF Team Report: A Visit to Iraq*. New York: WHO and UNICEF, 16–21 February 1991.

World Military Expenditures and Arms Transfers: 1990. Washington, D.C.: United States Arms Control and Disarmament Agency, November 1991.

Zaidi, Sarah, and Mary C. Smith-Fawzi. "Health of Baghdad's Children." *Lancet* 346, no. 8988 (2 December 1995).

Zimmerman, Warren. *Origins of a Catastrophe: Yugoslavia and Its Destroyers—America's Last Ambassador Tells What Happened and Why*. New York: Times Books, 1996.

Index

263

Black market, 75, 99
Blondin Beye, Alioune, 154, 156
Borders, sealing, 3, 71, 191
Bosnia, 63, 65, 67, 68, 73, 74, 76, 80;
 effectiveness of sanctions on, 9
Boutros-Ghali, Boutros, 23, 138, 141,
 152, 229, 238
Brown, Frederick, 144
Bulgaria, 69, 174
Burkina Faso, 174, 189
Burundi, 198
Bush, George, 91, 95, 102

Cambodia, 136*map;* Cambodian
 People's Party, 137; China and, 139;
 displaced persons in, 135; economic
 sanctions on, 1; effectiveness of
 sanctions on, 137, 204, 205*tab,* 208;
 elections in, 135, 142, 143; France
 and, 139; military demobilization in,
 135, 143; monitoring sanctions on,
 140–142; peacekeeping missions in,
 9; reconstruction assistance in, 135,
 138; refugees in, 135; sanctions
 against, 135–144; sanctions enforcement in, 140–142; Supreme National
 Council, 139, 140; United National
 Front for an Independent, Neutral,
 Peaceful, Cooperative Cambodia,
 137; United Nations resolutions in,
 135–144
Canada: Governors Island agreement
 and, 92; Haiti and, 92, 94, 100; Iraq
 and, 57
Caputo, Dante, 92
CARE, 97
Carnegie Commission on Preventing
 Deadly Conflict, 30, 201*n26,*
 222
Carter, Jimmy, 95
Cedras, Raoul, 87, 92, 93, 95
Center for Strategic and International
 Studies, 52
China, 6, 24; Angola and, 163*n2;*
 Cambodia and, 139; Iraq and, 58
Christopher, Warren, 80
Clinton, Bill, 18, 56, 91, 93, 94
Compliance: conciliation and, 30–31;
 diplomatic settlements, 31; elements
 for ensuring, 223; partial, 5, 31;
 political, 3

Conakry agreement, 172, 173
Conference on Security and
 Cooperation in Europe, 65, 69
Conflict: inducement strategies and, 29,
 30; negotiating, 56, 81; prevention,
 29; regionalization, 149; resolution,
 27, 28, 29, 56
Congressional Black Caucus, 93,
 94
Contact Group peace plan, 68, 78, 80,
 86*n77*
Cooperation: changing, 6; encouraging,
 56; inducements for, 29, 30; interna-
 tional, 1, 63, 216–217; member
 state, 233–234; theory, 30
Copenhagen Roundtable on the
 Sanctions against Yugoslavia,
 222
Corruption, 75, 95, 158
Cotonou agreement, 192
Crawford, Neta, 21
Croatia, 63, 69, 73, 80
CSCE. *See* Conference on Security and
 Cooperation in Europe
Cuba, 149
Cyprus, 71

Dahlgren, Hans, 174
Dallaire, Romeo, 195
Damrosch, Lori, 21
Danube Commission, 83
Danube Patrol, 69, 70
Dayton peace accord, 31, 63, 65, 68, 77,
 79–80, 86*n77*
DeBeers Company, 159, 161
Delevic, Milica, 76, 77
Dellums, Ronald, 105*n65*
Democratic Republic of Congo, 149,
 198
Diplomacy: carrot-and-stick, 28, 29–32,
 45, 56, 223; coercive, 29, 56, 223;
 flexible, 109; forceful, 7; patient,
 138–139, 141, 156; preventive, 27;
 quiet, 139
Disarmament, 2, 51
Dominican Republic, 92, 94, 99–101,
 105*n65,* 216
Dos Santos, Jose Eduardo, 147
Dow, Samuel, 187, 189
Dowty, Alan, 16
Doxey, Margaret, 13

Macedonia, 69, 70, 71
Maguire, Robert, 92
Mahdi, Ali, 186
Mahugu, Njuguna, 160, 163
Malary, Guy, 94
Malnutrition, 24, 47, 74, 96, 97, 157, 176, 177
Malone, David, 100
Mandela, Nelson, 118
Martin, Lisa, 6, 18, 238
Médecins Sans Frontières-Holland, 176
Mercenaries, 159, 170, 174
Military operations, 16; effectiveness of, 14–17; in Haiti, 2, 6, 87, 89, 95; in Iraq, 2, 6; in Sierra Leone, 172; in Yugoslavia, 2, 6
Milosevic, Slobodan, 3, 31, 63, 67, 68, 71, 74, 75, 76, 77, 78, 79, 80, 86*n77*, 210
Mitterrand, François, 77
Mobuto Sese Seko, 149, 197, 198
Monitoring, 161; efforts, 103; of embargoes, 184; institutional capacity for, 69; regional, 70; sanctions, 9, 42, 99–101; stations, 140; United Nations, 31
Montenegro, 31, 67, 75, 78
Mubarak, Hosni, 121, 125

Nationalism, 20
National Patriotic Front of Liberia, 174, 187, 189, 191, 192
National Union for the Total Independence of Angola. *See* UNITA
NATO. *See* North Atlantic Treaty Organization
Netherlands: Haiti and, 100; Iraq and, 58; Libya and, 110, 118, 119
Nigeria, 167, 172, 173, 189, 190, 192, 193
North Atlantic Treaty Organization, 69, 79, 82, 83
Nossal, Kim, 22
Nunn, Sam, 95

Omar, Mohammad, 130
Operation Lifeline Sudan, 125
Organization for Economic Cooperation and Development, 234, 240
Organization of African Unity, 109, 118, 121, 132*n40*, 183, 192, 193

Organization of American States, 87, 89, 218; Charter, 105*n54;* Inter-American Commission on Human Rights, 90; Permanent Council, 89; sanctions, 89, 90, 95, 99–101, 101
Organization of the Islamic Conference, 39, 132*n40*
Organizations: international, 75; nongovernmental, 56, 97, 162, 214; relief, 97, 175; religious, 193
Organizations, regional, 70; Conference on Security and Cooperation in Europe, 65, 69; Economic Community of West African States, 183; European Community, 39, 65, 69; European Union, 13, 82, 83; Gulf Cooperation Council, 39; inducement strategies and, 30; League of Arab States, 39; opposition to sanctions, 118, 132*n40;* Organization of American States, 89, 101; Organization of the Islamic Conference, 39; sanctions implementation and, 174; sanction success and, 5, 15; Western European Union, 69
Owen, David, 70, 71, 77, 78
Oxfam America, 142

PAHO. *See* Pan American Health Organization
Pakistan, 129, 130
Pan American Health Organization, 97–98
Pape, Robert, 14
Paris Accords, 135, 137, 138, 139, 140
PDK. *See* Khmer Rouge, Party of Democratic Kampuchea
Peacekeeping missions, 1, 2; in Angola, 153; in Cambodia, 9, 135, 142, 143; in Liberia, 191; in Sierra Leone, 170; in Somalia, 183, 186
Pérez de Cuéllar, Javier, 45
Policy: change, 17, 18, 20; continuum, 28; counterproductivity in, 29; framework setting, 223–224; influence on sanctions, 17; lobbying, 160; sanction, 221–249; strengthening, 231–239
Political: change, 19, 44; choices, 19; compliance, 3; compromise, 31;

About the Book

Since the end of the Cold War, economic sanctions have been a frequent instrument of UN authority, imposed by the Security Council against nearly a dozen targets. Some efforts appear to have been successful, others are more doubtful—all, though, have been controversial. This book, based on more than two hundred interviews with officials from the UN and sanctioned countries, and other involved actors, provides the first comprehensive assessment of the effectiveness of UN sanctions during the 1990s.

The authors develop a set of criteria for judging the full impact of sanctions—political, economic, and humanitarian—and then provide detailed studies of specific cases. They conclude with far-reaching recommendations for increasing the viability of sanctions as a productive diplomatic tool.

George A. Lopez is professor of government and international studies and also a faculty fellow at the Joan B. Kroc Institute for International Peace Studies, University of Notre Dame. **David Cortright** is president of the Fourth Freedom Forum and a research fellow at the Kroc Institute.

WITHDRAWN